On Law, Morality, and Politics

Saint Thomas Aquinas

Edited, with Introduction, by

William P. Baumgarth and

Richard J. Regan, S.J.

Hackett Publishing Company
Indianapolis/Cambridge

Cover design by Listenberger Design and Associates

Interior design by Baskerville Book and Editorial Services

For further information, please contact

Hackett Publishing Company
P.O. Box 44937
Indianapolis, Indiana 46204

Library of Congress Cataloging-in-Publication Data

Thomas, Aquinas, Saint, 1225?–1274.
   On law, morality, and politics / edited, with introduction, by
Richard J. Regan and William P. Baumgarth.
     p.   cm.
   Bibliography: p.
   Includes index.
   ISBN 0-87220-032-9   ISBN 0-87220-031-0 (pbk.)
   1. Natural law. 2. Law and ethics. 3. Law and politics.
I. Baumgarth, William P. II. Regan, Richard J. III. Title.
K447.T45A2 1988
340'.11—dc19   87-28272
                                         CIP

Contents

5 War and Killing 220

6 Sedition and Obedience 231

7 Tolerance and Church-State Relations 249

8 Statesmanship 263

Preface

The writings of St. Thomas Aquinas on morals and politics deserve
wide circulation for a host of reasons. No student of political
thought can be considered well grounded in the Western tradition if
the contribution of the Middle Ages to that tradition is ignored. All
too often, courses in political philosophy skip rapidly from the
ancients to the moderns, with very little comment on the Medieval
period. St. Thomas, of course, is not the only or even, perhaps, the
most characteristic theorist of that era in the Christian West. However, his ideas ought to be more familiar than those of others, because of our inheritance of the notion of natural law, to the formulation of which Thomas gave so much of his labor. A full, inexpensive
anthology on the parts of the *Summa Theologiae* dealing with the
natural law will enable the student to judge firsthand the vitality of
that inheritance and the degree to which we are still faithful to it. In
our selections from the Treatise on Law (ST I–II, QQ. 90–108), we
reproduce the bulk of Thomas's argument, omitting only those sections that deal with specifics of the Old and New Laws.

In addition, the relationship of religion to politics is one which
nobody concerned with matters of public policy today can afford to
ignore. From all segments of the political spectrum, but especially
the extremes, come demands, whose origins are said to be religious,
upon the body politic. St. Thomas thought deeply and comprehen-
sively about the relationship between reason and revelation. In this
volume we offer, beyond our selections on law, questions from the
Summa Theologiae dealing with political and moral concerns as
Thomas viewed them in the light of both the Scriptures and tradition, as well as from the perspective of philosophy.

In every case, we present the full argument that St. Thomas
makes, generally following the order of the *Summa* itself, as literally as we can. The Introduction and Notes are meant as background
aids for the reader, but we have tried to let the work of interpretation and judgment fall as squarely as possible on the reader's shoulders. Our editing, therefore, centered on choosing the texts to include, and we have respected the integrity of St. Thomas's well-
formulated arguments.

We are indebted to many people. In particular, we wish to thank
Professor Patrick Corrigan of St. Anselm's College (Manchester,

New Hampshire) and Professor Paul Seaton of St. John's Seminary (Brighton, Massachusetts) for their thorough reading of the translation and their helpful suggestions. We thank William Wray, Esq., for his patient proofreading of the manuscript. We thank the Reverend Francis P. Canavan, S.J., for his assistance in translating some key Latin texts (especially the *De regno* selection). We thank the Reverend W. Norris Clarke, S.J., and the Reverend Louis B. Pascoe, S.J., for providing much in the way of background advice and criticism. Finally, we thank Ms. Eileen McCauley, without whose skilled deciphering of handwritten copy the manuscript would not have seen the light of day. Needless to add, none of the above shares any responsibility for defects in this volume.

Note on the Text

The translation of the *Summa Theologiae* is that of the Fathers of the English Dominican Province (3 vols.; New York: Benzinger Bros., 1948). The Glencoe Publishing Co. of Encino, California, has graciously granted permission to use that translation for our selections from the *Summa.*

The Dominican Fathers' translation is a generally precise and literal rendition of the text of Aquinas. We have checked that translation against the Latin text of the Leonine edition and have substituted our own renderings where we felt the Dominican text obscure or inaccurate.

We include original translations of sections of the *Commentary on the Sentences of Peter Lombard* (Mathis edition, Marietti, Turin, 1942) and the *De regno*. The Latin text for the latter is the Mathis edition, with corrected manuscript readings by the Reverend I. Th. Eschmann, O.P. (St. Thomas Aquinas, *On Kingship*, trans. Phelan and Eschmann, Pontifical Institute of Mediaevel Studies, Toronto, Canada, 1949, pp. 83–84).

Although we have followed St. Thomas's use of the Vulgate numbering for the Psalter, the names for the books of the Bible are those of the Revised Standard Version. Where possible, we give Migne's *Patrologia* references, the Bekker citations for Aristotle, and the Stephanus citations for Plato.

Bronx, New York

William P. Baumgarth
Richard J. Regan

Introduction

Philosophy may be hazardous: if not to health, at least to reputation. In the year 1277, Etienne Tempier, Bishop of Paris, issued a condemnation of 219 propositions, several of which, it is believed, were connected with the philosophical teachings of Thomas Aquinas (1225–1274).[1] The bishop took this action in an attempt to squelch a revival of classical Greek—and especially Aristotelian—philosophy, which he feared would be hazardous to the faith of his flock. However, he was unsuccessful. Less than fifty years later, in 1323, Thomas Aquinas, on the basis of his life and writings, was declared a saint, and in 1879 his philosophy was made the official teaching on matters theological and philosophical in the seminaries of the Catholic Church.

Why did a revival of classical Greek philosophy and the teachings of St. Thomas cause such controversy? What fueled the controversy? And why, centuries later, are the teachings of St. Thomas still relevant to contemporary issues of political philosophy? The answers to these questions lie in the historical debate between philosophers and theologians about the relative roles that reason and faith should play in the Christian quest for truth. To understand St. Thomas's theories of politics and law, we need to examine this debate in light of the philosophical and theological traditions that informed his thinking.

The Philosophical and Theological Background

Let us begin by recalling a few salient points regarding the historical attitude of the Christian Church toward philosophy. Christianity, like Judaism and Islam, lays claim to truths about God and His designs for the human race, truths inaccessible to human reason without divine revelation. Christianity, however, stresses belief in ways that the other two great religions do not. The core of Christianity is belief in the person and mission of Jesus Christ. Critical to Christian belief are affirmations about the identity of Jesus, the meaning of His life and death for humankind, the way He wanted His followers to live, and the reward He promised to those who follow His way faithfully.

Christianity, then, claims to possess all-important truths which are inaccessible to reason without God's revelation of these truths in the person of Jesus Christ. The spirit of classical Greek philosophy, on the other hand, claims that "there is no rationally disputable question that the philosopher ought not to dispute or determine, because reasons are derived from things."[2] Christianity makes comprehensive claims to ultimate truths about God, man, and the world—but so does philosophy. To the Christian believer, philosophy may seem at best irrelevant and at worst a threat; to the philosopher, supernatural religion may seem at best superfluous and at worst contrary to reason.

Yet, despite this tension, Christianity has been, since its earliest days, receptive, if not always hospitable, to philosophy. The most authoritative text of the Christian Church, the New Testament, provides no code of conduct for the faithful in their day-to-day lives beyond the Ten Commandments and love of neighbor. Moreover, the New Testament provides no systematic guidelines for the organization of human society. How are human beings to act in this or that situation? What is just in this or that situation? How should Christians form their conscience? What are the purposes of human society? How should human society be organized? What is the role of law in human society? To help answer these questions, the Christian Church of necessity turned to philosophers, to those who systematically reason about morals, politics, and law.

Before assimilating St. Thomas's work into its teachings, the Christian Church largely relied on the Neo-Platonic tradition. For example, St. Augustine (354–430) applied this philosophical approach to issues of morals and politics, as he did to other issues of theology. The Neo-Platonists viewed the visible world, the realm of flux and flow, as a symbol of the divine reality that remained hidden within. Everything in the visible world appeared to them to be related to God, just as objects of the visible world, in some interpretations of Plato's philosophy, were related to ideal forms of these objects. For the Neo-Platonists, the everyday world, the material world, was largely symbolic; only the immaterial (for the Neo-Platonists: God, the Ideas) was real.[3]

Philosophy, as practiced by the Neo-Platonists therefore seemed not only compatible with Christian doctrine but also useful for it. Indeed, for hundreds of years, the Christian Church was content to contemplate philosophical matters in the context of the Neo-Platonic tradition. In the late 12th and early 13th centuries, however, Aristotle's writings on natural philosophy, psychology, ethics, and politics were introduced to the West. The appearance of the *Physics*, *Metaphysics*, *De Anima*, *Nicomachean Ethics*, and *Politics* changed

Christianity's view towards politics and law for centuries. From the writings of St. Thomas Aquinas came an Aristotelian interpretation of the world that replaced the Church's Neo-Platonic outlook. Aristotle presented to Western Christians a view which, unlike that of the Neo-Platonists, fully accepted the reality of the visible world and sought to understand it as such.

St. Thomas's attraction to Aristotle is due in part to Aristotle's approach to politics and ethics and also to the ways in which it differed from Plato's. For Plato, political virtue, at best, was an image of virtue proper. Virtue, properly speaking, was wisdom.[4] Wisdom, in turn, was a comprehensive knowledge of the universe. There could be only one science that was genuine: knowledge of the whole, of the cosmos. For Aristotle, there was more than one science. Each science had principles proper to it, and no science could be simply reduced to a more fundamental science (such as metaphysics). The science that embraced political inquiry was therefore distinct from the science of cosmology: matters of politics and law could be examined separately from those of physics.[5] Aristotle distinguished between moral virtues (such as courage, moderation, and justice) and intellectual virtues. The intellectual virtues concerned both speculative knowledge (philosophy and science) and practical knowledge (prudence or practical wisdom). Practical knowledge was knowledge of how to act well. To know how to live well, how to direct oneself toward the goal of happiness, one needed to observe and follow the example of prudent persons rather than to learn scientific truths.

St. Thomas acknowledged that the world had a reality of its own and that matters of everyday life could be understood separately from matters proper to the sphere of revealed theology. This made it possible for him to formulate a political philosophy that seemed descriptive of the reality of politics as experienced by the Christian community, politics characterized by the coexistence of canonical and civil law.[6] But the Church at large was not so quick to draw St. Thomas's conclusion. For most of its life, Christianity had relied on the Neo-Platonic tradition for its philosophy and theology. Little or no comprehensive grappling with broad questions of philosophy in general or of political philosophy in particular had gone on since the time of St. Augustine. Neo-Platonism had become venerable with age and had strong defenders; habitual ways of thinking had inured theologians to fresh philosophical reflection. Indeed, except in England, church authorities banned the use of Aristotle's texts on natural philosophy in the universities of the West, including the University of Paris, where St. Thomas lectured. In addition to those who defended the old order on the basis of tradition, there were those who objected to St. Thomas's teachings because they believed the Aristotelianism he taught contained elements incompatible with Christian belief. The latter were unable to distinguish St. Thomas's teachings from those of the so-called Latin Averroists, and that is why Bishop Templer, for one, condemned theses connected with St. Thomas.

The Latin Averroists were radical followers of Aristotle who accepted Averroës's (1126–1198) interpretation of Aristotle. They were attempting to revive the spirit of classical Greek philosophy as a whole. They apparently argued that reason could arrive at truths at variance with Christian faith and that the philosopher should not defer in any way to the theologian.[7] On the political level, Marsilius of Padua (c. 1275–1342), prominent among later Latin Averroists, argued not only for the complete autonomy of the temporal power of princes from the spiritual power of Pope and bishops, but even for the subordination of the latter power to the former.[8]

Christian officials and theologians could not accept certain teachings of Aristotle, especially as interpreted by Averroës, because these teachings were clearly contrary to Christian doctrine.[9] First, Aristotle taught that God contemplated only Himself, but the Christian believes that God also knows and provides for His creatures. Second, Aristotle taught that God moves other things to act only insofar as His perfection attracts the others to perfect themselves, but the Christian believes in an active God (one Who sometimes even performs miracles). The Christian believes that God is the ultimate source as well as the ultimate goal of the activities of His creatures. Third, Aristotle taught that the world is eternal, but the Christian believes that the world had a beginning, i.e., a first moment. Fourth, Averroist Aristotelians taught that the human soul is only the form of the body and so perishes at death, but the Christian believes that the human soul is immortal. Lastly, Aristotle taught that human beings would be happy to their full satisfaction in this world if they developed intellectual and moral virtues and rightly organized their society, but the Christian believes that humans can be perfectly happy only in the next world, with the vision of God.

Thus, in formulating his approach to philosophical inquiry, St. Thomas had to contend with two strong-minded sets of opponents. Against the traditionalists, he needed to defend the reality and integrity of the visible world. After the introduction of Aristotelian works on metaphysics, psychology, natural science, ethics, and politics, the other-worldly philosophy of Neo-Platonism would never again dominate Western thought. Against the Aristotelianism of the Latin Averroists, Thomas needed to reaffirm the truth of revelation and its complete compatibility with truths discovered by reason.

Religious truth, for St. Thomas, was neither a symbol of what philosophers knew from reason with certainty nor a myth useful for
social control. What he arrived at was, in the words of Josef Pieper,
a conceptual framework for a "theologically founded worldliness."[10]

The Moral and Political Philosophy
of St. Thomas: An Overview

Aristotle's epistemology, metaphysics, and psychology provided the
philosophical framework for Aquinas's moral and political theory.
Unlike modern empiricists, Aquinas accepted as fact that the human intellect can be certain about the existence of sensible objects,
can understand the natures or essences of those things, and can
reason from effects to the causes of things. Unlike his contemporary
Neo-Platonists, Aquinas acknowledged that the human intellect can
form concepts about sensible things only if it has sensible experience of those things or if it derives concepts about things not sensi-
bly experienced from those things that are. The function of philosophy is to understand reality in terms of its first principles or
causes.

Above all, Aristotelian and Thomistic metaphysics are concerned
with the final causes of things. The natures or structures of things
determine their type of activity, and, conversely, types of activities
are determined by the natures or structures of things. Activities
develop and perfect things according to their structures and so bring
things to their specific ends. Trees achieve their perfection by activities whereby acorns, for example, mature to oaks; horses achieve
their perfection by activities whereby foals mature to fully developed horses; human beings achieve their perfection by activities
whereby babies mature to adulthood. Related to this principle is the
distinction between potentiality and actuality. The acorn is not actually an oak, but it has the potentiality to become one; the foal is
not actually a grown horse, but it has the potentiality to become
one. Finite things are thus a composite of what they actually are and
what they are capable of becoming.

Aristotelian psychology stresses rationality in all its dimensions
as the characteristic which distinguishes human beings from other
species. It is, of course, true that human beings have animal appetites and that they act to satisfy them, but when human beings act
consciously, they have to decide when and how to act: human beings
rationally perceive pleasure as good for them and pain as bad for
them, but the former as only partially good and the latter as only
partially bad. Not only are human beings capable of understanding
the world they live in, they are capable of deciding how they will

behave in that world. Moreover, Aristotle and Aquinas recognized that human intelligence and freedom open to human beings the possibilities of friendship and love.

Fundamental to the thought of St. Thomas, however, is the existence of a supernatural order beyond the natural. The natural order, for St. Thomas, depends upon God in a way that Aristotle's universe does not: St. Thomas's God created the world and maintains its existence and activity. The supernatural realm consists of those things above nature, those things human beings could not know, had not God so informed them. This realm includes grace, the gift of God which saves humanity. Grace, however, does not abolish nature; it adds to it. Human beings, like all creatures, are ordered to a natural end, and that end is happiness in this life. By virtue of grace, human beings are ordered to a further end to which nature alone does not entitle them: the contemplation of God in the next life. The task St. Thomas set for himself was to work out the relationship between the natural order and the supernatural order without minimizing or depreciating either.

Thomas's conception of virtue is key to his theory of politics and reflects not only his working out of this relationship but also Aristotle's influence on his philosophical thought. Unlike modern political thinkers, such as Hobbes (1588–1679), St. Thomas views the cultivation of virtue as *the* political end. Virtue, in Greek, is synonymous with excellence. Excellence is connected with a way of life, a way of life that for both individual and community has happiness as its goal. The study of ethics teachs us how to be happy. The best community is that which has actualized excellence (virtue).

Happiness, for Aristotle and for St. Thomas, is not mindless, momentary euphoria, but rather the consciousness we have of long-term, successful, intelligent human activity. If, for example, the human eye were conscious of doing its activity well—of seeing properly—that awareness would constitute, for the eye, happiness. Pleasure and pain are clues given by nature about what we ought to do to be happy. However, such clues are not infallible guides; they need to be scrutinized by reason. Reason, as we have seen, can be interpreted in two ways: it can be understood as contemplation, as the pursuit of knowledge for the joy of knowing, or it can be understood as the sense of knowing how to conduct ourselves in our practical lives. The perfection of reason as contemplation yields the intellectual virtue of wisdom. The perfection of reason as knowledge of how to conduct ourselves practically yields the intellectual virtue of prudence (or practical wisdom).

Within the sphere of proper conduct, we can be said to be virtuous when we have developed a firm disposition to do the right thing for the right reason. As children we do the right thing at best because we have a right opinion, at worst because of the extrinsic rewards or punishments promised by adults. It is only when we take proper satisfaction in doing things correctly, however, that we can be said to be truly virtuous. To be truly virtuous is to have acquired the proper habitual disposition to act in a certain way. In learning to play the piano, for example, we first attend to mechanical details, such as knowing where to place our fingers. Once we gain a mastery over the instrument, our knowledge of mechanical things becomes second nature. We acquire the proper habitual disposition, if you will, to play the piano. Having acquired the necessary disposition, we shift our consciousness from precept to performance for its own sake, from awareness of secondary details of a technical or mechanical nature to awareness of the beauty of the act itself and the pleasures that accompany it. Just so, in the wider practical arena, this shift signals the development of moral virtue. We are always creatures of habit, either good or bad. Nature inclines us toward good habits, but it is not without our own efforts, the promptings of our parents, and the precepts of the law that we are able to acquire the proper habitual disposition. Success in doing so puts us in possession of moral virtue.

In the selections from St. Thomas's works which follow, we will encounter arguments which embrace the teachings of Aristotle, whom St. Thomas calls the Philosopher, arguments which qualify Aristotle's teachings, and arguments which contradict them. Each argument serves to support St. Thomas's formulation of his political philosophy. On the question of justice, for example, St. Thomas maintains in his discussion some of the tension and ambiguity that characterizes Aristotle's discussion of justice in the *Nicomachean Ethics*. This tension involves the relationship of legal justice (general justice, as St. Thomas calls it) to the other virtues. On this subject, St. Thomas is far less ambivalent than the Philosopher. Aristotle says about magnanimity that this virtue appears to be a crown for all other virtues. Yet the magnanimous or great-souled man does not remember favors done to him. He does not, therefore, give to each what is owed to him. He is not, therefore, just. For St. Thomas, however, justice is unequivocally higher than magnanimity. About this ranking, however, Aristotle makes no explicit judgment. Likewise, for Aristotle, only statesmen and potential statesmen are granted the full possession of the virtue of prudence.[11] St. Thomas, to the contrary, extends at least a modified form of this virtue to all the citizens of a political association.[12] Both Aristotle and St. Thomas agree that the goal of human activity is happiness; however, Aristotle limits that goal to this life. St. Thomas argues that the ultimate human goal is the vision of God after death. The goal of happiness therefore has a place in both the supernatural order and the natural order. Thus, although Aristotelian thought informs and, in places, lends structure to his philosophy, in the end, St. Thomas's theory of politics must be judged on the basis of its own original synthesis.[13]

St. Thomas's Writings

Some of Thomas's writings take the form of commentaries. These include those on the *Sentences of Peter Lombard* and those on Aristotle's *Ethics* and *Politics*. Thomas remained exceptionally sensitive to the structure of the given works; so much so, that it is difficult for the reader to separate comment from the text.[14]

Other modes of exposition in Thomas's corpus include writings expressing Thomas's own reasoning on certain themes. The treatise *On Kingship* and the *Summa Contra Gentiles*, Thomas's reply to the arguments of the pagan philosophers and their Eastern commentators, are examples of such writings. Also included in this genre is the *Summa Theologiae*, sections of which constitute the overwhelming majority of texts in this volume. The *Summa Theologiae* is divided into four parts: Part I deals with God and creation; Part I–II is on human action and the virtues in general; Part II–II considers such actions and virtues in particular detail; Part III deals with Christ. The *Summa* was left unfinished.

Each part of this large work consists of a number of Questions, each of which is divided into several investigations, called Articles. The arrangement of the material in the Articles reflects the nature of academic disputes as they were carried on in the universities of St. Thomas's day. Thomas spent a great deal of time during his lectures responding to objections to his theoretical positions. The rules of dispute demanded that the objector's refutation be first restated by the respondent in a way that the objector found true to his own sense.[15] Each article in the *Summa Theologiae* begins with a series of such Objections to the point Thomas will be defending. After stating the Objections, Thomas asserts what he believes to be the correct answer to the Question considered in the Article, sometimes citing the Philosopher, or a recognized theological authority or some other source. He next explains his position in his Response, then returns to the original Objections and addresses each in order (omitting those which have been answered in his Response).

As Pieper has observed, the structure of an Article has much in common with the Socratic approach illustrated in a Platonic dialogue.[16] Thomas attempts to pose the objections to his position as strongly as he can. At times what he uses to support these objections—the apparent judgment of a pagan or patristic authority, for example—later reappears in support of his own position. Unlike the reader of Platonic dialogues, however, the reader of the *Summa* knows exactly what position the author holds. This does not mean, however, that the *Summa Theologiae* requires no interpretation. The reasons Thomas raises certain objections and not others are not immediately clear. Such matters as the ordering of the Questions, of the Articles, and of the Objections within the Articles should provoke thought on the reader's part. St. Thomas usually cites an authority for his position in his "On the contrary" summation of the Question, but there are cases in which he simply posits his own answer. Observing whether he chooses to cite an authority or to posit his own answer may be important in comprehending the significance of certain Articles for St. Thomas. These and other aspects of Thomas's mode of exposition serve to encourage the reader to weigh carefully the issues at hand and to enter into the debate.

Conclusion

The issues that concerned St. Thomas in his political philosophy—the nature of the political order, the force of reason, the function of the law, the meaning of justice, the relationship between everyday life and divine order—reflect the concerns of a society and a theology in transition. After their introduction to Aristotle's work in the late 12th and early 13th centuries, Western philosophers and theologians were forced to rethink the foundation of their beliefs. Studying St. Thomas in the context of his era is essential to understanding the motivation for his teachings, but relegating him to that era overlooks the impact of his work.

Questions as to how to interpret law, as to what constitutes justice, as to whether or not our actions reflect divine guidance are posed almost daily today in world politics. In the United States, in recent years, both liberation theologians on the left and fundamentalist preachers on the right have aroused interest in political and moral issues. Both groups argue on religious grounds, though, like their Aristotelian and Neo-Platonic counterparts of the 13th century, they interpret these religious grounds in dramatically different ways. Thus, working out the relationship between reason and revelation in morals and politics continues to trouble modern thinkers. For today's student of moral and political theory, the study of St. Thomas's philosophy can provide reasoned insight into central problems of political life.

Notes to Introduction

1. Ralph Lerner and Mushin Mahdi, eds., *Medieval Political Philosophy: A Sourcebook* (New York: Free Press of Glencoe, 1963), p. 336 (hereafter cited as Lerner and Mahdi).

2. "Condemnation of 219 Propositions," Proposition 6, Lerner and Mahdi, p. 338. (The numbering follows the order of the Mandonnet edition.)

3. Josef Pieper, *Guide to Thomas Aquinas* (New York: Pantheon Books, 1962), p. 47 (hereafter cited as Pieper).

4. Plato, *Republic*, 430c; 518e.

5. Leo Strauss, *The City and Man* (Chicago: Rand McNally, 1964), pp. 21, 25.

6. Lerner and Mahdi, p. 17.

7. Cf. Averroës, "The Decisive Treatise," in Lerner and Mahdi, pp. 164–85.

8. Marsilius of Padua, "The Defender of the Peace," in Lerner and Mahdi, pp. 441–88.

9. Aristotle, *Metaphysics* XII, 9, 1074b30–34.

10. Pieper, p. 132.

11. Aristotle, *Ethics* VI, 7, 1141b23–27. For great-souledness as a seeming crown of all the virtues, see *Ethics* IV, 3. 1123a33–1125a35.

12. ST II–II, Q. 50, A. 2.

13. Among other themes of political importance, compare Thomas's treatment of the family with, for example, Avempace, "The Governance of the Solitary," in Lerner and Mahdi, p. 125.

14. Lerner and Mahdi, p. 273.

15. Pieper, p. 13.

16. Ibid., p. 79.

Signs & Abbreviations

Conf.	Augustine, *Confessions*
Contra Adimant.	Augustine, *Contra Adimantum, Manichaei discipulum*
Contra duas epist. Pelag.	Augustine, *Contra duas epistolas Pelagianorum*
Contra Faust.	Augustine, *Contra Faustum, Manichaeum*
CS	Aquinas, *Commentary on the Sentences*
De bello Gal.	Julius Caesar, *Commentarii de bello Gallico*
De bono conjug.	Augustine, *De bono conjugali*
De catech. rud.	Augustine, *De catechizandis rudibus*
De doctr. Christ.	Augustine, *De doctrina Christiana*
De fide	Ambrose, *De fide, ad Gratianum*
De fide orth.	John Damascene, *De fide orthodoxa*
De haeres.	Augustine, *De haeresibus*
De hebdom.	Boethius, *De hebdomadibus*
De invent. rhet.	M. Tullius Cicero, *De inventione rhetorica*
De lib. arb.	Augustine, *De libero arbitrio*
De mor. Eccl.	Augustine, *De moribus Ecclesiae Catholicae*
De nat. boni	Augustine, *De natura boni contra Manichaeos*
De offic.	M. Tullius Cicero, *De officiis*
De Trin.	Augustine, *De Trinitate*
De vera relig.	Augustine, *De vera religione*
De veritat.	Anselm, *Dialogus de veritate*
Decretals	Gregory IX, *Decreta*
Decretum	Gratian, *Decretum magistri Gratiani*
Div. nom.	Dionysius the Pseudo-Areopagite, *De divinis nominibus*
Epist.	Augustine, *Epistolae*
Eth.	Aristotle, *Nicomachean Ethics*
Etym.	Isidore, *Etymologiarum libri*
Expos. in Psalt.	Cassiodorus, *In Psalterum expositio*
Gen. ad lit.	Augustine, *De Genesi ad litteram*
Glossa	Peter Lombard, *Glossa*

Glossa ordin.	*Glossa ordinaria*
Hom. in Evang.	Gregory I, *Quadraginta homiliarum in Evangelia*
Hom. in Exod.	Origen, *Homiliae in Exodum*
Hom. in Luc.	Basil, *Homilia in illud Lucae [12:18]*
Hom. in princ. Proverb.	Basil, *Homiliae in principium Proverbiorum*
Homil.	Chrysostom, *Homiliae in Epistolam ad Romanos*
In Eth.	Aquinas, *Commentary on the Nicomachean Ethics*
In Ezech.	Jerome, *Commentariorum in Ezechielem*
In Galat.	Jerome, *In Epistolam ad Galatas*
In Hexaem.	Basil, *Homiliae in Hexaemeron*
In Joan.	Augustine, *In Joannis Evangelium*
In Lev.	Hesychius, *In Leviticum*
In Matt. hom.	Chrysostom, *In Matthaeum homiliae*
In Osee	Jerome, *In Osee commentariorum libri tres*
In Pol.	Aquinas, *Commentary on the Politics of Aristotle*
In Ps.	Augustine, *Enarrationes in Psalmos*
Interlin.	*Biblia Sacra cum glossis, interlineari, et ordinaria.* 6 vols. Venice: 1558
Instit. rei militar.	Vigetius, *Ad Valentinianum Augustum institutorum rei militaris*
K	P. Kruger, ed., *Corpus Juris Civilis.* Berlin: I (15th ed.), 1928; II (9th ed.), 1915
Libri	Isidore, *Libri tres sententiarum*
Metaph.	Aristotle, *Metaphysics*
Moral.	Gregory I, *Moralia*
PG	J. P. Migne, ed., *Patrologia Graeca*
Phys.	Aristotle, *Physics*
PL	J. P. Migne, ed., *Patrologia Latina*
Pol.	Aristotle, *Politics*
Quaest.	Augustine, *De diversis quaestionibus LXXXIII*
Quaest. in Exod.	Augustine, *Quaestionum in Exodum*
Quaest. in Heptat.	Augustine, *Quaestionum in Heptateuchum*

RF	E. Richter and E. Friedberg, eds., *Corpus Juris Canonici*. 2nd ed. Leipzig: 1879
Rhet.	Aristotle, *Rhetoric*
Rhetor.	M. Tullius Cicero, *Rhetorica*
Sent.	Peter Lombard, *Libri quattuor sententiarum*
ST	Thomas Aquinas, *Summa theologiae*
Summa	Alexander of Hales, *Summa theologiae*
Synon.	Isidore, *Synonoma de lamentatione animae peccatricis*

Biblical Abbreviations

Col.	Colossians
Cor.	Corinthians
Dan.	Daniel
Dt.	Deuteronomy
Ec.	Ecclesiastes
Eph.	Ephesians
Ex.	Exodus
Ezech.	Ezechiel
Gal.	Galatians
Gen.	Genesis
Heb.	Hebrews
Hos.	Hosea
Is.	Isaiah
Jer.	Jeremiah
Jn.	John
Judg.	Judges
Lev.	Leviticus
Lk.	Luke
Macc.	Maccabees
Mk.	Mark
Mt.	Matthew
Num.	Numbers
Pet.	Peter
Pr.	Proverbs
Ps.	Psalms
Rev.	Revelation
Rom.	Romans
Sam.	Samuel

Sir.	Sirach (Ecclesiasticus)
Th.	Thessalonians
Tim.	Timothy
Tit.	Titus
Wis.	Wisdom
Zech.	Zechariah

Authors Cited by St. Thomas

Alexander of Hales (A.D. 1170?–1245)

Ambrose, St. (A.D. 340?–97)

Anselm, St. (A.D. 1033–1109)

Aristotle, "the Philosopher" (384–327 B.C.)

Augustine, St. (A.D. 354–430)

Ausonius, Decius (A.D. 310?–93?)

Basil the Great, St. (A.D. 330?–79?)

Boethius (A.D. 480?–524?)

Caesar, Julius (100–44 B.C.)

Cassidorus (A.D. 490?–583)

Celsus, Publius Juventius (A.D. 67?–130?)

Chrysostom, St. John (A.D. 345?–407)

Cicero, M. Tullius (106–43 B.C.)

Damascene, St. John (A.D. 700?–754?)

Dionysius, the Pseudo-Areopagite (early 6th c. A.D.)

Gaius (2nd c. A.D.)

Gratian (1st half 12th c. A.D.)

Gregory I, Pope St. (A.D. 540?–604)

Gregory IX, Pope (A.D. 1147?–1241)

Hesychius of Jerusalem (early 5th c. A.D.)

Hugh of St. Victor (A.D. 1096?–1141)

Isidore of Seville, St. (A.D. 560?–636)

Jerome, St. (A.D. 340?–420)

Lombard, Peter (A.D. 1100?–1160?)

Nicholas I, Pope (A.D. 819?–67)

Origen (A.D. 185?–254?)

Paul, St., "the Apostle" (1st c. A.D.)

Seneca, Lucius Annaeus (4? B.C.–A.D. 65)

Tully=Cicero

Ulpian, Domitius, "the Jurist" (A.D. 170?–228)

Conscience

ST I

Question 79
Of the Intellectual Powers

*[In Thirteen Articles, of Which
Articles Twelve and Thirteen Are Included]*

TWELFTH ARTICLE
Is *Synderesis* a Special Power of the Soul?

We proceed thus to the Twelfth Article:

Objection 1. It would seem that *synderesis* is a special power distinct from the others. For those things which fall under one division seem to be of one genus. But in the gloss of Jerome on Ezech. 1:6, *synderesis* is divided over against the irascible, the concupiscible, and the rational, which are powers.[1] Therefore, *synderesis* is a power.

Obj. 2. Further, opposite things are of one genus. But *synderesis* and sensuality seem to be opposed to one another because *synderesis* always incites to good, while sensuality always incites to evil and is therefore signified by the serpent, as is clear from Augustine.[2] It seems, therefore, that *synderesis* is a power, just as sensuality is.

Obj. 3. Further, Augustine says that, in the natural powers of judging, there are certain "rules and seeds of virtue, both true and unchangeable."[3] And this is what we call *synderesis.* Since, therefore, the unchangeable rules which guide our judgment pertain to reason as to its superior part, as Augustine says,[4] it seems that *synderesis* is the same as reason, and thus it is a power.

On the contrary, According to the Philosopher, "rational powers pertain to opposite things."[5] But *synderesis* does not pertain to opposites but inclines to good only. Therefore, *synderesis* is not a power. For if it were a power, it would be a rational power, since it is not found in brute animals.

I answer that Synderesis is not a power but a habit, though some held that it is a power higher than reason, and others

1

said that it is reason itself, not as reason but as nature.⁶ In order to make this clear, we must observe that, as we have said above,⁷ the human act of reasoning, since it is a certain movement, proceeds from the understanding of certain things—namely, those which are naturally known without any investigation on the part of reason, as from an immovable principle—and ends also at understanding, inasmuch as, by means of those principles naturally known of themselves, we judge of those things we have discovered by reasoning. Now, it is clear that, as the speculative reason argues about speculative things, so practical reason argues about practical things. Therefore, it is fitting that we have bestowed on us by nature not only speculative principles but also practical principles. Now, the first speculative principles bestowed on us by nature do not belong to a special power but to a special habit, which is called "the understanding of principles,"⁸ as the Philosopher explains. Wherefore, the first practical principles bestowed on us by nature, do not belong to a special power but to a special natural habit, which we call *synderesis*. Thus *synderesis* is said to incite to good and to murmur at evil, inasmuch as we proceed from first principles to discover and judge of what we have discovered. It is therefore clear that *synderesis* is not a power but a natural habit.

Reply Obj. 1. The division given by Jerome is taken from the variety of acts rather than the variety of powers, and various acts can belong to one power.

Reply Obj. 2. In like manner, the opposition of sensuality to *synderesis* is an opposition of acts, not of different species of one genus.

Reply Obj. 3. Those unchangeable notions are the first practical principles, concerning which no one errs, and they are attributed to reason as a power and to *synderesis* as a habit. Therefore, we judge naturally both by our reason and by *synderesis*.

THIRTEENTH ARTICLE
Is Conscience a Power?

We proceed thus to the Thirteenth Article:

Obj. 1. It would seem that conscience is a power; for Origen says that "conscience is a correcting and guiding spirit accompanying the soul, by which it is led away from evil and made to cling to good."[9] But in the soul, spirit designates a power—either the mind itself, according to the text, "Be you renewed in the spirit of your mind"[10]—or the imagination, whence imaginary vision is called spiritual, as Augustine says.[11] Therefore conscience is a power.

Obj. 2. Further, nothing is a subject of sin except a power of the soul. But conscience is a subject of sin; for it is said of some that "their mind and conscience are defiled."[12] Therefore, it seems that conscience is a power.

Obj. 3. Further, conscience must of necessity be either an act, a habit, or a power. But it is not an act, for thus it would not always exist in man. Nor is it a habit, for conscience is not one thing but many, since we are directed in our actions by many habits of knowledge. Therefore, conscience is a power.

On the contrary, Conscience can be laid aside. But a power cannot be laid aside. Therefore conscience is not a power.

I answer that, Properly speaking, conscience is not a power, but an act. This is evident both from the very name and from those things which in the common way of speaking are attributed to conscience. For conscience, according to the very nature of the word, implies the relation of knowledge to something: for conscience may be resolved into *cum alio scientia,* i.e., knowledge applied to an individual case. But the application of knowledge to something is done by some act. Wherefore, from this explanation of the name, it is clear that conscience is an act.

The same is manifest from those things which are attributed to conscience. For conscience is said to witness, to bind or incite, and also to accuse, torment, or rebuke. And all these follow the application of knowledge or science to what we do, which application is made in three ways. One way, insofar as we recognize that we have done or not done something: "Your conscience knows that you have often spoken evil of others,"[13] and according to this, conscience is said to witness. In another way, so far as through the conscience we judge that something should be done or not done, and in this sense, conscience is said to incite or to bind. In the third way, so far as by conscience we judge that something done is well done or ill done, and in this sense conscience is said to excuse, accuse, or torment. Now, it is clear that all these things follow the actual application of knowledge to what we do. Wherefore, properly speaking, conscience denominates an act. But since habit is a principle of act, sometimes the name "conscience" is given to the first natural habit—namely, *synderesis*; thus Jerome calls *synderesis* "conscience,"[14] Basil calls conscience the "natural power of judgment,"[15] and Damascene says that conscience is the "law of our intellect."[16] For it is customary for causes and effects to be called after one another.

Reply Obj. 1. Conscience is called a spirit, so far as spirit is the same as mind, because conscience is a certain pronouncement of the mind.

Reply Obj. 2. The conscience is said to be defiled, not as a subject, but as the thing known is in knowledge, so far as someone knows he is defiled.

Reply Obj. 3. Although an act does not always remain in itself, yet it always remains in its cause, which is power and habit. Now, all the habits by which conscience is formed, although many, nevertheless have their efficacy from one first habit, the habit of first principles, which is called *synderesis*. And for this special reason, this habit is sometimes called conscience, as we have said above.

ST I–II

Question 19

Of the Goodness and Malice of the Interior Act of the Will

*[In Ten Articles of Which
Articles Five and Six Are Included]*

FIFTH ARTICLE

Is the Will Evil When It Is at Variance with Erring Reason?

We proceed thus to the Fifth Article:

Obj. 1. It would seem that the will is not evil when it is at variance with erring reason. Because reason is the rule of the human will, insofar as it is derived from the eternal law, as stated above.[1] But erring reason is not derived from the eternal law. Therefore, erring reason is not the rule of the human will. Therefore, the will is not evil if it be at variance with erring reason.

Obj. 2. Further, according to Augustine, the command of a lower authority does not bind if it be contrary to the command of a higher authority; for instance, if a provincial governor command something that is forbidden by the emperor.[2] But erring reason sometimes proposes what is against the command of a higher power, namely, God, Whose power is supreme. Therefore, the decision of an erring reason does not bind. Consequently, the will is not evil if it be at variance with erring reason.

Obj. 3. Further, every evil will is reducible to some species of malice. But the will that is at variance with erring reason is not reducible to some species of malice. For instance, if a man's reason err in telling him to commit fornication, his will in not willing to do so cannot be reduced to any species of malice. Therefore, the will is not evil when it is at variance with erring reason.

On the contrary, As stated in the First Part, conscience is nothing else than the application of knowledge to some action.[3] Now knowledge is in reason. Therefore when the will is at variance with erring reason, it is against conscience. But every such will is evil; for it is written: "All that is not of faith"—i.e., all that is against conscience—"is sin".[4] Therefore, the will is evil when it is at variance with erring reason.

I answer that, Since conscience is a kind of dictate of the reason (for it is an application of knowledge to action, as was stated in the First Part[5]), to inquire whether the will is evil when it is at variance with erring reason is the same as to inquire whether an erring conscience binds. On this matter, some distinguished three kinds of actions: some are good generically; some are indifferent; some are evil generically. And they say that if reason or conscience tell us to do something which is good generically, there is no error, and in like manner, if it tell us not to do something which is evil generically; since it is the same reason that prescribes what is good and forbids what is evil. On the other hand, if a man's reason or conscience tells him that he is bound by precept to do

what is evil in itself, or that what is good in itself is forbidden, then his reason or conscience errs. In like manner, if a
man's reason or conscience tell him that what is indifferent
in itself, for instance to raise a straw from the ground, is
forbidden or commanded, his reason or conscience errs. They
say, therefore, that reason or conscience when erring in matters of indifference, either by commanding or by forbidding
them, binds, so that the will which is at variance with that
erring reason is evil and sinful. But they say that when reason
or conscience errs in commanding what is evil in itself, or in
forbidding what is good in itself and necessary for salvation,
it does not bind; wherefore, in such cases the will which is at
variance with erring reason or conscience is not evil.

But this is unreasonable. For in matters of indifference, the
will that is at variance with erring reason or conscience is
evil in some way on account of the object, on which the
goodness or malice of the will depends, not indeed on account of the object according as it is in its own nature but as
it is accidentally apprehended by reason as something evil to
do or to avoid. And since the object of the will is that which
is proposed by reason, as stated above,[6] from the very fact
that a thing is proposed by reason as being evil, the will by
tending thereto becomes evil. And this is the case not only in
indifferent matters but also in those that are good or evil in
themselves. For not only indifferent matters can receive the
character of goodness or malice accidentally, but also that
which is good can receive the character of evil, or that which
is evil can receive the character of goodness, on account of
reason apprehending it as such. For instance, to refrain from
fornication is good, yet the will does not tend to this good
except insofar as it is proposed by the reason. If, therefore,
erring reason propose it as an evil, the will tends to it as to
something evil. Consequently, the will is evil because it wills
evil, not indeed that which is evil in itself, but that which is
evil accidentally, through being apprehended as such by reason. In like manner, to believe in Christ is good in itself and
necessary for salvation, but the will does not tend thereto,
except inasmuch as it is proposed by reason. Consequently if
it be proposed by reason as something evil, the will tends to
it as to something evil, not as if it were evil in itself, but
because it is evil accidentally, through the apprehension of

reason. Hence, the Philosopher says that "properly speaking, the incontinent man is one who does not follow right reason, but accidentally, he is also one who does not follow false reason."[7] We must, therefore, conclude that, absolutely speaking, every will at variance with reason, whether right or erring, is always evil.

Reply Obj. 1. Although the judgment of an erring reason is not derived from God, yet the erring reason puts forward its judgment as being true, and consequently as being derived from God, from Whom is all truth.

Reply Obj. 2. The saying of Augustine holds good when it is known that the inferior authority prescribes something contrary to the command of the higher authority. But if a man were to believe the command of the proconsul to be the command of the emperor, in scorning the command of the proconsul he would scorn the command of the emperor. In like manner, if a man were to know that human reason was dictating something contrary to God's commandment, he would not be bound to abide by reason; but then reason would not be entirely erroneous. But when erring reason proposes something as being commanded by God, then to scorn the dictate of reason is to scorn the commandment of God.

Reply Obj. 3. Whenever reason apprehends something as evil, it apprehends it under some species of evil, for instance, as being something contrary to a divine precept, or as giving scandal, or for some such like reason. And then that evil is reduced to that species of malice.

SIXTH ARTICLE
Is the Will Good When It Abides by Erring Reason?

We proceed thus to the Sixth Article:

Obj. 1. It would seem that the will is good when it abides by erring reason. For just as the will, when at variance with reason, tends to that which reason judges to be evil, so, when in accord with reason, it tends to what reason judges to be good. But the will is evil when it is at variance with reason, even when erring. Therefore, even when it abides by erring reason, the will is good.

Obj. 2. Further, the will is always good when it abides by the commandment of God and the eternal law. But the eternal law and God's commandment are proposed to us by the apprehension of reason, even when it errs. Therefore, the will is good, even when it abides by erring reason.

Obj. 3. Further, the will is evil when it is at variance with erring reason. If, therefore, the will is evil also when it abides by erring reason, it seems that the will is always evil when in conjunction with erring reason, so that in such a case a man would be in a dilemma and, of necessity, would sin, which is unreasonable. Therefore, the will is good when it abides by erring reason.

On the contrary, The will of those who slew the apostles was evil. And yet it was in accord with erring reason, according to Jn.:[8] "The hour comes that whosoever kills you will think that he does a service to God." Therefore, the will can be evil when it abides by erring reason.

I answer that, Whereas the previous question is the same as inquiring whether an erring conscience binds, so this question is the same as inquiring whether an erring conscience excuses. Now, this question depends on what has been said about ignorance.[9] For it was said that ignorance sometimes causes an act to be involuntary and sometimes not. And since moral good and evil consist in action insofar as it is voluntary, as was stated above,[10] it is evident that when ignorance causes an act to be involuntary, it takes away the character of moral good and evil, but not when it does not cause the act to be involuntary. Again, it has been stated above that when ignorance is in any way willed, either directly or indirectly, it does not cause the act to be involuntary.[11] And I call that ignorance directly voluntary to which the act of the will tends, and that indirectly voluntary which is due to negligence, by reason of a man not wishing to know what he ought to know, as stated above.[12]

If then reason or conscience err with an error that is voluntary, either directly or through negligence, so that one errs about what one ought to know, then such an error of reason or conscience does not excuse the will that abides by that erring reason or conscience from being evil. But if the error arises from ignorance of some circumstance and without any negligence, so that it cause the act to be involuntary, then that error of reason or conscience excuses the will that abides by that erring reason from being evil. For instance, if erring reason tell a man that he should have intercourse with another man's wife, the will that abides by that erring reason is evil, since this error arises from ignorance of the divine law, which he is bound to know. But if a man's reason errs in mistaking another for his wife, and if he wishes to give her her right when she asks for it, his will is excused from being evil because this error arises from ignorance of a circumstance, which ignorance excuses and causes the act to be involuntary.

Reply Obj. 1. As Dionysius says, "Good results from the entire cause, evil from each particular defect."[13] Consequently, in order that the thing to which the will tends be called evil, it suffices either that it be evil in itself or that it be apprehended as evil. But in order for it to be good, it must be good in both ways.

Reply Obj. 2. The eternal law cannot err, but human reason can. Consequently, the will that abides by human reason is not always right, nor is it always in accord with the eternal law.

Reply Obj. 3. Just as in syllogistic arguments, granted one absurdity, others must needs follow, so in moral matters, given one absurdity, others must follow too. Thus suppose a man to seek vainglory, he will sin, whether he does his duty for vainglory or whether he omit to do it. Nor is he in a dilemma about the matter, because he can put aside his evil intention. In like manner, suppose a man's reason or conscience to err through inexcusable ignorance, then evil must needs result in the will. Nor is this man in a dilemma, because he can lay aside his error, since his ignorance is vincible and voluntary.

Notes to Chapter 1
ST I, Q. 79, AA. 12–13

1. *In Ezech.* I, 1, 10. PL 25, 22.

2. *De Trin.* XII, 12. PL 42, 1007.

3. *De lib. arb.* II, 10. PL 32, 1256.

4. *De Trin.* XII, 2. PL 42, 999.

5. *Metaph.* IX, 2. 1046b4.

6. Cf. *Summa* II, Q. 73.

7. A. 8.

8. *Eth.* VI, 6. 1140b3–1141a8.

9. *Commentary* on Rom. 2:15. PG 14, 893.

10. Eph. 4:13.

11. *Gen. ad lit.* XII, 7, 24. PL 34, 459 and 475.

12. Tit. 1:15.

13. Ec. 7:23.

14. *In Ezech.*, on 1:6. PL 25, 22.

15. *Hom. in princ. Proverb.* PG 31, 405.

16. *De fide orth.* IV, 22. PG 94, 1200.

ST I–II, Q. 19, AA. 5–6

1. A. 4.

2. *Sermones ad populum.* 8. PL 38, 421.

3. Q. 79, A. 13.

4. Rom. 14:23.

5. Q. 79, A. 13.

6. A. 3.

7. Aristotle, *Eth* VIII, 9. 1151a33.

8. 16:2.

9. I–II, Q. 6, A. 8.

10. A. 2.

11. I–II, Q. 6, A. 8.

12. Ibid.

13. *Div. nom.* IV. PG 63, 729.

2
Law

ST I–II

Question 90
Of the Essence of Law

[In Four Articles]

We have now to consider the extrinsic principles of acts. Now the extrinsic principle inclining to evil is the devil, of whose temptations we have spoken in the First Part.[1] But the extrinsic principle moving to good is God, Who both instructs us by means of His law and assists us by His grace; wherefore, in the first place, we must speak of law; in the second place, of grace.

Concerning law, we must consider (1) law itself in general; (2) its parts. Concerning law in general, three points offer themselves for our consideration: (1) its essence; (2) the different kinds of law; (3) the effects of law.

Under the first head, there are four points of inquiry: (1) Whether law is something pertaining to reason? (2) concerning the end of law; (3) its cause; (4) the promulgation of law.

FIRST ARTICLE
Is Law Something Pertaining to Reason?

We proceed thus to the First Article:

Objection 1. It would seem that law is not something pertaining to reason. For the Apostle says: "I see another law in my members," etc.[2] But nothing pertaining to reason is in the members, since the reason does not make use of a bodily organ. Therefore, law is not something pertaining to reason.

Obj. 2. Further, in the reason there is nothing else but power, habit, and act. But law is not the power itself of reason. In like manner, neither is it a habit of reason, because the habits of reason are the intellectual virtues of which we have spoken above.[3] Nor, again, is it an act of reason because then law would cease when the act of reason ceases, for instance,

11

while we are asleep. Therefore, law is nothing pertaining to reason.

Obj. 3. Further, the law moves those who are subject to it to act aright. But it belongs properly to the will to move to act, as is evident from what has been said above.[4] Therefore, law pertains not to the reason but to the will, according to the words of the Jurist: "Whatever pleases the ruler has the force of law."[5]

On the contrary, It belongs to the law to command and to forbid. But it belongs to reason to command, as stated above.[6] Therefore, law is something pertaining to reason.

I answer that Law is a certain rule and measure of acts whereby man is induced to act or is restrained from acting; for *lex* (law) is derived from *ligare* (to bind) because it binds one to act. Now the rule and measure of human acts is reason, which is the first principle of human acts, as is evident from what has been stated above,[7] since it belongs to reason to direct to the end, which is the first principle in all matters of action, according to the Philosopher.[8] Now, that which is the principle in any genus is the rule and measure of that genus, for instance, unity in the genus of numbers, and the first movement in the genus of movements. Consequently, it follows that law is something pertaining to reason.

Reply Obj. 1. Since law is a kind of rule and measure, it may be in something in two ways. First, as in that which measures and rules; and since this is proper to reason, it follows that, in this way, law is in reason alone. Second, as in that which is measured and ruled. In this way, law is in all those things that are inclined to something by reason of some law, so that any inclination arising from a law may be called a law, not essentially but by participation as it were. And thus the inclination of the members to concupiscence is called "the law of the members."

Reply Obj. 2. Just as, in external action, we may consider the work and the work done—for instance, the work of building and the house built, so in the acts of reason we may consider the act itself of reason, i.e., to understand and to reason, and something produced by this act. With regard to the speculative reason, this is first of all the definition; secondly, the proposition; thirdly, the syllogism or argument. And since also the practical reason makes use of a kind of syllogism in respect to the work to be done, as stated above[9] and as the Philosopher teaches,[10] hence we find in the practical reason something that holds the same position in regard to operations as, in the speculative intellect, the proposition holds in regard to conclusions. Suchlike universal propositions of the practical intellect that are directed to actions have the nature of law. And these propositions are sometimes under our actual consideration, while sometimes they are retained in the reason by means of a habit.

Reply Obj. 3. Reason has its power of moving from the will, as stated above,[11] for it is due to the fact that one wills the end that the reason issues its commands as regards things ordained to the end. But in order that the volition of what is commanded may have the nature of law, it needs to be in accord with some rule of reason. And in this sense is to be understood the saying that the will of the ruler has the force of law; otherwise, the ruler's will would savor of lawlessness rather than of law.

SECOND ARTICLE
Is the Law Always Directed to the Common Good?

We proceed thus to the Second Article:

Obj. 1. It would seem that the law is not always directed to the common good as to its end. For it belongs to law to command and to forbid. But commands are directed to certain individual goods. Therefore, the end of the law is not always the common good.

Obj. 2. Further, the law directs man in his actions. But human actions are concerned with particular matters. Therefore, the law is directed to some particular good.

Obj. 3. Further, Isidore says, "If the law is based on reason, whatever is based on reason will be a law."[12] But reason is the foundation not only of what is ordained to the common good but also of that which is directed to private good. Therefore, the law is not only directed to the common good but also to the private good of an individual.

On the contrary, Isidore says that "Laws are enacted for no private profit but for the common benefit of the citizens."[13]

I answer that, As stated above, the law belongs to that

which is a principle of human acts because it is their rule and measure.[14] Now, as reason is a principle of human acts, so in reason itself there is something which is the principle in respect of all the rest; wherefore to this principle chiefly and mainly law must needs be referred. Now the first principle in practical matters, which are the object of the practical reason, is the last end, and the last end of human life is bliss or happiness, as stated above.[15] Consequently, the law must needs regard principally the relationship to happiness. Moreover, since every part is ordained to the whole as imperfect to perfect, and since a single man is a part of the perfect community, the law must needs regard properly the relationship to universal happiness. Wherefore the Philosopher, in the above definition of legal matters, mentions both happiness and the body politic, for he says that we call those legal matters just "which are adapted to produce and preserve happiness and its parts for the body politic"[16] since the political community is a perfect community, as he says in *Politics* I, 1.[17]

Now, in every genus, that which belongs to it most of all is the principle of the others, and the others belong to that genus in subordination to that thing; thus fire, which is chief among hot things, is the cause of heat in mixed bodies, and these are said to be hot insofar as they have a share of fire. Consequently, since the law is chiefly ordained to the common good, any other precept in regard to some individual work must needs be devoid of the nature of a law, save insofar as it is ordered to the common good. Therefore, every law is ordained to the common good.

Reply Obj. 1. A command denotes an application of a law to matters regulated by the law. Now the order to the common good, at which the law aims, is applicable to particular ends. And in this way, commands are given even concerning particular matters.

Reply Obj. 2. Actions are indeed concerned with particular matters, but those particular matters are referable to the common good, not as to a common genus or species, but as to a common final cause, according as the common good is said to be the common end.

Reply Obj. 3. Just as nothing stands firm with regard to the speculative reason except that which is traced back to the first indemonstrable principles, so nothing stands firm with regard to the practical reason unless it be directed to the last end which is the common good, and whatever stands to reason in this sense has the nature of a law.

THIRD ARTICLE

Is the Reason of Any Person Competent to Make Laws?

We proceed thus to the Third Article:

Obj. 1. It would seem that the reason of any person is competent to make laws. For the Apostle says that "when the Gentiles, who have not the law, do by nature those things that are of the law, . . . they are a law to themselves."[18] Now he says this of all in general. Therefore, anyone can make a law for himself.

Obj. 2. Further, as the Philosopher says, "The intention of the lawgiver is to lead men to virtue."[19] But every man can lead another to virtue. Therefore, the reason of any man is competent to make laws.

Obj. 3. Further, just as the ruler of a political community governs the political community, so every father of a family governs his household. But the ruler of a political community can make laws for the political community. Therefore, every father of a family can make laws for his household.

On the contrary, Isidore says, "A law is an ordinance of the people, whereby something is sanctioned by nobles together with commoners."[20] Not everyone, therefore, is competent to make law.

I answer that Law, properly speaking, regards first and chiefly an ordering to the common good. Now to order anything to the common good belongs either to the whole people or to someone who is the vicegerent of the whole people. And, therefore, the making of law belongs either to the whole people or to a public personage who has care of the whole people, since, in all other matters, the directing of anything to the end concerns him to whom the end belongs.

Reply Obj. 1. As stated above, law is in a person not only as in one that rules but also by participation as in one that is ruled.[21] In the latter way, each one is a law to himself, insofar as he shares the direction that he receives from one who rules him. Hence the same text goes on, "who show the work of the law written in their hearts."

Reply Obj. 2. A private person cannot lead another to virtue efficaciously, for he can only advise, and if his advice be not taken, it has no coercive power, such as the law should have in order to prove an efficacious inducement to virtue, as the Philosopher says.[22] But this coercive power is vested in the whole people or in some public personage to whom it belongs to inflict penalties, as we shall state further on.[23] Wherefore, the framing of laws belongs to him alone.

Reply Obj. 3. As one man is a part of the household, so a household is a part of the political community, and the political community is a perfect community, according to *Politics* I, 1.[24] And, therefore, as the good of one man is not the last end but is ordained to the common good, so too the good of one household is ordained to the good of a single political community, which is a perfect community. Consequently, he that governs a family can indeed make certain commands or ordinances but not such as to have properly the nature of law.

FOURTH ARTICLE
Is Promulgation Essential to a Law?

We proceed thus to the Fourth Article:

Obj. 1. It would seem that promulgation is not essential to a law. For the natural law above all has the nature of law. But the natural law needs no promulgation. Therefore, it is not essential to a law that it be promulgated.

Obj. 2. Further, it belongs properly to a law to bind one to do or not to do something. But the obligation of fulfilling a law touches not only those in whose presence it is promulgated but also others. Therefore, promulgation is not essential to a law.

Obj. 3. Further, the obligation of a law extends even to the future since "laws are binding in matters of the future," as the jurists say.[25] But promulgation is made to those who are present. Therefore, it is not essential to a law.

On the contrary, It is laid down in the *Decretum,* dist. 4, that "Laws are established when they are promulgated."

I answer that, As stated above, a law is imposed on others by way of a rule and measure.[26] Now a rule or measure is imposed by being applied to those who are to be ruled and measured by it. Wherefore, in order that a law obtain the binding force which is proper to a law, it must needs be applied to the men who have to be ruled by it. Such application is made by its being notified to them by promulgation. Wherefore promulgation is necessary for the law to obtain its force.

Thus, from the four preceding articles, the definition of law may be gathered, and it is nothing else than a certain ordinance of reason for the common good, made by him who has care of the community, and promulgated.

Reply Obj. 1. The natural law is promulgated by the very fact that God instilled it into men's minds so as to be known by them naturally.

Reply Obj. 2. Those who are not present when a law is promulgated are bound to observe the law, insofar as it is notified or can be notified to them by others after it has been promulgated.

Reply Obj. 3. The promulgation that takes place now extends to future time by reason of the durability of written characters, by which means it is continually promulgated. Hence Isidore says that "*lex* (law) is derived from *legere* (to read) because it is written."[27]

Question 91
Of the Various Kinds of Law

[In Six Articles]

We must now consider the various kinds of law, under which head there are six points of inquiry: (1) Whether there is an eternal law? (2) Whether there is a natural law? (3) Whether there is a human law? (4) Whether there is a divine law? (5) Whether there is one divine law or several? (6) Whether there is a law of sin?

FIRST ARTICLE

Is There an Eternal Law?

We proceed thus to the First Article:

Obj. 1. It would seem that there is no eternal law because every law is imposed on someone. But there was not someone from eternity on whom a law could be imposed since God alone was from eternity. Therefore, no law is eternal.

Obj. 2. Further, promulgation is essential to law. But promulgation could not be from eternity because there was no one to whom it could be promulgated from eternity. Therefore, no law can be eternal.

Obj. 3. Further, a law implies order to an end. But nothing ordained to an end is eternal, for the last end alone is eternal. Therefore, no law is eternal.

On the contrary, Augustine says, "That law which is the supreme reason cannot be understood to be otherwise than unchangeable and eternal."[1]

I answer that, As stated above, a law is nothing else but a dictate of practical reason in the ruler who governs a perfect community.[2] Now it is evident, granted that the world is ruled by divine providence, as was stated in the First Part,[3] that the whole community of the universe is governed by divine reason. Wherefore, the very idea of the government of things in God the Ruler of the universe has the nature of a law. And since the divine reason's conception of things is not subject to time but is eternal, according to Pr. 8:23, therefore it is that this kind of law must be called eternal.

Reply Obj. 1. Those things that are not in themselves exist with God inasmuch as they are foreknown and preordained by Him, according to Rom. 4:17, "Who calls those things that are not, as those that are." Accordingly, the eternal concept of the divine law bears the nature of an eternal law insofar as it is ordained by God to the government of things foreknown by Him.

Reply Obj. 2. Promulgation is made by word of mouth or in writing, and in both ways the eternal law is promulgated, because both the divine word and the writing of the Book of Life are eternal. But the promulgation cannot be from eternity on the part of the creature that hears or reads.

Reply Obj. 3. The law implies order to an end actively, insofar as it directs certain things to an end, but not passively—that is to say, the law itself is not ordained to an end—except accidentally, in a governor whose end is extrinsic to him, and to which end his law must needs be ordained. But the end of the divine government is God Himself, and His law is not distinct from Himself. Wherefore the eternal law is not ordained to another end.

SECOND ARTICLE

Is There a Natural Law in Us?

We proceed thus to the Second Article:

Obj. 1. It would seem that there is no natural law in us because man is governed sufficiently by the eternal law; for Augustine says that "the eternal law is that by which it is right that all things should be most orderly."[4] But nature does not abound in superfluities, as neither does it fail in necessaries. Therefore, there is no natural law in man.

Obj. 2. Further, by the law man is directed in his acts to the end, as stated above.[5] But the directing of human acts to their end is not by nature, as is the case in irrational creatures, which act for an end solely by their natural appetite, whereas man acts for an end by his reason and will. Therefore, there is no natural law for man.

Obj. 3. Further, the more a man is free, the less is he under the law. But man is freer than all other animals on account of his free will, with which he is endowed above all other animals. Since, therefore, other animals are not subject to a natural law, neither is man subject to a natural law.

On the contrary, A gloss on Rom. 2:14 ("When the Gentiles, who have not the law, do by nature those things that are of the law") comments as follows: "Although they have no written law, yet they have the natural law, whereby each one knows, and is conscious of, what is good and what is evil."[6]

I answer that, As stated above, law, being a rule and measure, can be in a person in two ways: in one way, as in him that rules and measures; in another way, as in that which is ruled and measured, since a thing is ruled and measured insofar as it partakes of the rule or measure.[7] Wherefore, since all things subject to divine providence are ruled and measured by the eternal law, as was stated above,[8] it is evident that all things partake somewhat of the eternal law insofar as, namely, from its being imprinted on them, they derive their respective inclinations to their proper acts and ends. Now among all others, the rational creature is subject to divine providence in a more excellent way, insofar as it partakes of a share of providence, by being provident both for itself and for others. Wherefore it has a share of the eternal reason, whereby it has a natural inclination to its proper act and end, and this participation of the eternal law in the rational creature is called the natural law. Hence the Psalmist, after saying "offer up the sacrifice of justice," as though someone asked what the works of justice are, adds: "Many say, 'Who shows us good things?'," in answer to which question he says: "The light of Your countenance, O Lord, is signed upon us"[9]; thus implying that the light of natural reason, whereby we discern what is good and what is evil, which pertains to the natural law, is nothing else than an imprint on us of the divine light. It is therefore evident that the natural law is nothing else than the rational creature's participation of the eternal law.

Reply Obj. 1. This argument would hold if the natural law were something different from the eternal law, whereas it is nothing but a participation thereof, as stated above.

Reply Obj. 2. Every act of reason and will in us is derived from that which is according to nature, as stated above;[10] for every act of reasoning is based on principles that are known naturally, and every act of appetite in respect of the means is derived from the natural appetite in respect of the last end. Accordingly, the first direction of our acts to their end must needs be in virtue of the natural law.

Reply Obj. 3. Even irrational animals partake in their own way of the eternal reason, just as the rational creature does. But because the rational creature partakes thereof in an intellectual and rational manner, therefore the participation of the eternal law in the rational creature is properly called a law, since a law is something pertaining to reason, as stated above.[11] Irrational creatures, however, do not partake thereof in a rational manner; wherefore, there is no participation of the eternal law in them, except by way of similitude.

THIRD ARTICLE

Is There a Human Law?

We proceed thus to the Third Article:

Obj. 1. It would seem that there is not a human law. For the natural law is a participation of the eternal law, as stated above.[12] Now, through the eternal law, "all things are most orderly," as Augustine states.[13] Therefore, the natural law suffices for the ordering of all human affairs. Consequently, there is no need for a human law.

Obj. 2. Further, a law has the nature of a measure, as stated above.[14] But human reason is not a measure of things, but vice versa, as stated in *Metaphysics* IX, 1.[15] Therefore, no law can emanate from human reason.

Obj. 3. Further, a measure should be most certain, as stated in *Metaphysics* 10. But the dictates of human reason in matters of conduct are uncertain, according to Wisdom 9:14: "The thoughts of mortal men are fearful, and our counsels uncertain." Therefore, no law can emanate from human reason.

On the contrary, Augustine distinguishes two kinds of law: the one eternal; the other temporal, which he calls human.[16]

I answer that, As stated above, a law is a certain dictate of practical reason.[17] Now it is to be observed that the same procedure takes place in the practical and in the speculative reason, for each proceeds from principles to conclusions, as stated above (ibid.). Accordingly, we conclude that just as, in the speculative reason, from naturally know indemonstrable principles we draw the conclusions of the various sciences, the knowledge of which is not imparted to us by nature but acquired by the efforts of reason, so too it is from the precepts of the natural law, as from general and indemonstrable principles, that the human reason needs to proceed to certain particular determinations of the laws. These particular determinations, devised by human reason, are called human laws, provided the other essential conditions of law be observed, as stated above.[18] Wherefore, Tully says in his *Rhetoric* that "justice has its source in nature; thence certain things came into custom by reason of their utility; afterward these things which emanated from nature and were approved by custom were sanctioned by fear and reverence for the law."[19]

Reply Obj. 1. The human reason cannot have a full participation of the dictate of the divine reason but according to its
own mode and imperfectly. Consequently, as on the part of
the speculative reason, by a natural participation of divine
wisdom, there is in us the knowledge of certain general principles but not proper knowledge of each single truth, such as
that contained in the divine wisdom, so too on the part of the
practical reason, man has a natural participation of the eternal law according to certain general principles but not as
regards the particular determinations of individual cases,
which are, however, contained in the eternal law. Hence the
need for human reason to proceed further to particular legal
sanctions.

Reply Obj. 2. Human reason is not of itself the rule of
things, but the principles impressed on it by nature are general rules and measures of all things relating to human conduct, whereof the natural reason is the rule and measure,
although it is not the measure of things that are from nature.

Reply Obj. 3. The practical reason is concerned with practical matters, which are singular and contingent, but not with
necessary things, with which the speculative reason is concerned. Wherefore human laws cannot have that inerrancy
that belongs to the demonstrated conclusions of sciences.
Nor is it necessary for every measure to be altogether unerr-
ing and certain but according as it is possible in its own
particular genus.

FOURTH ARTICLE
Was There Any Need for a Divine Law?

We proceed thus to the Fourth Article:

Obj. 1. It would seem that there was no need for a divine
law because, as stated above, the natural law is a participation in us of the eternal law.[20] But the eternal law is a divine
law, as stated above.[21] Therefore, there is no need for a divine
law in addition to the natural law and human laws derived
therefrom.

Obj. 2. Further, it is written that "God left man in the hand
of his own counsel."[22] Now counsel is an act of reason, as

stated above.[23] Therefore, man was left to the direction of his reason. But a dictate of human reason is a human law, as stated above.[24] Therefore, there is no need for man to be governed also by a divine law.

Obj. 3. Further, human nature is more self-sufficing than irrational creatures. But irrational creatures have no divine law besides the natural inclination impressed on them. Much less, therefore, should the rational creature have a divine law in addition to the natural law.

On the contrary, David prayed God to set His law before him, saying: "Set before me for a law the way of Your justifications, O Lord."[25]

I answer that, Besides the natural and the human law, it was necessary for the directing of human life to have a divine law. And this for four reasons. First, because it is by law that man is directed how to perform his proper acts in view of his last end. And, indeed, if man were ordained to no other end than that which is proportionate to his natural faculty, there would be no need for man to have any further direction on the part of his reason beyond the natural law and human law which is derived from it. But since man is ordained to an end of eternal happiness which is inproportionate to man's natural faculty, as stated above,[26] therefore it was necessary that, besides the natural and the human law, man should be directed to his end by a law given by God.

Secondly, because, on account of the uncertainty of human judgment, especially on contingent and particular matters, different people form different judgments on human acts, whence also different and contrary laws result. In order, therefore, that man may know without any doubt what he ought to do and what he ought to avoid, it was necessary for man to be directed in his proper acts by a law given by God, for it is certain that such a law cannot err.

Thirdly, because man can make laws in those matters of which he is competent to judge. But man is not competent to judge of interior movements that are hidden but only of exterior acts which appear, and yet, for the perfection of virtue, it is necessary for man to conduct himself aright in both kinds of acts. Consequently, human law could not sufficiently curb and direct interior acts, and it was necessary for this purpose that a divine law should supervene.

Fourthly, because, as Augustine says, human law cannot punish or forbid all evil deeds, since, while aiming at doing away with all evils, it would do away with many good things and would hinder the advance of the common good, which is necessary for human intercourse.[27] In order, therefore, that no evil might remain unforbidden and unpunished, it was necessary for the divine law to supervene, whereby all sins are forbidden.

And these four causes are touched upon in Ps. 118:8, where it is said: "The law of the Lord is unspotted," i.e., allowing no foulness of sin, "converting souls" because it directs not only exterior but also interior acts, "the testimony of the Lord is faithful" because of the certainty of what is true and right, "giving wisdom to little ones" by directing man to an end supernatural and divine.

Reply Obj. 1. By natural law, the eternal law is participated in in proportion to the capacity of human nature. But to his supernatural end, man needs to be directed in a yet higher way. Hence the additional law given by God whereby man shares more perfectly in the eternal law.

Reply Obj. 2. Counsel is a kind of inquiry; hence it must proceed from some principles. Nor is it enough for it to proceed from principles imparted by nature, which are the precepts of the natural law, for the reasons given above, but there is need for certain additional principles, namely, the precepts of the divine law.

Reply Obj. 3. Irrational creatures are not ordained to an end higher than that which is proportionate to their natural powers; consequently, the comparison fails.

FIFTH ARTICLE
Is There But One Divine Law?

We proceed thus to the Fifth Article:

Obj. 1. It would seem that there is but one divine law because, where there is one king in one kingdom, there is but one law. Now the whole of mankind is compared to God as to one king, according to Ps. 46:8: "God is the King of all the earth." Therefore, there is but one divine law.

Obj. 2. Further, every law is directed to the end which the lawgiver intends for those for whom he makes the law. But God intends one and the same thing for all men, since, according to 1 Tim. 2:4, "He will have all men to be saved and to come to the knowledge of the truth." Therefore, there is but one divine law.

Obj. 3. Further, the divine law seems to be closer to the eternal law, which is one, than the natural law, according as the revelation of grace is of a higher order than natural knowledge. Therefore, much more is the divine law only one.

On the contrary, The Apostle says, "The priesthood being translated, it is necessary that a translation also be made of the law."[28] But the priesthood is twofold, as stated in the same passage, viz., the levitical priesthood and the priest-, hood of Christ. Therefore, the divine law is twofold, namely, the Old Law and the New Law.

I answer that, As stated in the First Part, distinction is the cause of number.[29] Now, things may be distinguished in two ways. First, as those things that are altogether specifically different, e.g., a horse and an ox. Secondly, as perfect and imperfect in the same species, e.g., a boy and a man, and in this way the divine law is divided into Old and New. Hence the Apostle compares the state of man under the Old Law to that of a child "under a pedagogue" but the state under the New Law to that of a full-grown man who is "no longer under a pedagogue."[30]

Now the perfection and imperfection of these two laws is to be taken in connection with the three conditions pertaining to law, as stated above. For, in the first place, it belongs to law to be directed to the common good as to its end, as stated above.[31] This good may be twofold. It may be a sensible and earthly good, and to this, man was directly ordained by the Old Law; wherefore, at the very outset of the law, the people were invited to the earthly kingdom of the Canaanites.[32] Again, it may be an intelligible and heavenly good, and to this man is ordained by the New Law. Wherefore, at the very beginning of His preaching, Christ invited men to the kingdom of heaven, saying: "Do penance, for the kingdom of heaven is at hand."[33] Hence Augustine says that "promises of temporal goods are contained in the Old Testament, for which reason it is called old, but the promise of eternal life belongs to the New Testament."[34]

Secondly, it belongs to the law to direct human acts according to the order of righteousness,[35] wherein also the New Law surpasses the Old Law since it directs our internal acts, according to Mt. 5:20: "Unless your justice abound more than that of the Scribes and Pharisees, you shall not enter into the kingdom of heaven." Hence the saying that "the Old Law restrains the hand, but the New Law controls the mind."[36]

Thirdly, it belongs to the law to induce men to observe its commandments. This the Old Law did by the fear of punishment, but the New Law by love, which is poured into our hearts by the grace of Christ bestowed in the New Law but foreshadowed in the Old. Hence Augustine says that "there is little difference between the Law and the Gospel—fear and love."[37]

Reply Obj. 1. As the father of a family issues different commands to children and to adults, so also the one King, God, in His one kingdom, gave one law to men while they were yet imperfect and another more perfect law when, by the preceding law, they had been led to a greater capacity for divine things.

Reply Obj. 2. The salvation of man could not be achieved otherwise than through Christ, according to Acts 4:12: "There is no other name . . . given to men whereby we must be saved." Consequently, the law that brings all to salvation could not be given perfectly until after the coming of Christ. But, before His coming, it was necessary to give to the people of whom Christ was to be born a law containing certain rudiments of righteousness unto salvation in order to prepare them to receive Him.

Reply Obj. 3. The natural law directs man by way of certain general precepts common to both the perfect and the imperfect; wherefore it is one and the same for all. But the divine law directs man also in certain particular matters to which the perfect and imperfect do not stand in the same relation. Hence the necessity for the divine law to be twofold, as already explained.

SIXTH ARTICLE

Is There a Law of Concupiscence (*Fomes*)?[38]

We proceed thus to the Sixth Article:

Obj. 1. It would seem that there is no law of concupiscence. For Isidore says that the "law is based on reason."[39] But concupiscence is not based on reason but deviates from it. Therefore, concupiscence has not the nature of a law.

Obj. 2. Further, every law is binding, so that those who do not obey it are called transgressors. But man is not called a transgressor from not following the instigations of concupiscence but rather from his following them. Therefore, concupiscence has not the nature of a law.

Obj. 3. Further, the law is ordained to the common good, as stated above.[40] But concupiscence inclines us, not to the common good, but to our own private good. Therefore, concupiscence does not have the nature of a law.

On the contrary, The Apostle says, "I see another law in my members fighting against the law of my mind."[41]

I answer that, As stated above,[42] the law, as to its essence, resides in him that rules and measures, but, by way of participation, in that which is ruled and measured, so that every inclination or ordination which may be found in things subject to the law is called a law by participation, as stated above (ibid.). Now those who are subject to a law may receive a twofold inclination from the lawgiver. First, insofar as he directly inclines his subjects to something, sometimes indeed different subjects to different acts; in this way, we may say that there is a military law and a mercantile law. Secondly, indirectly; thus by the very fact that a lawgiver deprives a subject of some dignity, the latter passes into another order so as to be under another law, as it were; thus if a soldier is discharged from the army, he becomes a subject of rural or mercantile legislation.

Accordingly, under the divine lawgiver, various creatures have various natural inclinations, so that what is, as it were, a law for one is against the law for another; thus I might say that fierceness is, in a way, the law of a dog but against the law of a sheep or another meek animal. And so the law of man, which, by the divine ordinance, is allotted to him according to his proper condition, is that he should act in accordance with reason, and this law was so effective in the first state that nothing either beside or against reason could take man unawares. But when man turned his back on God, he fell under the influence of his sensual impulses—in fact, this happens to each one individually the more he deviates from the path of reason—so that, after a fashion, he is likened to the beasts that are led by the impulse of sensuality, according to Ps. 58:21: "Man, when he was in honor, did not understand; he has been compared to senseless beasts and made like to them."

So, then, this very inclination of sensuality, which is called concupiscence, in other animals has simply the nature of a law (yet only insofar as a law may be said to be in such things) by reason of a direct inclination. But in man, it has not the nature of law in this way; rather is it a deviation from the law of reason. But since, by divine justice, man is destitute of original justice, and his reason bereft of its vigor, this impulse of sensuality whereby he is led, insofar as it is a penalty following from the divine law depriving man of his proper dignity, has the nature of a law.

Reply Obj. 1. This argument considers concupiscence in itself as an incentive to evil. It is not thus that it has the nature of a law, as stated above, but according as it results from the justice of the divine law; it is as though we were to say that the law allows a nobleman to be condemned to servile tasks for some misdeed.

Reply Obj. 2. This argument considers law in the light of a rule or measure, for it is in this sense that those who deviate from the law become transgressors. But concupiscence is not a law in this respect but by a kind of participation, as stated above.

Reply Obj. 3. This argument considers concupiscence as to its proper inclination and not as to its origin. And yet, if the inclination of sensuality be considered as it is in other animals, thus it is ordained to the common good, namely, to the preservation of nature in the species or in the individual. And this is in man also, insofar as sensuality is subject to reason. But it is called concupiscence insofar as it strays from the order of reason.

Question 92
Of the Effects of Law

[In Two Articles]

We must now consider the effects of law, under which head there are two points of inquiry: (1) Whether an effect of law is to make men good? (2) Whether the effects of law are to command, to forbid, to permit, and to punish, as the Jurist states?[1]

FIRST ARTICLE
Is an Effect of Law to Make Men Good?

We proceed thus to the First Article:

Obj. 1. It seems that it is not an effect of law to make men good. For men are good through virtue, since virtue, as stated in *Ethics* II, 6, is "that which makes its subject good."[2] But virtue is in man from God alone, because He it is Who "works it in us without us," as we stated above in giving the definition of virtue.[3] Therefore, the law does not make men good.

Obj. 2. Further, law does not profit a man unless he obeys it. But the very fact that a man obeys a law is due to his being good. Therefore, in man, goodness is presupposed to the law. Therefore, the law does not make men good.

Obj. 3. Further, law is ordained to the common good, as stated above.[4] But some behave well in things regarding the community who behave ill in things regarding themselves. Therefore, it is not the business of the law to make men good.

Obj. 4. Further, some laws are tyrannical, as the Philosopher says.[5] But a tyrant does not intend the good of his subjects but considers only his own profit. Therefore, law does not make men good.

On the contrary, The Philosopher says that the "intention of every lawgiver is to make men good."[6]

I answer that, As stated above, a law is nothing else than a dictate of reason in the ruler by which his subjects are governed.[7] Now the virtue of any subordinate thing consists in its being well subordinated to that by which it is regulated; thus we see that the virtue of the irascible and concupisible faculties consists in their being obedient to reason, and accordingly, "the virtue of every subject consists in his being well subjected to his ruler," as the Philosopher says.[8] But every law aims at being obeyed by those who are subject to it. Consequently, it is evident that the proper effect of law is to lead its subjects to their proper virtue, and since virtue is "that which makes its subjects good," it follows that the proper effect of law is to make those to whom it is given good, either simply or in some particular respect. For if the intention of the lawgiver is fixed on true good, which is the common good regulated according to divine justice, it follows that the effect of the law is to make men good simply. If, however, the intention of the lawgiver is fixed on that which is not simply good but useful or pleasurable to himself or in opposition to divine justice, then the law does not make men good simply but in respect to that particular government. In this way, good is found even in things that are bad of themselves; thus a man is called a good robber because he works in a way that is adapted to his end.

Reply Obj. 1. Virtue is twofold, as explained above,[9] viz., acquired and infused. Now the fact of being accustomed to an action contributes to both, but in different ways; for it causes the acquired virtue, while it disposes to infused virtue and preserves and fosters it when it already exists. And since law is given for the purpose of directing human acts, as far as human acts conduce to virtue, so far does law make men good. Wherefore the Philosopher says in the second book of the *Politics* that "lawgivers make men good by habituating them to good works."[10]

Reply Obj. 2. It is not always through perfect virtue that one obeys the law, but sometimes it is through fear of punishment, and sometimes from the mere dictate of reason, which is a beginning of virtue, as stated above.[11]

Reply Obj. 3. The goodness of any part is considered in comparison with the whole; hence Augustine says that "unseemly is the part that harmonizes not with the whole."[12] Since, then, every man is a part of the political community, it is impossible that a man be good unless he be well propor-

tionate to the common good, nor can the whole be well con-
sistent unless its parts be proportionate to it. Consequently,
the common good of the political community cannot flourish
unless the citizens be virtuous, at least those whose business
it is to govern. But it is enough for the good of the community that the other citizens be so far virtuous that they obey the
commands of their rulers. Hence the Philosopher says that
"the virtue of a ruler is the same as that of a good man, but
the virtue of any common citizen is not the same as that of a
good man."[13]

Rely Obj. 4. A tyrannical law, through not being according
to reason, is not a law, absolutely speaking, but rather a
perversion of law, and yet insofar as it is something in the
nature of a law, it aims at the citizens being good. For all it
has in the nature of a law consists in its being an ordinance
made by a superior to his subjects and aims at being obeyed
by them, which is to make them good, not simply but with
respect to that particular government.

SECOND ARTICLE
Are the Acts of Law Suitably Assigned?

We proceed thus to the Second Article:
  Obj. 1. It would seem that the acts of law are not suitably
assigned as consisting in "command," "prohibition," "permission," and "punishment." For "every law is a general precept,"
as the Jurist states.[14] But command and precept are the same.
Therefore, the other three are superfluous.
  Obj. 2. Further, the effect of a law is to induce its subjects
to good, as stated above.[15] But counsel aims at a higher good
than a command does. Therefore, it belongs to law to counsel
rather than to command.
  Obj. 3. Further, just as punishment stirs a man to good
deeds, so does reward. Therefore, if to punish is reckoned an
effect of law, so also is to reward.
  Obj. 4. Further, the intention of a lawgiver is to make men
good, as stated above.[16] But he that obeys the law merely
through fear of being punished is not good, because, "although a good deed may be done through servile fear, i.e.,
fear of punishment, it is not done well," as Augustine says.[17]

Therefore, punishment is not a proper effect of law.

On the contrary, Isidore says, "Every law either permits something, as: 'A brave man may demand his reward,' or forbids something, as: 'No man may ask a consecrated virgin in marriage,' or punishes, as: 'Let him that commits a murder be put to death.' "[18]

I answer that, Just as an assertion is a dictate of reason asserting something, so is a law a dictate of reason commanding something. Now it is proper to reason to lead from one thing to another. Wherefore, just as, in demonstrative sciences, the reason leads us from certain principles to assent to the conclusion, so it induces us by some means to assent to the precept of the law.

Now the precepts of law are concerned with human acts, in which the law directs, as stated above.[19]

Again, there are three kinds of human acts; for, as stated above,[20] some acts are good generically, viz., acts of virtue, and in respect of these, the act of the law is a precept or command, for "the law commands all acts of virtue."[21] Some acts are evil generically, viz., acts of vice, and in respect of these, the law forbids. Some acts are generically indifferent, and in respect of these, the law permits; and all acts that are either not distinctly good or not distinctly bad may be called indifferent. And it is the fear of punishment that law makes use of in order to ensure obedience, in which respect punishment is an effect of law.

Reply Obj. 1. Just as to cease from evil is a kind of good, so a prohibition is a kind of precept, and accordingly, taking precept in a wide sense, every law is a kind of precept.

Reply Obj. 2. To advise is not a proper act of law but may be within the competency even of a private person, who cannot make a law. Wherefore, too, the Apostle, after giving a certain counsel says: "I speak, not the Lord."[22] Consequently, it is not reckoned as an effect of law.

Reply Obj. 3. To reward may also pertain to anyone, but to punish pertains to none but the framer of the law, by whose authority the pain is inflicted. Wherefore, to reward is not reckoned an effect of law, but only to punish.

Reply Obj. 4. From becoming accustomed to avoid evil and fulfill what is good, through fear of punishment, one is sometimes led on to do so likewise with delight and of one's own accord. Accordingly, law, even by punishing, leads men on to being good.

Question 93
Of the Eternal Law

[In Six Articles]

We must now consider each law by itself, and (1) the eternal law, (2) the natural law, (3) the human law, (4) the Old Law, (5) the New Law, which is the law of the Gospel. Of the sixth law, which is the law of concupiscence, suffice what we have said when treating of original sin.

Concerning the first, there are six points of inquiry: (1) What is the eternal law? (2) Whether it is known to all? (3) Whether every law is derived from it? (4) Whether necessary things are subject to the eternal law? (5) Whether natural contingencies are subject to the eternal law? (6) Whether all human things are subject to it?

FIRST ARTICLE
Is the Eternal Law a Sovereign Type Existing in God?

We proceed thus to the First Article:

Obj. 1. It would seem that the eternal law is not a sovereign type existing in God. For there is only one eternal law. But there are many types of things in the divine mind, for Augustine says that God "made each thing according to its type."[1] Therefore, the eternal law does not seem to be a type existing in the divine mind.

Obj. 2. Further, it is essential to a law that it be promulgated by word, as stated above.[2] But Word is a personal name in God, as stated in the First Part,[3] whereas type refers to the essence. Therefore, the eternal law is not the same as a divine type.

Obj. 3. Further, Augustine says, "We see a law above our minds, which is called truth."[4] But the law which is above our minds is the eternal law. Therefore, truth is the eternal law. But the idea of truth is not the same as the idea of a type. Therefore, the eternal law is not the same as the sovereign type.

On the contrary, Augustine says that "the eternal law is the sovereign type, to which we must always conform."[5]

I answer that, Just as in every artificer there pre-exists a type of the things that are made by his art, so too in every governor there must pre-exist the type of the order of those things that are to be done by those who are subject to his government. And just as the type of the things yet to be made by an art is called the art or exemplar of the products of that art, so too the type in him who governs the acts of his subjects has the nature of a law, provided the other conditions be present which we have mentioned above.[6] Now God, by His wisdom, is the creator of all things, in relation to which He stands as the artificer to the products of His art, as stated in the First Part.[7] Moreover, He governs all the acts and movements that are to be found in each single creature, as was also stated in the First Part.[8] Wherefore, as the type of the divine wisdom, inasmuch as by it all things are created, has the nature of art, exemplar, or idea, so the type of divine wisdom, as moving all things to their due end, has the nature of law. Accordingly, the eternal law is nothing else than the type of divine wisdom, as directing all actions and movements.

Reply Obj. 1. Augustine is speaking in that passage of the ideal types which regard the proper nature of each single thing, and consequently, in them there is a certain distinction and plurality according to their different relations to things, as stated in the First Part.[9] But law is said to direct acts by ordaining them to the common good, as stated above.[10] And things which are in themselves different may be considered as one according as they are ordained to one common thing. Wherefore the eternal law is one since it is the type of this order.

Reply Obj. 2. With regard to any sort of word, two points may be considered: viz., the word itself and that which is expressed by the word. For the spoken word is something uttered by the mouth of man and expresses that which is signified by the human word. The same applies to the human mental word, which is nothing else than something conceived by the mind, by which man expresses his thoughts mentally. So, then, in God, the Word conceived by the intel-

lect of the Father is the name of a person, but all things that
are in the Father's knowledge, whether they refer to the essence or to the persons or to the works of God are expressed
by this Word, as Augustine declares.[11] And among other
things expressed by this Word, the eternal law itself is expressed thereby. Nor does it follow that the eternal law is a
personal name in God, yet it is appropriated to the Son on
account of the kinship between type and word.

Reply Obj. 3. The types of the divine intellect do not stand
in the same relation to things as the types of the human
intellect. For the human intellect is measured by things, so
that a human concept is not true by reason of itself but by
reason of its being consonant with things, since an opinion is
true or false depending on whether a thing is or is not. But
the divine intellect is the measure of things since each thing
has so far truth in it as it represents the divine intellect, as
was stated in the First Part.[12] Consequently, the divine intellect is true in itself, and its type is truth itself.

SECOND ARTICLE
Is the Eternal Law Known to All?

We proceed thus to the Second Article:

Obj. 1. It would seem that the eternal law is not known to
all because, as the Apostle says, "the things that are of God
no man knows, but the Spirit of God."[13] But the eternal law
is a type existing in the divine mind. Therefore, it is un-
known to all save God alone.

Obj. 2. Further, as Augustine says, "the eternal law is that
by which it is right that all things should be most orderly."[14]
But all do not know how all things are most orderly. Therefore, all do not know the eternal law.

Obj. 3. Further, Augustine says that "the eternal law is not
subject to the judgment of man."[15] But according to *Ethics* I,
"Any man can judge well of what he knows."[16] Therefore, the
eternal law is not known to us.

On the contrary, Augustine says that "knowledge of the
eternal law is imprinted on us."[17]

I answer that A thing may be known in two ways: first, in
itself; secondly, in its effect, wherein some likeness of that
thing is found; thus someone not seeing the sun in its sub-

stance may know it by its rays. So, then, no one can know the eternal law as it is in itself except God and the blessed who see Him in His essence. But every rational creature knows it in its reflection, greater or less. For every knowledge of truth is a kind of reflection and participation of the eternal law, which is the unchangeable truth, as Augustine says.[18] Now, all men know the truth to a certain extent, at least as to the common principles of the natural law, and as to the others, they partake of the knowledge of truth, some more, some less, and in this respect are more or less cognizant of the eternal law.

Reply Obj. 1. We cannot know the things that are of God as they are in themselves, but they are made known to us in their effects, according to Rom. 1:20: "The invisible things of God . . . are clearly seen, being understood by the things that are made."

Reply Obj. 2. Although each one knows the eternal law according to his own capacity, in the way explained above, yet no one can comprehend it, for it cannot be made perfectly known by its effects. Therefore, it does not follow that anyone who knows the eternal law in the way aforesaid knows also the whole order of things whereby they are most orderly.

Reply Obj. 3. To judge of a thing may be understood in two ways. First, as when a cognitive power judges of its proper object, according to Job 12:11: "Does not the ear discern words, and the palate of him that eats, the taste?" It is to this kind of judgment that the Philosopher alludes when he says that "anyone can judge well of what he knows,"[19] by judging, namely, whether what is put forward is true. In another way, we speak of a superior judging of a subordinate by a kind of practical judgment as to whether he should be such and such or not. And thus none can judge of the eternal law.

THIRD ARTICLE

Is Every Law Derived from the Eternal Law?

We proceed thus to the Third Article:

Obj. 1. It would seem that not every law is derived from the eternal law. For there is a law of concupiscence, as stated above,[20] which is not derived from that divine law which is the eternal law, since thereunto pertains the "prudence of the flesh," of which the Apostle says that "it cannot be subject to the law of God."[21] Therefore, not every law is derived from the eternal law.

Obj. 2. Further, nothing unjust can be derived from the eternal law, because, as stated above, "the eternal law is that according to which it is right that all things should be most orderly."[22] But some laws are unjust, according to Is. 10:1: "Woe to them that make wicked laws." Therefore, not every law is derived from the eternal law.

Obj. 3. Further, Augustine says that "the law which is framed for ruling the people rightly permits many things which are punished by divine providence."[23] But the type of divine providence is the eternal law, as stated above.[24] Therefore, not even every good law is derived from the eternal law.

On the contrary, Divine wisdom says, "By Me kings reign, and lawgivers decree just things."[25] But the type of divine wisdom is the eternal law, as stated above.[26] Therefore, all laws proceed from the eternal law.

I answer that, As stated above,[27] law denotes a kind of plan directing acts toward an end. Now wherever there are movers ordained to one another, the power of the second mover must needs be derived from the power of the first mover, since the second mover does not move except insofar as it is moved by the first. Wherefore we observe the same in all those who govern, so that the plan of government is derived by secondary governors from the governor-in-chief; thus the plan of what is to be done in a political community flows from the king's command to his inferior administrators, and again in things of art, the plan of whatever is to be done by art flows from the chief craftsman to the undercraftsmen who work with their hands. Since, then, the eternal law is the plan of government in the Chief Governor, all the plans of government in the inferior governors must be derived from the eternal law. But these plans of inferior governors are all other laws besides the eternal law. Therefore, all laws, insofar as they partake of right reason, are derived from the eternal law. Hence Augustine says that, "in temporal law, there is nothing just and lawful but what man has drawn from the eternal law."[28]

Reply Obj. 1. Concupiscence has the nature of law in man insofar as it is a punishment resulting from divine justice, and in this respect, it is evident that it is derived from the eternal law. But insofar as it denotes a proneness to sin, it is contrary to the divine law and has not the nature of law, as stated above.[29]

Reply Obj. 2. Human law has the nature of law insofar as it partakes of right reason, and it is clear that, in this respect, it is derived from the eternal law. But insofar as it deviates from reason, it is called an unjust law and has the nature, not of law, but of violence. Nevertheless, even an unjust law, insofar as it retains some appearance of law through being framed by one who is in power, is derived from the eternal law, since all power is from the Lord God, according to Romans.[30]

Reply Obj. 3. Human law is said to permit certain things, not as approving of them, but as being unable to direct them. And many things are directed by the divine law, which human law is unable to direct, because more things are subject to a higher than to a lower cause. Hence the very fact that human law does not meddle with matters it cannot direct comes under the ordination of the eternal law. It would be different were human law to sanction what the eternal law condemns. Consequently, it does not follow that human law is not derived from the eternal law, but that it is not on a perfect equality with it.

FOURTH ARTICLE

Are Necessary and Eternal Things Subject to the Eternal Law?

We proceed thus to the Fourth Article:

Obj. 1. It would seem that necessary and eternal things are subject to the eternal law, for whatever is reasonable is subject to reason. But the divine will is reasonable, for it is just. Therefore, it is subject to reason. But the eternal law is the divine reason. Therefore, God's will is subject to the eternal law. But God's will is eternal. Therefore, eternal and necessary things are subject to the eternal law.

Obj. 2. Further, whatever is subject to the King is subject to the King's law. Now the Son, according to 1 Cor.[31] "shall be subject . . . to God the Father . . . when He shall have delivered up the Kingdom to Him." Therefore, the Son, Who is eternal, is subject to the eternal law.

Obj. 3. Further, the eternal law is divine providence as a type. But many necessary things are subject to divine providence; for instance, the stability of incorporeal substances and of the heavenly bodies. Therefore, even necessary things are subject to the eternal law.

On the contrary, Things that are necessary cannot be otherwise and consequently need no restraining. But laws are imposed on men in order to restrain them from evil, as explained above.[32] Therefore, necessary things are not subject to the law.

I answer that, As stated above, the eternal law is the type of the divine government.[33] Consequently, whatever is subject to the divine government is subject to the eternal law, while if anything is not subject to the divine government, neither is it subject to the eternal law. The application of this distinction may be gathered by looking around us. For those things are subject to human government which can be done by man, but what pertains to the nature of man is not subject to human government, for instance, that he should have a soul, hands, or feet. Accordingly, all that is in things created by God, whether it be contingent or necessary, is subject to the eternal law, while things pertaining to the divine nature or essence are not subject to the eternal law but are the eternal law itself.

Reply Obj. 1. We may speak of God's will in two ways. First, as to the will itself, and thus, since God's will is His very essence, it is subject neither to the divine government nor to the eternal law but is the same thing as the eternal law. Secondly, we may speak of God's will as to the things themselves that God wills about creatures, which things are subject to the eternal law insofar as they are planned by divine wisdom. In reference to these things, God's will is said to be reasonable, though, regarded in itself, it should rather be called their type.

Reply Obj. 2. God the Son was not made by God but was naturally born of God. Consequently, He is not subject to divine providence or to the eternal law but rather is Himself the eternal law by a kind of appropriation, as Augustine explains.[34] But He is said to be subject to the Father by reason of His human nature, in respect of which also the Father is said to be greater than He.

The Third Objection we grant, because it deals with those necessary things that are created.

Reply Obj. 4.[35] As the Philosopher says,[36] some necessary things have a cause of their necessity, and thus they derive from something else the fact that they cannot be otherwise. And this is in itself a most effective restraint, for whatever is restrained is said to be restrained insofar as it cannot do otherwise than it is allowed to.

FIFTH ARTICLE

Are Natural Contingents Subject to the Eternal Law?

We proceed thus to the Fifth Article:

Obj. 1. It would seem that natural contingents are not subject to the eternal law because promulgation is essential to law, as stated above.[37] But a law cannot be promulgated except to rational creatures to whom it is possible to make an announcement. Therefore, only rational creatures are subject to the eternal law, and consequently, natural contingents are not.

Obj. 2. Further, "Whatever obeys reason partakes somewhat of reason," as stated in *Ethics* I, 13.[38] But the eternal law is the supreme type, as stated above.[39] Since, then, natural contingents do not partake of reason in any way but are altogether void of reason, it seems that they are not subject to the eternal law.

Obj. 3. Further, the eternal law is most efficient. But, in natural contingents, defects occur. Therefore, they are not subject to the eternal law.

On the contrary, It is written: "When He compassed the sea with its bounds and set a law to the waters, that they should not pass their limits."[40]

I answer that We must speak otherwise of the law of man than of the eternal law, which is the law of God. For the law of man extends only to rational creatures subject to man. The reason of this is because law directs the actions of those that are subject to the government of someone; wherefore, properly speaking, none imposes a law on his own actions. Now, whatever is done regarding the use of irrational things subject to man is done by the act of man himself moving those things, for these irrational creatures do not move themselves but are moved by others, as stated above.[41] Consequently, man cannot impose laws on irrational beings, however much they may be subject to him. But he can impose laws on rational beings subject to him insofar as, by his command or pronouncement of any kind, he imprints on their minds a rule which is a principle of action.

Now, just as man, by such pronouncement, impresses a kind of inward principle of action on the man that is subject to him, so God imprints on the whole of nature the principles of its proper actions. And so, in this way, God is said to command the whole of nature, according to Ps. 148:6: "He has made a decree, and it shall not pass away." And thus all actions and movements of the whole of nature are subject to the eternal law. Consequently, irrational creatures are subject to the eternal law through being moved by divine providence, but not, as rational creatures are, through understanding the divine commandment.

Reply Obj. 1. The impression of an inward active principle is to natural things what the promulgation of law is to men because law, by being promulgated, imprints on man a directive principle of human actions, as stated above.

Reply Obj. 2. Irrational creatures neither partake of, nor are obedient to, human reason, whereas they do partake of the divine reason by obeying it, because the power of divine reason extends over more things than human reason does. And as the members of the human body are moved at the command of reason and yet do not partake of reason, since they have no apprehension subordinate to reason, so too irrational creatures are moved by God without on that account being rational.

Reply Obj. 3. Although the defects which occur in natural things are outside the order of particular causes, they are not outside the order of universal causes, especially of the First Cause, i.e., God, from Whose providence nothing can escape, as stated in the First Part.[42] And since the eternal law is the type of divine providence, as stated above,[43] hence the defects of natural things are subject to the eternal law.

SIXTH ARTICLE
Are All Human Affairs Subject to the Eternal Law?

We proceed thus to the Sixth Article:

Obj. 1. It would seem that not all human affairs are subject to the eternal law, for the Apostle says, "If you are led by the spirit you are not under the law."[44] But the righteous, who are the sons of God by adoption, are led by the spirit of God, according to Romans: "Whosoever are led by the Spirit of God, they are the sons of God."[45] Therefore, not all men are under the eternal law.

Obj. 2. Further, the Apostle says, "The prudence of the flesh is an enemy to God, for it is not subject to the law of God."[46] But many are those in whom the prudence of the flesh dominates. Therefore, all men are not subject to the eternal law, which is the law of God.

Obj. 3. Further, Augustine says that "the eternal law is that by which the wicked deserve misery, the good a life of blessedness."[47] But those who are already blessed, and those who are already lost, are not in the state of merit. Therefore, they are not under the eternal law.

On the contrary, Augustine says, "Nothing evades the laws of the most high Creator and Governor, for by Him the peace of the universe is administered."[48]

I answer that There are two ways in which a thing is subject to the eternal law, as explained above,[49] first, by partaking of the eternal law by way of knowledge; secondly, by way of action and passion, i.e., by partaking of the eternal law by way of an inward motive principle, and in this second way, irrational creatures are subject to the eternal law, as stated above (ibid.). But since the rational nature, together with that which it has in common with all creatures, has something proper to itself inasmuch as it is rational, consequently it is subject to the eternal law in both ways; because while each rational creature has some knowledge of the eternal law, as stated above,[50] it also has a natural inclination to that which is in harmony with the eternal law, for "we are naturally adapted to be the recipients of virtue."[51]

Both ways, however, are imperfect and to a certain extent corrupted in the wicked, because in them the natural inclination to virtue is corrupted by vicious habits, and, moreover, the natural knowledge of good is darkened by passions and habits of sin. But, in the good, both ways are found more perfect, because in them, besides the natural knowledge of good, there is the added knowledge of faith and wisdom, and again, besides the natural inclination to good, there is the added interior motive of grace and virtue.

Accordingly, the good are perfectly subject to the eternal law, as always acting according to it, whereas the wicked are subject to the eternal law imperfectly as to their actions, since both their knowledge of good and their inclination thereto are imperfect. But this imperfection on the part of action is supplied on the part of passion insofar as they suffer what the eternal law decrees concerning them, according as they fail to act in harmony with that law. Hence Augustine says, "I esteem that the righteous act according to the eternal law,"[52] and: "Out of the just misery of the souls which deserted Him, God knew how to furnish the inferior parts of His creation with most suitable laws."[53]

Reply Obj. 1. This saying of the Apostle may be understood in two ways. First, so that a man is said to be under the law through being pinned down thereby against his will, as by a load. Hence, on the same passage, a gloss says that "he is under the law who refrains from evil deeds through fear of the punishment threatened by the law and not from love of virtue."[54] In this way, the spiritual man is not under the law because he fulfills the law willingly, through charity which is poured into his heart by the Holy Spirit. Secondly, it can be understood as meaning that the works of a man who is led by the Holy Spirit are works of the Holy Spirit rather than his own. Therefore, since the Holy Spirit is not under the law, as neither is the Son, as stated above,[55] it follows that such works, insofar as they are of the Holy Spirit, are not under the law. The Apostle witnesses to this when he says, "Where the Spirit of the Lord is, there is liberty."[56]

Reply Obj. 2. The prudence of the flesh cannot be subject to the law of God as regards action since it inclines to actions contrary to the divine law; yet it is subject to the law of God as regards passion since it deserves to suffer punishment according to the law of divine justice. Nevertheless, in no man does the prudence of the flesh dominate so far as to destroy the whole good of his nature, and consequently, there remains in man the inclination to act in accordance with the eternal law. For we have seen above that sin does not destroy entirely the good of nature.[57]

Reply Obj. 3. A thing is maintained in the end and moved toward the end by one and the same cause; thus gravity which makes a heavy body rest in the lower place is also the cause of its being moved thither. We, therefore, reply that as it is according to the eternal law that some deserve happiness, others unhappiness, so is it by the eternal law that some are maintained in a happy state, others in an unhappy state. Accordingly, both the blessed and the damned are under the eternal law.

Question 94
Of the Natural Law

[In Six Articles]

We must now consider the natural law, concerning which there are six points of inquiry: (1) What is the natural law? (2) What are the precepts of the natural law? (3) Whether all acts of virtue are prescribed by the natural law? (4) Whether the natural law is the same in all? (5) Whether it is changeable? (6) Whether it can be abolished from the heart of man?

FIRST ARTICLE
Is the Natural Law a Habit?

We proceed thus to the First Article:

Obj. 1. It would seem that the natural law is a habit because, as the Philosopher says, "there are three things in the soul: power, habit, and passion."[1] But the natural law is not one of the soul's powers, nor is it one of the passions, as we may see by going through them one by one. Therefore, the natural law is a habit.

Obj. 2. Further, Basil says that the conscience or "*syndere-*

sis is the law of our mind,"[2] which can only apply to the natural law. But *synderesis* is a habit, as was shown in the First Part.[3] Therefore, the natural law is a habit.

Obj. 3. Further, the natural law abides in man always, as will be shown further on.[4] But man's reason, to which the law pertains, does not always think about the natural law. Therefore, the natural law is not an act but a habit.

On the contrary, Augustine says that "a habit is that whereby something is done when necessary."[5] But such is not the natural law since it is in infants and in the damned who cannot act by it. Therefore, the natural law is not a habit.

I answer that A thing may be called a habit in two ways. First, properly and essentially, and thus the natural law is not a habit. For it has been stated above that the natural law is something appointed by reason, just as a proposition is a work of reason.[6] Now, that which a man does is not the same as that whereby he does it, for he makes a becoming speech by the habit of grammar. Since, then, a habit is that by which we act, a law cannot be a habit properly and essentially.

Secondly, the term "habit" may be applied to that which we hold by a habit; thus faith may mean that which we hold by faith. And accordingly, since the precepts of the natural law are sometimes considered by reason actually, while sometimes they are in the reason only habitually, in this way the natural law may be called a habit. Thus, in speculative matters, the indemonstrable principles are not the habit itself whereby we hold those principles but are the principles the habit of which we possess.

Reply Obj. 1. The Philosopher proposes there to discover the genus of virtue, and since it is evident that virtue is a principle of action, he mentions only those things which are principles of human acts, viz., powers, habits, and passions. But there are other things in the soul besides these three: there are acts; thus to will is in the one that wills; again, things known are in the knower. Moreover, its own natural properties are in the soul, such as immortality and the like.

Reply Obj. 2. Synderesis is said to be the law of our mind because it is a habit containing the precepts of the natural law, which are the first principles of human actions.

Reply Obj. 3. This argument proves that the natural law is held habitually, and this is granted.

To the argument advanced in the contrary sense we reply

that sometimes a man is unable to make use of that which is in him habitually on account of some impediment; thus, on account of sleep, a man is unable to use the habit of reasoning. In like manner, through the deficiency of his age, a child cannot use the habit of understanding principles, or the natural law, which is in him habitually.

SECOND ARTICLE
Does the Natural Law Contain Several Precepts or One Only?

We proceed thus to the Second Article:

Obj. 1. It would seem that the natural law contains, not several precepts, but one only. For law is a kind of precept, as stated above.[7] If, therefore, there were many precepts of the natural law, it would follow that there are also many natural laws.

Obj. 2. Further, the natural law is consequent to human nature. But human nature as a whole is one, though, as to its parts, it is manifold. Therefore, either there is but one precept of the law of nature, on account of the unity of nature as a whole, or there are many by reason of the number of parts of human nature. The result would be that even things relating to the inclination of the concupiscible faculty belong to the natural law.

Obj. 3. Further, law is something pertaining to reason, as stated above.[8] Now, reason is but one in man. Therefore, there is only one precept of the natural law.

On the contrary, The precepts of the natural law in man stand in relation to practical matters as the first principles to matters of demonstration. But there are several first indemonstrable principles. Therefore, there are also several precepts of the natural law.

I answer that, As stated above, the precepts of the natural law are to the practical reason what the first principles of demonstrations are to the speculative reason because both are self-evident principles.[9] Now a thing is said to be self-evident in two ways: first, in itself; secondly, in relation to us. Any proposition is said to be self-evident in itself if its predicate is contained in the notion of the subject, although, to one who knows not the definition of the subject, it happens that such a proposition is not self-evident. For instance, this proposition, "Man is a rational being," is in its very nature self-evident, since who says "man" says "a rational being," and yet to one who knows not what a man is, this proposition is not self-evident. Hence it is that, as Boethius says,[10] certain axioms or propositions are universally self-evident to all, and such are those propositions whose terms are known to all, as, "Every whole is greater than its part," and, "Things equal to one and the same are equal to one another." But some propositions are self-evident only to the wise who understand the meaning of the terms of such propositions; thus to one who understands that an angel is not a body, it is self-evident that an angel is not circumspectively in a place, but this is not evident to the unlearned, for they cannot grasp it.

Now, a certain order is to be found in those things that are apprehended universally. For that which, before aught else, falls under apprehension, is "being," the notion of which is included in all things whatsoever a man apprehends. Wherefore the first indemonstrable principle is that the same thing cannot be affirmed and denied at the same time, which is based on the nature of "being" and "not-being," and on this principle all others are based, as it is stated in *Metaphysics* IV.[11] Now, as "being" is the first thing that falls under the apprehension simply, so "good" is the first thing that falls under the apprehension of the practical reason, which is directed to action, since every agent acts for an end under the aspect of good. Consequently, the first principle in the practical reason is one founded on the notion of good, viz., that good is that which all things seek after. Hence this is the first precept of law, that good is to be done and pursued, and evil is to be avoided. All other precepts of the natural law are based upon this, so that whatever the practical reason naturally apprehends as man's good (or evil) belongs to the precepts of the natural law as something to be done or avoided.

Since, however, good has the nature of an end, and evil the nature of a contrary, hence it is that all those things to which man has a natural inclination are naturally apprehended by reason as being good and, consequently, as objects of pursuit, and their contraries as evil and objects of avoidance. Where-

fore the order of the precepts of the natural law is according
to the order of natural inclinations. Because in man there is
first of all an inclination to good in accordance with the
nature which he has in common with all substances, inasmuch as every substance seeks the preservation of its own
being according to its nature, and by reason of this inclination, whatever is a means of preserving human life and of
warding off its obstacles belongs to the natural law. Secondly,
there is in man an inclination to things that pertain to him
more specially according to that nature which he has in common with other animals, and in virtue of this inclination,
those things are said to belong to the natural law "which
nature has taught to all animals,"[12] such as sexual intercourse, education of offspring, and so forth. Thirdly, there is
in man an inclination to good according to the nature of his
reason, which nature is proper to him; thus man has a natural
inclination to know the truth about God and to live in society, and in this respect, whatever pertains to this inclination
belongs to the natural law, for instance, to shun ignorance, to
avoid offending those among whom one has to live, and other
such things regarding the above inclination.

Reply Obj. 1. All these precepts of the law of nature have
the character of one natural law inasmuch as they flow from
one first precept.

Reply Obj. 2. All the inclinations of any parts whatsoever
of human nature, e.g., of the concupiscible and irascible
parts, insofar as they are ruled by reason, belong to the natural law and are reduced to one first precept, as stated above,
so that the precepts of the natural law are many in themselves but are based on one common foundation.

Reply Obj. 3. Although reason is one in itself, yet it directs
all things regarding man, so that whatever can be ruled by
reason is contained under the law of reason.

THIRD ARTICLE

Are All Acts of Virtue Prescribed
by the Natural Law?

We proceed thus to the Third Article:

Obj. 1. It would seem that not all acts of virtue are prescribed by the natural law because, as stated above, it is

essential to a law that it be ordained to the common good.[13] But some acts of virtue are ordained to the private good of the individual, as is evident especially in regard to acts of temperance. Therefore, not all acts of virtue are the subject of natural law.

Obj. 2. Further, every sin is opposed to some virtuous act. If, therefore, all acts of virtue are prescribed by the natural law, it seems to follow that all sins are against nature, where-as this applies to certain special sins.

Obj. 3. Further, those things which are according to nature are common to all. But acts of virtue are not common to all, since a thing is virtuous in one and vicious in another. There-fore, not all acts of virtue are prescribed by the natural law.

On the contrary, Damascene says that "virtues are natu-ral."[14] Therefore, virtuous acts also are a subject of the natu-ral law.

I answer that We may speak of virtuous acts in two ways: first, under the aspect of virtuous; secondly, as such and such acts considered in their proper species. If, then, we speak of acts of virtue considered as virtuous, thus all virtuous acts belong to the natural law. For it has been stated that to the natural law belongs everything to which a man is inclined according to his nature.[15] Now each thing is inclined natural-ly to an operation that is suitable to it according to its form; thus fire is inclined to give heat. Wherefore, since the ration-al soul is the proper form of man, there is in every man a natural inclination to act according to reason, and this is to act according to virtue. Consequently, considered thus, all acts of virtue are prescribed by the natural law, since each one's reason naturally dictates to him to act virtuously. But if we speak of virtuous acts considered in themselves, i.e., in their proper species, thus not all virtuous acts are prescribed by the natural law; the many things are done virtuously to which nature does not incline at first, but which, through the inquiry of reason, have been found by men to be conducive to well-living.

Reply Obj. 1. Temperance is about the natural concupis-cences of food, drink, and sexual matters, which are indeed ordained to the natural common good, just as other matters of law are ordained to the moral common good.

Reply Obj. 2. By human nature we may mean either that which is proper to man—and in this sense all sins, as being against reason, are also against nature, as Damascene states[16]—or we may mean that nature which is common to man and other animals, and in this sense certain special sins are said to be against nature; thus, contrary to heterosexual intercourse, which is natural to all animals, is male homosexual union, which has received the special name of the unnatural vice.

Reply Obj. 3. This argument considers acts in themselves. For it is owing to the various conditions of men that certain acts are virtuous for some as being proportionate and becoming to them, while they are vicious for others as being out of proportion to them.

FOURTH ARTICLE
Is the Natural Law the Same in All Men?

We proceed thus to the Fourth Article:

Obj. 1. It would seem that the natural law is not the same in all. For it is stated in the *Decretum* that "the natural law is that which is contained in the Law and the Gospel."[17] But this is not common to all men because, as it is written, "all do not obey the gospel."[18] Therefore, the natural law is not the same in all men.

Obj. 2. Further, "Things which are according to the law are said to be just," as stated in *Ethics* V.[19] But it is stated in the same book that nothing is so universally just as not to be subject to change in regard to some men. Therefore, even the natural law is not the same in all men.

Obj. 3. Further, as stated above, to the natural law belongs everything to which a man is inclined according to his nature.[20] Now, different men are naturally inclined to different things, some to the desire of pleasures, others to the desire of honors, and other men to other things. Therefore, there is not one natural law for all.

On the contrary, Isidore says, "The natural law is common to all nations."[21]

I answer that, As stated above, to the natural law belong those things to which a man is inclined naturally, and among these, it is proper to man to be inclined to act according to reason.[22] Now the process of reason is from the common to the proper, as stated in *Phys.* I.[23] The speculative reason, however, is differently situated in this matter from the practical reason. For, since the speculative reason is concerned chiefly with necessary things, which cannot be otherwise than they are, its proper conclusions, like the universal principles, contain the truth without fail. The practical reason, on the other hand, is concerned with contingent matters, about which human actions are concerned, and consequently, although there is necessity in the general principles, the more we descend to matters of detail, the more frequently we encounter deviations. Accordingly, then, in speculative matters, truth is the same for all men both as to principles and as to conclusions, although the truth is not known to all as regards the conclusions but only as regards the principles which are called common notions. But in matters of action, truth or practical rectitude is not the same for all as to matters of detail but only as to the general principles, and where there is the same rectitude in matters of detail, it is not equally known to all.

It is, therefore, evident that, as regards the general principles, whether of speculative or practical reason, truth or rectitude is the same for all and is equally known by all. As to the proper conclusions of the speculative reason, the truth is the same for all but is not equally known to all; thus it is true for all that the three angles of a triangle are together equal to two right angles, although it is not known to all. But as to the proper conclusions of the practical reason, neither is the truth or rectitude the same for all, nor, where it is the same, is it equally known by all. Thus it is right and true for all to act according to reason, and from this principle, it follows as a proper conclusion that goods entrusted to another should be restored to their owner. Now this is true for the majority of cases, but it may happen in a particular case that it would be injurious, and therefore unreasonable, to restore goods held in trust, for instance, if they are claimed for the purpose of fighting against one's country. And this principle will be found to fail the more according as we descend further into detail, e.g., if one were to say that goods held in trust should be restored with such and such a guarantee or in such and such a way, because the greater the number of conditions added, the greater the number of ways in which the principle may fail, so that it be not right to restore or not to restore.

Consequently, we must say that the natural law as to general principles is the same for all both as to rectitude and as to knowledge. But as to certain matters of detail, which are conclusions, as it were, of those general principles, it is the same for all in the majority of cases both as to rectitude and as to knowledge, and yet, in some few cases, it may fail both as to rectitude by reason of certain obstacles (just as natures subject to generation and corruption fail in some few cases on account of some obstacle) and as to knowledge, since, in some, the reason is perverted by passion or evil habit or an evil disposition of nature; thus, formerly, theft, although it is expressly contrary to the natural law, was not considered wrong among the Germans, as Julius Caesar relates.[24]

Reply Obj. 1. The meaning of the sentence quoted is not that whatever is contained in the Law and the Gospel belongs to the natural law, since they contain many things that are above nature, but that whatever belongs to the natural law is fully contained in them. Wherefore Gratian, after saying that "the natural law is what is contained in the Law and the Gospel," adds at once, by way of example, "by which everyone is commanded to do to others as he would be done by."

Reply Obj. 2. The saying of the Philosopher is to be understood of things that are naturally just, not as general principles but as conclusions drawn from them, having rectitude in the majority of cases but failing in a few.

Reply Obj. 3. As, in man, reason rules and commands the other powers, so all the natural inclinations belonging to the other powers must needs be directed according to reason. Wherefore it is universally right for all men that all their inclinations should be directed according to reason.

FIFTH ARTICLE
Can the Natural Law Be Changed?

We proceed thus to the Fifth Article:

Obj. 1. It would seem that the natural law can be changed because, on Sir. 17:9, "He gave them instructions, and the law of life," a gloss says: "He wished the law of the letter to be written in order to correct the law of nature."[25] But that which is corrected is changed. Therefore, the natural law can be changed.

Obj. 2. Further, the slaying of the innocent, adultery, and theft are against the natural law. But we find these things changed by God, as when God commanded Abraham to slay his innocent son,[26] and when He ordered the Jews to borrow and purloin the vessels of the Egyptians,[27] and when He commanded Hosea to take to himself "a wife of fornications."[28] Therefore, the natural law can be changed.

Obj. 3. Further, Isidore says that "the possession of all things in common and universal freedom are matters of natural law."[29] But these things are seen to be changed by human laws. Therefore, it seems that the natural law is subject to change.

On the contrary, It is said in the *Decretum:* "The natural law dates from the creation of the rational creature. It does not vary according to time but remains unchangeable."[30]

I answer that A change in the natural law may be understood in two ways. First, by way of addition. In this sense, nothing hinders the natural law from being changed, since many things, for the benefit of human life, have been added over and above the natural law both by the divine law and by human laws.

Secondly, a change in the natural law may be understood by way of subtraction, so that what previously was according to the natural law ceases to be so. In this sense, the natural law is altogether unchangeable in its first principles, but in its secondary principles, which, as we have said, are like certain proper conclusions closely related to the first principles, the natural law is not changed so that what it prescribes be not right in most cases. But it may be changed in some particular cases of rare occurrence[31] through some special causes hindering the observance of such precepts, as stated above.[32]

Reply Obj. 1. The written law is said to be given for the correction of the natural law, either because it supplies what was wanting to the natural law or because the natural law was perverted in the hearts of some men as to certain matters, so that they esteemed those things good which are naturally evil, which perversion stood in need of correction.

Reply Obj. 2. All men alike, both guilty and innocent, die the death of nature, which death of nature is inflicted by the power of God on account of original sin, according to 1 Kings: "The Lord kills and makes alive."[33] Consequently, by the command of God, death can be inflicted on any man, guilty or innocent, without any injustice whatever. In like manner, adultery is intercourse with another's wife, who is allotted to him by the law handed down by God. Consequently, intercourse with any woman, by the command of God, is neither adultery nor fornication. The same applies to theft, which is the taking of another's property. For whatever is taken by the command of God, to Whom all things belong, is not taken against the will of its owner, whereas it is in this that theft consists. Nor is it only in human things that whatever is commanded by God is right but also in natural things—whatever is done by God is, in some way, natural, as stated in the First Part.[34]

Reply Obj. 3. A thing is said to belong to the natural law in two ways. First, because nature inclines thereto, e.g., that one should not do harm to another. Secondly, because nature did not bring in the contrary; thus we might say that for man to be naked is of the natural law because nature did not give him cl thes, but art invented them. In this sense, "the possession of all things in common and universal freedom" are said to be of the natural law because, to wit, the distinction of possessions and slavery were not brought in by nature but devised by human reason for the benefit of human life. Accordingly, the law of nature was not changed in this respect except by addition.

SIXTH ARTICLE

Can the Law of Nature Be Abolished from the Heart of Man?

We proceed thus to the Sixth Article:

Obj. 1. It would seem that the natural law can be abolished from the heart of man because, on Rom. 2:14, "When the Gentiles who have not the law," etc., a gloss says that "the

law of righteousness, which sin had blotted out, is graven on
the heart of man when he is restored by grace."[35] But the law
of righteousness is the law of nature. Therefore, the law of
nature can be blotted out.

Obj. 2. Further, the law of grace is more efficacious than
the law of nature. But the law of grace is blotted out by sin.
Much more, therefore, can the law of nature be blotted out.

Obj. 3. Further, that which is established by law is made
just. But many things are legally established which are contrary to the law of nature. Therefore, the law of nature can be
abolished from the heart of man.

On the contrary, Augustine says, "Thy law is written in the
hearts of men, which iniquity itself effaces not."[36] But the
law which is written in men's hearts is the natural law. Therefore, the natural law cannot be blotted out.

I answer that, As stated above, there belong to the natural
law, first, certain most general precepts that are known to all;
and secondly, certain secondary and more detailed precepts
which are, as it were, conclusions following closely from first
principles.[37] As to those general principles, the natural law, in
the abstract, can nowise be blotted out from men's hearts.
But it is blotted out in the case of particular action insofar as
reason is hindered from applying the general principles to a
particular point of practice on account of concupiscence or
some other passion, as stated above.[38] But as to the other, i.e.,
the secondary precepts, the natural law can be blotted out
from the human heart either by evil persuasions, just as in
speculative matters errors occur in respect of necessary conclusions, or by vicious customs and corrupt habits, as among
some men theft and even unnatural vices, as the Apostle
states,[39] were not esteemed sinful.

Reply Obj. 1. Sin blots out the law of nature in particular
cases, not universally, except perchance in regard to the secondary precepts of the natural law, in the way stated above.

Reply Obj. 2. Although grace is more efficacious than nature, yet nature is more essential to man and therefore more
enduring.

Reply Obj. 3. The argument is true of the secondary precepts of the natural law, against which some legislators have
framed certain enactments which are unjust.

Question 95
Of Human Law

[In Four Articles]

We must now consider human law, and (1) this law considered in itself; (2) its power; (3) its mutability. Under the first head, there are four points of inquiry: (1) its utility; (2) its origin; (3) its quality; (4) its divisions.

FIRST ARTICLE
Was It Useful for Laws to Be Framed by Men?

We proceed thus to the First Article:

Obj. 1. It would seem that it was not useful for laws to be framed by men because the purpose of every law is that man be made good thereby, as stated above.[1] But men are more to be induced to be good willingly by means of admonitions than against their will by means of laws. Therefore, there was no need to frame laws.

Obj. 2. Further, as the Philosopher says, "men have recourse to a judge as to justice in the flesh."[2] But justice in the flesh is better than inanimate justice, which is contained in laws. Therefore, it would have been better for the execution of justice to be entrusted to the decision of judges than to frame laws in addition.

Obj. 3. Further, every law is framed for the direction of human actions, as is evident from what has been stated above.[3] But since human actions are about singulars, which are infinite in number, matters pertaining to the direction of human actions cannot be taken into sufficient consideration except by a wise man who looks into each one of them. Therefore, it would have been better for human acts to be directed by the judgment of wise men than by the framing of laws. Therefore, there was no need of human laws.

On the contrary, Isidore says, "Laws were made that, in fear thereof, human audacity might be held in check, that innocence might be safeguarded in the midst of wickedness, and that the dread of punishment might prevent the wicked from doing harm."⁴ But these things are most necessary to mankind. Therefore, it was necessary that human laws should be made.

I answer that, As stated above,⁵ man has a natural aptitude for virtue, but the perfection of virtue must be acquired by man by means of some kind of training. Thus we observe that man is helped by industry in his necessities, for instance, in food and clothing. Certain beginnings of these he has from nature, viz., his reason and his hands, but he has not the full complement, as other animals have to whom nature has given sufficiency of clothing and food. Now, it is difficult to see how man could suffice for himself in the matter of this training, since the perfection of virtue consists chiefly in withdrawing man from undue pleasures, to which, above all, man is inclined, and especially the young, who are more capable of being trained. Consequently, a man needs to receive this training from another whereby to arrive at the perfection of virtue. And as to those young people who are inclined to acts of virtue by their good natural disposition or by custom, or rather by the gift of God, paternal training suffices, which is by admonitions. But since some are found to be depraved and prone to vice and not easily amenable to words, it was necessary for such to be restrained from evil by force and fear in order that they might at least desist from evil-doing and leave others in peace, and that they themselves, by being habituated in this way, might be brought to do willingly what hitherto they did from fear and thus become virtuous. Now this kind of training which compels through fear of punishment is the discipline of laws. Therefore, in order that man might have peace and virtue, it was necessary for laws to be framed, for, as the Philosopher says, "a man is the most noble of animals if he be perfect in virtue, so is he the lowest of all if he be severed from law and justice."⁶ Because man can use his reason to devise means of satisfying his lusts and evil passions, which other animals are unable to do.

Reply Obj. 1. Men who are well disposed are led willingly to virtue by being admonished better than by coercion, but men who are evilly disposed are not led to virtue unless they are compelled.

Reply Obj. 2. As the Philosopher says, "It is better that all things be regulated by law than left to be decided by judges,"[7] and this for three reasons. First, because it is easier to find a few wise men competent to frame right laws than to find the many who would be necessary to judge aright of each single case. Secondly, because those who make laws consider long beforehand what laws to make, whereas judgment on each single case has to be pronounced as soon as it arises, and it is easier for man to see what is right by taking many instances into consideration than by considering one solitary fact. Thirdly, because lawgivers judge in the abstract and of future events, whereas those who sit in judgment judge of things present, toward which they are affected by love, hatred, or some kind of cupidity; wherefore their judgment is perverted.

Since, then, the embodied justice of the judge is not found in every man, and since it can be deflected, therefore it was necessary, whenever possible, for the law to determine how to judge, and for very few matters to be left to the decision of men.

Reply Obj. 3. Certain individual facts which cannot be covered by the law "have necessarily to be committed to judges," as the Philosopher says in the same passage, for instance, "concerning something that has happened or not happened" and the like.

SECOND ARTICLE

Is Every Human Law Derived from the Natural Law?

We proceed thus to the Second Article:

Obj. 1. It would seem that not every human law is derived from the natural law. For the Philosopher says that "the legal just is that which originally was a matter of indifference."[8] But those things which arise from the natural law are not matters of indifference. Therefore, the enactments of human laws are not all derived from the natural law.

Obj. 2. Further, positive law is contrasted with natural law, as stated by Isidore[9] and the Philosopher.[10] But those things which flow as conclusions from the general principles of the natural law belong to the natural law, as stated above.[11]

Therefore, that which is established by human law does not belong to the natural law.

Obj. 3. Further, the law of nature is the same for all, since the Philosopher says that "the natural just is that which is equally valid everywhere."[12] If, therefore, human laws were derived from the natural law, it would follow that they too are the same for all, which is clearly false.

Obj. 4. Further, it is possible to give a reason for things which are derived from the natural law. But "it is not possible to give the reason for all the legal enactments of the lawgivers," as the Jurist says.[13] Therefore, not all human laws are derived from the natural law.

On the contrary, Tully says, "Things which emanated from nature and were approved by custom were sanctioned by fear and reverence for the laws."[14]

I answer that, As Augustine says, "that which is not just seems to be no law at all";[15] wherefore the force of a law depends on the extent of its justice. Now, in human affairs a thing is said to be just from being right according to the rule of reason. But the first rule of reason is the law of nature, as is clear from what has been stated above.[16] Consequently, every human law has just so much of the nature of law as it is derived from the law of nature. But if, in any point, it deflects from the law of nature, it is no longer a law but a perversion of law.

But it must be noted that something may be derived from the natural law in two ways: first, as a conclusion from premises; secondly, by way of determination of certain generalities. The first way is like to that by which, in the sciences, demonstrated conclusions are drawn from the principles, while the second mode is likened to that whereby, in the arts, general forms are particularized as to details; thus the craftsman needs to determine the general form of a house to some particular shape. Some things are, therefore, derived from the general principles of the natural law by way of conclusion, e.g., that "one must not kill" may be derived as a conclusion from the principle that "one should do harm to no man"; while some are derived therefrom by way of determination, e.g., the law of nature has it that the evildoer should be punished; but that he be punished in this or that way is not directly by natural law but is a certain determination of it.

Accordingly, both modes of derivation are found in the human law. But those things which are derived in the first way are contained in human law, not as emanating therefrom exclusively but having some force from the natural law also. But those things which are derived in the second way have no other force than that of human law.

Reply Obj. 1. The Philosopher is speaking of those enactments which are by way of determination or specification of the precepts of the natural law.

Reply Obj. 2. This argument avails for those things that are derived from the natural law by way of conclusions.

Reply Obj. 3. The general principles of the natural law cannot be applied to all men in the same way on account of the great variety of human affairs, and hence arises the diversity of positive laws among various people.

Reply Obj. 4. These words of the Jurist are to be understood as referring to decisions of rulers in determining particular points of the natural law, on which determinations the judgment of expert and prudent men is based as on its principles, insofar, to wit, as they see at once what is the best thing to decide.

Hence the Philosopher says that, in such matters, "we ought to pay as much attention to the undemonstrated sayings and opinions of persons who surpass us in experience, age, and prudence as to their demonstrations."[17]

THIRD ARTICLE

Is Isidore's Description of the Quality of Positive Law Appropriate?

We proceed thus to the Third Article:

Obj. 1. It would seem that Isidore's description of the quality of positive law is not appropriate when he says: "Law shall be virtuous, just, possible, according to nature, in agreement with the customs of the country, suitable to place and time, necessary, useful, clearly expressed lest by its obscurity it lead to misunderstanding, framed for no private benefit but for the common good."[18] Because he had previously expressed the quality of law in three conditions, saying that "law is anything founded on reason provided that it foster religion, be helpful to discipline, and further the common weal."[19] Therefore, it was needless to add any further conditions to these.

Obj. 2. Further, justice is included in virtue, as Tully says.[20] Therefore, after saying "virtuous," it was superfluous to add "just."

Obj. 3. Further, written law is distinct from custom, according to Isidore.[21] Therefore, it should not be stated in the definition of law that it is "in agreement with the customs of the country."

Obj. 4. Further, a thing may be necessary in two ways. It may be necessary simply because it cannot be otherwise, and that which is necessary in this way is not subject to human judgment. Wherefore human law is not concerned with necessity of this kind. Again, a thing may be necessary for an end, and this necessity is the same as usefulness. Therefore, it is superfluous to say both "necessary" and "useful."

On the contrary stands the authority of Isidore.

I answer that, Whenever a thing is for an end, its form must be determined proportionately to that end, as the form of a saw is such as to be suitable for cutting *(Physics* I, 9).[22] Again, everything that is ruled and measured must have a form proportionate to its rule and measure. Now both these conditions are verified of a human law since it is both something ordained to an end and is a rule or measure ruled or measured by a higher measure. And this higher measure is twofold, viz., the divine law and the natural law, as explained above.[23] Now, the end of human law is to be useful to man, as the Jurist states.[24] Wherefore Isidore, in determining the nature of law, lays down, at first, three conditions: viz., that it "foster religion," inasmuch as it is proportionate to the divine law; that it be "helpful to discipline," inasmuch as it is proportionate to the natural law; and that it "further the common weal," inasmuch as it is proportionate to the utility of mankind.

All the other conditions mentioned by him are reduced to these three. For it is called "virtuous" because it fosters religion. And when he goes on to say that it should be "just, possible, according to nature, in agreement with the customs of the country, adapted to place and time," he implies that it should be helpful to discipline. For human discipline depends, first, on the order of reason, to which he refers by saying "just"; secondly, it depends on the ability of the agent because discipline should be adapted to each one according to his ability, taking also into account the ability of nature (for the same burdens should be not laid on children as on adults), and should be according to human customs since man cannot live alone in society, paying no heed to others; thirdly, it depends on certain circumstances, in respect of which he says, "adapted to place and time." The remaining words, "necessary," "useful," etc., mean that law should further the common weal, so that "necessity" refers to the removal of evils, "usefulness" to the attainment of good, "clearness of expression" to the need of preventing any harm ensuing from the law itself. And since, as stated above,[25] law is ordained to the common good this is expressed in the last part of the description.

This suffices for the *Replies* to the *Objections.*

FOURTH ARTICLE
Is Isidore's Division of Human Laws Appropriate?

We proceed thus to the Fourth Article:

Obj. 1. It would seem that Isidore wrongly divided human statutes or human law. For, under this law, he includes the "law of nations," so called, because, as he says, "nearly all nations use it." But as he says, "natural law is that which is common to all nations."[26] Therefore, the law of nations is not contained under positive human law but rather under natural law.

Obj. 2. Further, those laws which have the same force seem to differ not formally but only materially. But "statutes, decrees of the commonality, senatorial decrees," and the like which he mentions, all have the same force.[27] Therefore, they do not differ except materially. But art takes no notice of such a distinction since it may go on to infinity. Therefore, this division of human laws is not appropriate.

Obj. 3. Further, just as, in the political community, there are princes, priests, and soldiers, so are there other human offices. Therefore, it seems that, as this division includes "military law," and "public law" referring to priests and magistrates, so also it should include other laws pertaining to other offices of the political community.

Obj. 4. Further, those things that are accidental should be passed over. But it is accidental to law that it be framed by this or that man. Therefore, it is unreasonable to divide laws according to the names of lawgivers, so that one be called the "Cornelian" law, another the "Falcidian" law, etc.

On the contrary, The authority of Isidore *(Obj. 1)* suffices.

I answer that A thing can of itself be divided in respect of something contained in the notion of that thing. Thus a soul, either rational or irrational, is contained in the notion of animal, and, therefore, animal is divided properly and of itself in respect of its being rational or irrational but not in the point of its being white or black, which are entirely beside the notion of animal. Now, in the notion of human law, many things are contained in respect of any of which human law can be divided properly and of itself. For in the first place, it belongs to the notion of human law to be derived from the law of nature, as explained above.[28] In this respect, positive right is divided into the "right among nations" and civil right according to the two ways in which something may be derived from the law of nature, as stated above.[29] Because to the right among nations belong those things which are derived from the law of nature as conclusions from premises, e.g., just buyings and sellings and the like, without which men cannot live together, which is a point of the law of nature since man is by nature a social animal, as is proved in *Politics* I, 1.[30] But those things which are derived from the law of nature by way of particular determination belong to the civil right according as each political community decides on what is best for itself.

Secondly, it belongs to the notion of human law to be ordained to the common good of the political community. In this respect, human law may be divided according to the different kinds of men who work in a special way for the common good, e.g., priests by praying to God for the people, princes by governing the people, soldiers by fighting for the safety of the people. Wherefore certain special kinds of law are adapted to these men.

Thirdly, it belongs to the notion of human law to be framed by that one who governs the political community, as shown above.[31] In this respect, there are various human laws according to the various forms of government. Of these, according to the Philosopher,[32] one is monarchy, i.e., when the state is governed by one, and then we have "royal ordinances." Another form is aristocracy, i.e., government by the best men or men of highest rank, and then we have the "authoritative legal opinions" ("*responsa prudentum*") and "decrees of the senate" ("*senatusconsulta*"). Another form is oligarchy, i.e., government by a few rich and powerful men, and then we have "praetorian," also called "honorary," law. Another form of government is that of the people, which is called democracy, and there we have "decrees of the commonalty" ("*plebiscita*"). There is also tyrannical government, which is altogether corrupt, which, therefore, has no corresponding law. Finally, there is a form of government made up of all these,[33] and which is the best; and in this respect, we have "law sanctioned by nobles together with commoners," as stated by Isidore.[34]

Fourthly, it belongs to the notion of human law to direct human actions. In this respect, according to the various matters of which the law treats, there are various kinds of laws, which are sometimes named after their authors: thus we have the *Lex Julia* about adultery, the *Lex Cornelia* concerning assassins, and so on, differentiated in this way not on account of the authors but on account of the matters to which they refer.

Reply Obj. 1. The law of nations is indeed in some way natural to man insofar as he is a reasonable being, because it is derived from the natural law by way of a conclusion that is not very remote from its premises. Wherefore men easily agreed thereto. Nevertheless, it is distinct from the natural law, especially from that natural law which is common to all animals.

The *Replies* to the other *Objections* are evident from what has been said.

Question 96
Of the Power of Human Law

[In Six Articles]

We must now consider the power of human law. Under this head, there are six points of inquiry: (1) Whether human law should be framed for the community? (2) Whether human law should repress all vices? (3) Whether human law is competent to direct all acts of virtue? (4) Whether it binds man in conscience? (5) Whether all men are subject to human law? (6) Whether those who are under the law may act beside the letter of the law?

FIRST ARTICLE

Should Human Law Be Framed for the Community Rather Than for the Individual?

We proceed thus to the First Article:

Obj. 1. It would seem that human law should be framed, not for the community, but rather for the individual. For the Philosopher says that "the legal just . . . includes all particular acts of legislation . . . and all those matters which are the subject of decrees,"[1] which are also individual matters, since decrees are framed about individual actions. Therefore, law is framed not only for the community but also for the individual.

Obj. 2. Further, law is the director of human acts, as stated above.[2] But human acts are about individual matters. Therefore, human laws should be framed, not for the community, but rather for the individual.

Obj. 3. Further, law is a rule and measure of human acts, as stated above.[3] But a measure should be most certain, as stated in *Metaphysics* X.[4] Since, therefore, in human acts no general proposition can be so certain as not to fail in some individual cases, it seems that laws should be framed not in general but for individual cases.

On the contrary, The Jurist says that "laws should be made to suit the majority of instances, and they are not framed according to what may possibly happen in an individual case."[5]

I answer that Whatever is for an end should be proportionate to that end. Now the end of law is the common good, because, as Isidore says, "Law should be framed, not for any private benefit, but for the common good of all the citizens."[6] Hence human laws should be proportionate to the common good. Now the common good comprises many things. Wherefore law should take account of many things, as to persons, as to occupations, and as to times, because the political community is composed of many citizens and its good is procured by many actions; nor is it established to endure for only a short time but to last for all time, by the citizens succeeding one another, as Augustine says.[7]

Reply Obj. 1. The Philosopher divides the "legal just," i.e., positive law, into three parts. For some things are laid down simply in a general way, and these are the general laws. Of these, he says that "the legal is that which originally was a matter of indifference, but which, when enacted, is so no longer," as the fixing of the ransom of a captive. Some things affect the community in one respect and individuals in another. These are called "privileges," i.e., "private laws," as it were, because they regard private persons, although their power extends to many matters, and in regard to these, he adds: "and further all prescriptions in particular cases." Other matters are legal, not through being laws but through being applications of general laws to particular cases; such are decrees which have the force of law, and in regard to these, he adds: "all matters subject to decrees."[8]

Reply Obj. 2. A principle of direction should be applicable to many; wherefore the Philosopher says that all things belonging to one genus are measured by one which is the first in that genus.[9] For if there were as many rules or measures as there are things measured or ruled, they would cease to be of use, since their use consists in being applicable to many things. Hence law would be of no use if it did not extend further than to one single act because the decrees of prudent men are made for the purpose of directing individual actions, whereas law is a general precept, as stated above.[10]

Reply Obj. 3. "We must not seek the same degree of certainty in all things."[11] Consequently, in contingent matters such as natural and human things, it is enough for a thing to be certain as being true in the greater number of instances, though at times and less frequently it fail.

SECOND ARTICLE

Does It Belong to Human Law to Repress All Vices?

We proceed thus to the Second Article:

Obj. 1. It would seem that it belongs to human law to repress all vices. For Isidore says that "laws were made in order that, in fear thereof, man's audacity might be held in check."[12] But it would not be held in check sufficiently unless all evils were repressed by law. Therefore, human law should repress all evils.

Obj. 2. Further, the intention of the lawgiver is to make the citizens virtuous. But a man cannot be virtuous unless he forbear from all kinds of vice. Therefore, it belongs to human law to repress all vices.

Obj. 3. Further, human law is derived from the natural law, as stated above.[13] But all vices are contrary to the law of nature. Therefore, human law should repress all vices.

On the contrary, We read in *De libero arbitrio:* "It seems to me that the law which is written for the governing of the people rightly permits these things, and that divine providence punishes them."[14] But divine providence punishes nothing but vices. Therefore, human law rightly allows some vices by not repressing them.

I answer that, As stated above,[15] law is imposed as a certain rule or measure of human actions. Now, a measure should be homogeneous with that which it measures, as stated in *Metaphysics* X,[16] since different things are measured by different measures. Wherefore laws imposed on men should also be in keeping with their condition, for, as Isidore says, law should be "possible both according to nature and according to the customs of the country."[17] Now, possibility or faculty of action is due to an interior habit or disposition, since the same thing is not possible to one who has not a virtuous habit as is possible to one who has. Thus, the same is not possible to a child as to a full-grown man, for which reason, the law for children is not the same as for adults, since many things are permitted to children which in an adult are punished by law or at any rate are open to blame. In like manner, many things are permissible to men not perfect in virtue which would be intolerable in a virtuous man.

Now, human law is framed for a number of human beings, the majority of whom are not perfect in virtue. Wherefore, human laws do not forbid all vices from which the virtuous abstain but only the more grievous vices from which it is possible for the majority to abstain and chiefly those that are to the hurt of others, without the prohibition of which human society could not be maintained; thus human law prohibits murder, theft, and suchlike.

Reply Obj. 1. Audacity seems to refer to the assailing of others. Consequently, it belongs to those sins chiefly whereby one's neighbor is injured, and these sins are forbidden by human law, as stated.

Reply Obj. 2. The purpose of human law is to lead men to virtue, not suddenly but gradually. Wherefore it does not lay upon the multitude of imperfect men the burdens of those who are already virtuous, viz., that they should abstain from all evil. Otherwise, these imperfect ones, being unable to bear such precepts, would break out into yet greater evils; thus it is written: "He that violently blows his nose, brings out blood,"[18] and that if "new wine," i.e., precepts of a perfect life, is "put into old bottles," i.e., into imperfect men, "the bottles break, and the wine runs out,"[19] i.e., the precepts are despised, and those men, from contempt, break out into evils worse still.

Reply Obj. 3. The natural law is a participation in us of the eternal law, while human law falls short of the eternal law. Now Augustine says: "The law which is framed for the government of political communities allows and leaves unpunished many things that are punished by divine providence. Nor, if this law does not attempt to do everything, is this a reason why it should be blamed for what it does."[20] Wherefore, too, human law does not prohibit everything that is forbidden by the natural law.

THIRD ARTICLE

Does Human Law Prescribe Acts of All the Virtues?

We proceed thus to the Third Article:

Obj. 1. It would seem that human law does not prescribe acts of all the virtues. For vicious acts are contrary to acts of virtue. But human law does not prohibit all vices, as stated above.[21] Therefore, neither does it prescribe all acts of virtue.

Obj. 2. Further, a virtuous act proceeds from a virtue. But virtue is the end of law, so that whatever is from a virtue cannot come under a precept of law. Therefore, human law does not prescribe all acts of virtue.

Obj. 3. Further, law is ordained to the common good, as stated above.[22] But some acts of virtue are ordained not to the common good but to private good. Therefore, the law does not prescribe all acts of virtue.

On the contrary, The Philosopher says that the law "prescribes the performance of the acts of a brave man . . . and the acts of the temperate man . . . and the acts of the meek man and in like manner as regards the other virtues and vices prescribing the former, forbidding the latter."[23]

I answer that The species of virtues are distinguished by their objects, as explained above.[24] Now all the objects of virtues can be referred either to the private good of an individual or to the common good of the multitude; thus matters of fortitude may be achieved either for the safety of the political community or for upholding the rights of a friend, and in like manner with the other virtues. But law, as stated above, is ordained to the common good.[25] Wherefore, there is no virtue whose acts cannot be prescribed by the law. Nevertheless, human law does not prescribe concerning all the acts of every virtue but only in regard to those that are ordained to the common good—either immediately, as when certain things are done directly for the common good, or mediately, as when a lawgiver prescribes certain things pertaining to good training whereby the citizens are disciplined in the upholding of the common good of justice and peace.

Reply Obj. 1. Human law does not forbid all vicious acts by the obligation of a precept, as neither does it prescribe all acts of virtue. But it forbids certain acts of each vice, just as it prescribes some acts of each virtue.

Reply Obj. 2. An act is said to be an act of virtue in two ways. First, from the fact that a man does something virtuous; thus the act of justice is to do what is right, and an act of fortitude is to do brave things—and in this way law prescribes certain acts of virtue. Secondly, an act of virtue is when a man does a virtuous thing in a way in which a virtuous man does it. Such an act always proceeds from virtue, and it does not come under a precept of law but is the end at which every lawgiver aims.

Reply Obj. 3. There is no virtue whose act is not ordainable to the common good, as stated above, either mediately or immediately.

FOURTH ARTICLE

Does Human Law Bind a Man in Conscience?

We proceed thus to the Fourth Article:

Obj. 1. It would seem that human law does not bind a man in conscience. For an inferior power has no jurisdiction in a court of higher power. But the power of man which frames human law is beneath the divine power. Therefore, human law cannot impose its precept in a divine court, such as is the court of conscience.

Obj. 2. Further, the judgment of conscience depends chiefly on the commandments of God. But sometimes God's commandments are made void by human laws, according to Mt. 15:6: "You have made void the commandment of God for your tradition." Therefore, human law does not bind a man in conscience.

Obj. 3. Further, human laws often bring loss of character and injury on man, according to Is. 10:1: "Woe to them that make wicked laws, and when they write, write injustice; to oppress the poor in judgment and do violence to the cause of the humble of My people." But it is lawful for anyone to avoid oppression and violence. Therefore, human laws do not bind man in conscience.

On the contrary, It is written: "This is thanksworthy, if for conscience . . . a man endure sorrows, suffering wrongfully."[26]

I answer that Laws framed by man are either just or unjust. If they be just, they have the power of binding in conscience from the eternal law whence they are derived, according to Pr. 8:15: "By Me kings reign, and lawgivers decree just things." Now laws are said to be just from the end, when, to wit, they are ordained to the common good, and from their author, that is to say, when the law that is made does not exceed the power of the lawgiver, and from their form, when, to wit, burdens are laid on the subjects according to an equality of proportion and with a view to the common good. For, since one man is a part of the community, each man, in all that he is and has, belongs to the community, just as a part, in all that it is, belongs to the whole; wherefore nature inflicts a loss on the part in order to save the whole, so that, on this account, such laws as these which impose proportionate burdens are just and binding in conscience and are legal laws.

On the other hand, laws may be unjust in two ways: first, by being contrary to human good, through being opposed to the things mentioned above—either in respect of the end, as when an authority imposes on his subjects burdensome laws conducive, not to the common good, but rather to his own cupidity or vainglory; or in respect of the author, as when a man makes a law that goes beyond the power committed to him; or in respect of the form, as when burdens are imposed unequally on the community, although with a view to the common good. The like are acts of violence rather than laws, because, as Augustine says, "A law that is not just, seems to be no law at all."[27] Wherefore such laws do not bind in conscience, except perhaps in order to avoid scandal or disturbance, for which cause a man should even yield his right, according to Mt. 5:40, 41: "If a man . . . take away your coat, let go your cloak also unto him, and whosoever will force you one mile, go with him other two."

Secondly, laws may be unjust through being opposed to the divine good; such are the laws of tyrants inducing to idolatry or to anything else contrary to the divine law, and laws of this kind must nowise be observed because, as stated in Acts 5:29, "we ought to obey God rather than men."

Reply Obj. 1. As the Apostle says, all human power is from God . . .; "therefore, he that resists the power" in matters that are within its scope "resists the ordinance of God,"[28] so that he becomes guilty according to his conscience.

Reply Obj. 2. This argument is true of laws that are contrary to the commandments of God, which is beyond the scope of (human) power. Wherefore in such matters human law should not be obeyed.

Reply Obj. 3. This argument is true of a law that inflicts unjust hurt on its subjects. The power that man holds from God does not extend to this; wherefore neither in such matters is man bound to obey the law, provided he avoid giving scandal or inflicting a more grievous hurt.

FIFTH ARTICLE

Are All Subject to the Law?

We proceed thus to the Fifth Article:

Obj. 1. It would seem that not all are subject to the law. For those alone are subject to a law for whom a law is made. But the Apostle says: "The law is not made for the just man."[29] Therefore, the just are not subject to the law.

Obj. 2. Further, Pope Urban says: "He that is guided by a private law need not for any reason be bound by the public law."[30] Now all spiritual men are led by the private law of the Holy Spirit, for they are the sons of God, of whom it is said: "Whosoever are led by the Spirit of God, they are the sons of God."[31] Therefore, not all men are subject to human law.

Obj. 3. Further, the Jurist says that "the ruler is exempt from the laws."[32] But he that is exempt from the law is not bound thereby. Therefore, not all are subject to the law.

On the contrary, The Apostle says, "Let every soul be subject to the higher powers."[33] But subjection to a power seems to imply subjection to the laws framed by that power. Therefore, all men should be subject to human law.

I answer that, As stated above, the notion of law contains two things: first, that it is a rule of human acts; secondly, that it has coercive power.[34] Wherefore a man may be subject to law in two ways. First, as the regulated is subject to the regulator, and, in this way, whoever is subject to a power is subject to the law framed by that power. But it may happen in two ways that one is not subject to a power. In one way, by being altogether free from its authority; hence the subjects of one city or kingdom are not bound by the laws of the sovereign of another city or kingdom, since they are not subject to his authority. In another way, by being under a yet higher law; thus the subject of a proconsul should be ruled by his command but not in those matters in which the subject receives his orders from the emperor, for in these matters he is not bound by the mandate of the lower authority since he is directed by that of a higher. In this way, one who is simply subject to a law may not be subject thereto in certain matters in respect of which he is ruled by a higher law.

Secondly, a man is said to be subject to a law as the coerced is subject to the coercer. In this way, the virtuous and righteous are not subject to the law but only the wicked. Because coercion and violence are contrary to the will, but the will of the good is in harmony with the law, whereas the will of the wicked is discordant from it. Wherefore, in this sense, the good are not subject to the law but only the wicked.

Reply Obj. 1. This argument is true of subjection by way of coercion, for, in this way, "the law is not made for the just men," because "they are a law to themselves" since they "show the work of the law written in their hearts," as the Apostle says.[35] Consequently, the law does not enforce itself upon them as it does on the wicked.

Reply Obj. 2. The law of the Holy Spirit is above all law framed by man, and, therefore, spiritual men, insofar as they are led by the law of the Holy Spirit, are not subject to the law in those matters that are inconsistent with the guidance of the Holy Spirit. Nevertheless, the very fact that spiritual men are subject to law is due to the leading of the Holy Spirit, according to 1 Pet.: "Be you subject . . . to every human creature for God's sake."[36]

Reply Obj. 3. The ruler is said to be "exempt from the law" as to its coercive power, since, properly speaking, no man is coerced by himself, and law has no coercive power save from the power of the ruler. Thus, then, is the ruler said to be exempt from the law because none is competent to pass sentence on him if he acts against the law. Wherefore on Ps. 50:6: "To You only have I sinned," a gloss says that "there is no man who can judge the deeds of a king."[37] But as to the directive force of law, the ruler is subject to the law by his own will, according to the statement that "whatever law a man makes for another, he should keep himself."[38] And a wise authority says: "Obey the law that you make yourself."[39] Moreover, the Lord reproaches those who "say and do not," and who "bind heavy burdens and lay them on men's shoulders, but with a finger of their own, they will not move them."[40] Hence, in the judgment of God, the ruler is not exempt from the law as to its directive force, but he should fulfill it of his own free will and not of constraint. Again, the ruler is above the law insofar as, when it is expedient, he can change the law and dispense from it according to time and place.

SIXTH ARTICLE

May He Who Is under a Law
Act beside the Letter of the Law?

We proceed thus to the Sixth Article:

Obj. 1. It seems that he who is subject to a law may not act beside the letter of the law. For Augustine says: "Although men judge about temporal laws when they make them, yet, when once they are made and confirmed, they must pass judgment, not on them but according to them."[41] But if anyone disregard the letter of the law, saying that he observes the intention of the lawgiver, he seems to pass judgment on the law. Therefore, it is not right for one who is under a law to disregard the letter of the law in order to observe the intention of the lawgiver.

Obj. 2. Further, he alone is competent to interpret the law who can make the law. But those who are subject to the law cannot make the law. Therefore, they have no right to interpret the intention of the lawgiver but should always act according to the letter of the law.

Obj. 3. Further, every wise man knows how to explain his intention by words. But those who framed the laws should be reckoned wise, for Wisdom says: "By Me kings reign, and lawgivers decree just things."[42] Therefore, we should not judge of the intention of the lawgiver otherwise than by the words of the law.

On the contrary, Hilary says, "The meaning of what is said is according to the motive for saying it, because things are not subject to speech, but speech to things."[43] Therefore, we should take more account of the motive of the lawgiver than to his very words.

I answer that, As stated above,[44] every law is directed to the common weal of men and derives the force and nature of law accordingly, but it has no power to oblige morally if it fails to be so directed. Hence the Jurist says: "By no reason of law or favor of equity is it allowable for us to interpret harshly and render burdensome those useful measures which have been enacted for the welfare of man."[45] Now, it happens often that the observance of some point of law conduces to the common weal in the majority of instances, and yet in some cases is very hurtful. Since, then, the lawgiver cannot have in view every single case, he shapes the law according to what happens most frequently, by directing his attention to the common good. Wherefore, if a case arise wherein the observance of that law would be hurtful to the general welfare, it should not be observed. For instance, suppose that, in a besieged city, it be an established law that the gates of the city are to be kept closed, this is good for public welfare as a general rule, but if it were to happen that the enemy are in pursuit of certain citizens who are defenders of the city, it would be a great loss to the city if the gates were not opened to them, and so, in that case, the gates ought to be opened, contrary to the letter of the law, in order to maintain the common weal, which the lawgiver had in view.

Nevertheless, it must be noted that if the observance of the law according to the letter does not involve any sudden risk needing instant remedy, it is not competent for everyone to expound what is useful and what is not useful to the political community; those alone can do this who are in authority, and who, on account of suchlike cases, have the power to dispense from the laws. If, however, the peril be so sudden as not to allow of the delay involved by referring the matter to authority, the mere necessity brings with it a dispensation, since necessity knows no law.

Reply Obj. 1. He who in a case of necessity acts beside the letter of the law does not judge of the law but of a particular case in which he sees that the letter of the law is not to be observed.

Reply Obj. 2. He who follows the intention of the lawgiver does not interpret the law indiscriminately but in a case in which it is evident, by reason of the manifest harm, that the lawgiver intended otherwise. For if it be a matter of doubt, he must either act according to the letter of the law or consult those in power.

Reply Obj. 3. No man is so wise as to be able to take account of every single case; wherefore he is not able sufficiently to express in words all those things that are suitable for the end he has in view. And even if a lawgiver were able to take all the cases into consideration, he ought not to mention them all, in order to avoid confusion, but should frame the law according to that which is of most common occurrence.

Question 97
Of Change in Laws

[In Four Articles]

We must now consider change in laws, under which head there are four points of inquiry: (1) Whether human law is changeable? (2) Whether it should always be changed whenever something better occurs? (3) Whether it is abolished by custom, and whether custom obtains the force of law? (4) Whether the application of human law should be changed by dispensation of those in authority?

FIRST ARTICLE
Should Human Law Be Changed in Any Way?

We proceed thus to the First Article:

Obj. 1. It would seem that human law should not be changed in any way at all because human law is derived from the natural law, as stated above.[1] But the natural law endures unchangeably. Therefore, human law should also remain without any change.

Obj. 2. Further, as the Philosopher says, a measure should be absolutely stable.[2] But human law is the measure of human acts, as stated above.[3] Therefore, it should remain without change.

Obj. 3. Further, it is of the essence of law to be just and right, as stated above.[4] But that which is right once is right always. Therefore, that which is law once should be always law.

On the contrary, Augustine says, "A temporal law, however just, may be justly changed in course of time."[5]

I answer that, As stated above, human law is a dictate of reason whereby human acts are directed.[6] Thus there may be two causes for the just change of human law: one on the part of reason; the other on the part of man, whose acts are regulated by law. The cause on the part of reason is that it seems natural to human reason to advance gradually from the imperfect to the perfect. Hence, in speculative sciences, we see that the teaching of the early philosophers was imperfect, and that it was afterward perfected by those who succeeded them. So also in practical matters; for those who first endeavored to discover something useful for the human community, not being able by themselves to take everything into consideration, set up certain institutions which were deficient in many ways, and these were changed by subsequent lawgivers who made institutions that might prove less frequently deficient in respect of the common weal.

On the part of man, whose acts are regulated by law, the law can be rightly changed on account of the changed condition of man, to whom different things are expedient according to the difference of his condition. An example is proposed by Augustine:

> If the people have a sense of moderation and responsibility and are most careful guardians of the common weal, it is right to enact a law allowing such a people to choose their own magistrates for the government of the commonwealth. But if, as time goes on, the same people become so corrupt as to sell their votes and entrust the government to scoundrels and criminals, then the right of appointing their public officials is rightly forfeit to such a people, and the choice devolves to a few good men.[7]

Reply Obj. 1. The natural law is a participation of the eternal law, as stated above,[8] and, therefore, endures without change, owing to the unchangeableness and perfection of the divine reason, the Author of nature. But the reason of man is changeable and imperfect; wherefore his law is subject to change. Moreover, the natural law contains certain universal precepts which are everlasting, whereas human law contains certain particular precepts according to various emergencies.

Reply Obj. 2. A measure should be as enduring as possible. But nothing can be absolutely unchangeable in things that are subject to change. And, therefore, human law cannot be altogether unchangeable.

Reply Obj. 3. Of corporeal objects, "right" ["straight"] is predicated absolutely and, therefore, as far as itself is concerned, always remains "right." But "right" is predicated of law with reference to the common weal, to which one and the same thing is not always adapted, as stated above; wherefore, rectitude of this kind is subject to change.

SECOND ARTICLE

Should Human Law Always Be Changed Whenever Something Better Occurs?

We proceed thus to the Second Article:

Obj. 1. It would seem that human law should be changed whenever something better occurs because human laws are devised by human reason, like other arts. But in the other arts, the tenets of former times give place to others if something better occurs. Therefore, the same should apply to human laws.

Obj. 2. Further, by taking note of the past, we can provide for the future. Now unless human laws had been changed when it was found possible to improve them, considerable inconvenience would have ensued because the laws of old were crude in many points. Therefore, it seems that laws should be changed whenever anything better occurs to be enacted.

Obj. 3. Further, human laws are enacted about single acts of man. But we cannot acquire perfect knowlege in singular matters except by experience, which "requires time," as stated in *Ethics* II, 1.[9] Therefore, it seems that, as time goes on, it is possible for something better to occur for legislation.

On the contrary, It is stated in the *Decretum:* "It is absurd and a detestable shame that we should suffer those traditions to be changed which we have received from the fathers of old."[10]

I answer that, As stated above, human law is rightly changed insofar as such change is conducive to the common weal.[11] But, to a certain extent, the mere change of law is of itself prejudicial to the common good because custom avails much for the observance of laws, seeing that what is done contrary to general custom, even in slight matters, is looked upon as grave. Consequently, when a law is changed, the binding power of the law is diminished insofar as custom is abolished. Wherefore, human law should never be changed unless, in some way or other, the common weal be compensated according to the extent of the harm done in this respect. Such compensation may arise either from some very great and very evident benefit conferred by the new enactment or from the extreme urgency of the case, due to the fact that either the existing law is clearly unjust or its observance extremely harmful. Wherefore the Jurist says that "in establishing new laws, there should be evidence of the benefit to be derived before departing from a law which has long been considered just."[12]

Reply Obj. 1. Rules of art derive their force from reason alone, and, therefore, whenever something better occurs, the rule followed hitherto should be changed. But "laws derive very great force from custom," as the Philosopher states;[13] consequently, they should not be quickly changed.

Reply Obj. 2. This argument proves that laws ought to be changed, not in view of any improvement but for the sake of a great benefit or in a case of great urgency, as stated above. This answer applies also to the *Third Objection.*

THIRD ARTICLE
Can Custom Obtain Force of Law?

We proceed thus to the Third Article:

Obj. 1. It would seem that custom cannot obtain force of law nor abolish a law because human law is derived from the natural law and from the divine law, as stated above.[14] But human custom cannot change either the law of nature or the divine law. Therefore, neither can it change human law.

Obj. 2. Further, many evils cannot make one good. But he who first acted against the law did evil. Therefore, by multiplying such acts, nothing good is the result. Now a law is something good, since it is a rule of human acts. Therefore, law is not abolished by custom so that the mere custom should obtain force of law.

Obj. 3. Further, the framing of laws belongs to those public men whose business it is to govern the community; wherefore private individuals cannot make laws. But custom grows by the acts of private individuals. Therefore, custom cannot obtain force of law so as to abolish the law.

On the contrary, Augustine says, "The customs of God's people and the institutions of our ancestors are to be considered as laws. And those who throw contempt on the customs of the Church ought to be punished as those who disobey the law of God."[15]

I answer that All law proceeds from the reason and will of the lawgiver: the divine and natural laws from the reasonable will of God, the human law from the will of man regulated by reason. Now just as human reason and will, in practical matters, may be made manifest by speech, so may they be made known by deeds, since, seemingly, a man chooses as good that which he carries into execution. But it is evident that, by human speech, law can be both changed and expounded insofar as it manifests the interior movement and thought of human reason. Wherefore, by actions also, especially if they be repeated so as to make a custom, law can be changed and expounded, and also something can be established which obtains force of law insofar as, by repeated external actions, the inward movement of the will and concepts of reason are most effectually declared; for when a thing is done again and again, it seems to proceed from a deliberate judgment of reason. Accordingly, custom has the force of law, abolishes law, and is the interpreter of law.

Reply Obj. 1. The natural and divine laws proceed from the divine will, as stated above. Wherefore, they cannot be changed by a custom proceeding from the will of man but only by divine authority. Hence it is that no custom can prevail over the divine or natural laws, for Isidore says: "Let custom yield to authority; evil customs should be eradicated by law and reason."[16]

Reply Obj. 2. As stated above, human laws fail in some cases;[17] wherefore, it is possible sometimes to act beside the law, namely, in a case where the law fails, yet the act will not be evil. And when such cases are multiplied, by reason of some change in man, then custom shows that the law is no longer useful, just as it might be declared by the verbal promulgation of a law to the contrary. If, however, the same reason remains for which the law was useful hitherto, then it is not the custom that prevails against the law but the law that overcomes the custom, unless perhaps the sole reason for the law seeming useless be that it is not "possible according to the custom of the country," which has been stated to be one of the conditions of law.[18] For it is not easy to set aside the custom of a whole people.

Reply Obj. 3. The people among whom a custom is introduced may be of two conditions. For if they are free and able to make their own laws, the consent of the whole people expressed by a custom counts far more in favor of a particular observance than does the authority of the ruler, who has not the power to frame laws except as representing the people. Wherefore, although single individuals cannot make laws, yet the whole people can. If, however, the people have not the free power to make their own laws or to abolish a law made by a higher authority, nevertheless, with such a people, a prevailing custom obtains force of law insofar as it is tolerated by those to whom it belongs to make laws for that people, because, by the very fact that they tolerate it, they seem to approve of that which is introduced by custom.

FOURTH ARTICLE

Can the Rulers of the People Dispense from Human Laws?

We proceed thus to the Fourth Article:

Obj. 1. It would seem that the rulers of the people cannot dispense from human laws. For the law is established for the "common weal," as Isidore says.[19] But the common good should not be set aside for the private convenience of an individual, because, as the Philosopher says, "the good of the nation is more godlike than the good of one man."[20] Therefore, it seems that a man should not be dispensed from acting in compliance with the general rule.

Obj. 2. Further, those who are placed over others are commanded as follows: "You shall hear the little as well as the great; neither shall you respect any man's person, because it is the judgment of God."[21] But to allow one man to do that which is equally forbidden to all seems to be respect of persons. Therefore, the rulers of a community cannot grant such dispensations, since this is against a precept of the divine law.

Obj. 3. Further, human law, in order to be just, should accord with the natural and divine laws, else it would not "foster religion nor be helpful to discipline," which is a requisite of law as laid down by Isidore.[22] But no man can dispense from the divine and natural laws. Neither, therefore, can he dispense from the human law.

On the contrary, The Apostle says, "A dispensation is committed to me."[23]

I answer that Dispensation, properly speaking, denotes a measuring out to individuals of some common goods; thus the head of a household is called a dispenser because, to each member of the household, he distributes work and necessaries of life in due weight and measure. Accordingly, in every community, a man is said to dispense from the very fact that he directs how some general precept is to be fulfilled by each individual. Now it happens at times that a precept which is conducive to the common weal as a general rule is not good for a particular individual or in some particular case, either because it would hinder some greater good or because it would be the occasion of some evil, as explained above.[24] But it would be dangerous to leave this to the discretion of each individual, except perhaps by reason of an evident and sudden emergency, as stated above (ibid.). Consequently, he who is placed over a community is empowered to dispense in a human law that rests upon his authority, so that, when the law fails in its application to persons or circumstances, he may allow the precept of the law not to be observed. If, however, he grant this permission without any such reason and of his mere will, he will be an unfaithful or an imprudent dispenser: unfaithful if he has not the common good in view; imprudent if he ignores the reasons for granting dispensations. Hence our Lord says: "Who, think you, is the faithful and wise dispenser, whom his lord sets over his family?"[25]

Reply Obj. 1. When a person is dispensed from observing the general law, this should not be done to the prejudice of, but with the intention of benefiting, the common good.

Reply Obj. 2. It is not "respect of persons" if unequal measures are served out to those who are themselves unequal. Wherefore, when the condition of any person requires that he should reasonably receive special treatment, it is not "respect of persons" if he be the object of a special favor.

Reply Obj. 3. Natural law, so far as it contains general precepts, which never fail, does not allow of dispensation. In the other precepts, however, which are as conclusions of the general precepts, man sometimes grants a dispensation: for instance, that a loan should not be paid back to the betrayer of his country, or something similar. But to the divine law, each man stands as a private person to the public law to which he is subject. Wherefore, just as none can dispense from public human law except the man from whom the law derives its authority or his delegate, so, in the precepts of the divine law, which are from God, none can dispense but God or the man to whom He may give special power for that purpose.

Questions 98–105

[Questions 98 to 105 deal with the Old Law. Aquinas there distinguishes three types of precepts of the Old Law: moral (Q. 100), ceremonial (QQ. 101–3), and judicial (QQ. 104–5). (The judicial precepts concern social institutions and relations.) In QQ. 106–8, Aquinas deals with the New Law and its relationship to the Old Law. Only Q. 100 and A. 1 of Q. 105 are reproduced here.]

Question 100
Of the Moral Precepts of the Old Law

[In Twelve Articles]

We must now consider each kind of precept of the Old Law: (1) the moral precepts; (2) the ceremonial precepts; (3) the judicial precepts. Under the first head, there are twelve points of inquiry: (1) Whether all the moral precepts of the Old Law belong to the law of nature? (2) Whether the moral precepts of the Old Law are about the acts of all the virtues? (3) Whether all the moral precepts of the Old Law are reducible to the ten precepts of the Decalogue? (4) How the precepts of the Decalogue are distinguished from one another? (5) their number; (6) their order; (7) the manner in which they

were given; (8) Whether they are dispensable? (9) Whether
the mode of observing a virtue comes under the precept of
the Law? (10) Whether the mode of charity comes under the
precept? (11) the distinction of other moral precepts; (12)
Whether the moral precepts of the Old Law justified man?

FIRST ARTICLE
Do All the Moral Precepts of the Old Law
Belong to the Law of Nature?

We proceed thus to the First Article:

Obj. 1. It would seem that not all the moral precepts belong
to the law of nature. For it is written, "Moreover, He gave
them instructions and the law of life for an inheritance."[1] But
instruction is in contradistinction to the law of nature, since
the law of nature is not learned but instilled by natural instinct. Therefore, not all the moral precepts belong to the
natural law.

Obj. 2. Further, the divine law is more perfect than human
law. But human law adds certain things concerning good
morals to those that belong to the law of nature, as is evidenced by the fact that the natural law is the same in all men,
while these moral precepts are various for various people.
Much more reason, therefore, was there why the divine law
should add to the law of nature ordinances pertaining to
good morals.

Obj. 3. Further, just as natural reason leads to good morals
in certain matters, so does faith; hence it is written that faith
"works by charity."[2] But faith is not included in the law of
nature, since that which is of faith is above nature. Therefore, not all the moral precepts of the divine law belong to
the law of nature.

On the contrary, The Apostle says that "the Gentiles, who
have not the Law, do by nature those things that are of the
Law,"[3] which must be understood of things pertaining to
good morals. Therefore, all the moral precepts of the Law
belong to the law of nature.

I answer that The moral precepts, distinct from the ceremonial and judicial precepts, are about things pertaining of
their very nature to good morals. Now, since human morals

depend on their relation to reason, which is the proper principle of human acts, those morals are called good which accord with reason, and those are called bad which are discordant from reason. And as every judgment of speculative reason proceeds from the natural knowledge of first principles, so every judgment of practical reason proceeds from principles known naturally, as stated above,[4] from which principles one may proceed in various ways to judge of various matters. For some matters connected with human actions are so evident that with a modicum of consideration, one is able at once to approve or disapprove of them by means of these general first principles, while some matters cannot be the subject of judgment without much consideration of the various circumstances, which all are not competent to do carefully but only those who are wise, just as it is not possible for all to consider the particular conclusions of sciences but only for those who are versed in philosophy; and lastly, there are some matters of which man cannot judge unless he be helped by divine instruction, such as the articles of faith.

It is, therefore, evident that, since the moral precepts are about matters which concern good morals, and since good morals are those which are in accord with reason, and since also every judgment of human reason must needs be derived in some way from natural reason, it follows of necessity that all the moral precepts belong to the law of nature, but not all in the same way. For there are certain things which the natural reason of every man of its own accord and at once judges to be done or not to be done: e.g., "Honor thy father and thy mother," and "Thou shalt not kill," "Thou shalt not steal,"[5] and these belong to the law of nature absolutely. And there are certain things which, after a more careful consideration, wise men deem obligatory. Such belong to the law of nature, yet so that they need to be inculcated, the wiser teaching the less wise: e.g., "Rise up before the hoary head, and honor the person of the aged man,"[6] and the like. And there are some things, to judge of which human reason needs divine instruction, whereby we are taught about the things of God: e.g., "Thou shalt not make to thyself a graven thing, nor the likeness of anything"; "Thou shalt not take the name of the Lord thy God in vain."[7]

This suffices for the *Replies* to the *Objections*.

SECOND ARTICLE

Are the Moral Precepts of the Law about All the Acts of Virtue?

We proceed thus to the Second Article:

Obj. 1. It would seem that the moral precepts of the Law are not about all the acts of virtue. For observance of the precepts of the Old Law is called justification, according to Ps. 118:8: "I will keep Your justifications." But justification is the execution of justice. Therefore, the moral precepts are only about acts of justice.

Obj. 2. Further, that which comes under a precept has the character of a duty. But the character of duty belongs to justice alone and to none of the other virtues, for the proper act of justice consists in rendering to each one his due. Therefore, the precepts of the moral law are not about the acts of the other virtues but only about the acts of justice.

Obj. 3. Further, every law is made for the common good, as Isidore says.[8] But of all the virtues, justice alone regards the common good, as the Philosopher says.[9] Therefore, the moral precepts are only about the acts of justice.

On the contrary, Ambrose says that "a sin is a transgression of the divine law and a disobedience to the commandments of heaven."[10] But there are sins contrary to all the acts of virtue. Therefore, it belongs to the divine law to direct all the acts of virtue.

I answer that, Since the precepts of the Law are ordained to the common good, as stated above,[11] the precepts of the law must needs be diversified according to the various kinds of community; hence the Philosopher teaches that the laws which are made in a political community which is ruled by a king must be different from the laws of a state which is ruled by the people or by a few powerful men in the state.[12] Now, human law is ordained for one kind of community, and the divine law for another kind, because human law is ordained for the civil community, implying mutual duties of man and his fellows, and men are ordained to one another by outward acts, whereby men live in communion with one another. This life in common of man with man pertains to justice, whose proper function consists in directing the human community. Wherefore human law makes precepts only about acts of justice, and if it commands acts of other virtues, this is only insofar as they assume the nature of justice, as the Philosopher explains.[13]

But the community for which the divine law is ordained is that of men in relation to God either in this life or in the life to come. And, therefore, the divine law proposes precepts about all those matters whereby men are well ordered in their relations to God. Now, man is united to God by his reason or mind, in which is God's image. Wherefore the divine law proposes precepts about all those matters whereby human reason is well ordered. But this is effected by the acts of all the virtues, since the intellectual virtues set in good order the acts of the reason in themselves, while the moral virtues set in good order the acts of the reason in reference to the interior passions and exterior actions. It is, therefore, evident that the divine law fittingly proposes precepts about the acts of all the virtues, yet so that certain matters, without which the order of virtue, which is the order of reason, cannot be observed come under an obligation of precept, while other matters, which pertain to the well-being of perfect virtue, come under an admonition of counsel.

Reply Obj. 1. The fulfilment of the commandments of the Law, even of those which are about the acts of the other virtues, has the character of justification inasmuch as it is just that man should obey God, or again, inasmuch as it is just that all that belongs to man should be subject to reason.

Reply Obj. 2. Justice, properly so called, regards the duty of one man to another, but all the other virtues regard the duty of the lower powers to reason. It is in relation to this latter duty that the Philosopher speaks of a kind of metaphorical justice.[14]

The *Reply* to the *Third Objection* is clear from what has been said about the different kinds of community.

THIRD ARTICLE

Are All the Moral Precepts of the Old Law Reducible to the Ten Precepts of the Decalogue?

We proceed thus to the Third Article:

Obj. 1. It would seem that not all the moral precepts of the Old Law are reducible to the ten precepts of the Decalogue.

For the first and principal precepts of the Law are: "Thou shalt love the Lord thy God" and "Thou shalt love thy neighbor," as stated in Mt.[15] But these two are not contained in the precepts of the Decalogue. Therefore, not all the moral precepts are contained in the precepts of the Decalogue.

Obj. 2. Further, the moral precepts are not reducible to the ceremonial precepts, but rather vice versa. But among the precepts of the Decalogue, one is ceremonial, viz., "Remember that thou keep holy the Sabbath-day."[16] Therefore, the moral precepts are not reducible to all the precepts of the Decalogue.

Obj. 3. Further, the moral precepts are about all the acts of virtue. But among the precepts of the Decalogue are only such as regard acts of justice, as may be seen by going through them all. Therefore, the precepts of the Decalogue do not include all the moral precepts.

On the contrary, The gloss on Mt. 5:11 ("Blessed are you when they shall revile you," etc.) says that "Moses, after propounding the ten precepts, set them out in detail."[17] Therefore, all the precepts of the Law are so many parts of the precepts of the Decalogue.

I answer that The precepts of the Decalogue differ from the other precepts of the Law in the fact that God Himself is said to have given the precepts of the Decalogue, whereas He gave the other precepts to the people through Moses. Wherefore the Decalogue includes those precepts the knowledge of which man has immediately from God. Such are those which with but slight reflection can be gathered at once from the first general principles and those also which become known to man immediately through divinely infused faith. Consequently, two kinds of precepts are not reckoned among the precepts of the Decalogue, viz., first general principles, for they need no further promulgation after being once imprinted on the natural reason to which they are nearly self-evident, as, for instance, that one should do evil to no man, and other similar principles, and again those which the careful reflection of wise men shows to be in accord with reason, since the people receive these principles from God through being taught by wise men. Nevertheless, both kinds of precepts are contained in the precepts of the Decalogue, yet in different ways. For the first general principles are contained in them as principles in their proximate conclusions, while those which are known through wise men are contained, conversely, as conclusions in their principles.

Reply Obj. 1. Those two principles are the first general principles of the natural law and are self-evident to human reason either through nature or through faith.[18] Wherefore all the precepts of the Decalogue are referred to these as conclusions to general principles.

Reply Obj. 2. The precept of the Sabbath observance is moral in one respect, insofar as it commands man to give some time to the things of God, according to Ps. 45:11: "Be still and see that I am God." In this respect, it is placed among the precepts of the Decalogue, but not as to the fixing of the time, in which respect it is a ceremonial precept.

Reply Obj. 3. The notion of duty is not so patent in the other virtues as it is in justice. Hence the precepts about the acts of the other virtues are not so well known to the people as are the precepts about acts of justice. Wherefore the acts of justice especially come under the precepts of the Decalogue, which are the primary elements of the Law.

FOURTH ARTICLE
Are the Precepts of the Decalogue Suitably Distinguished from One Another?

We proceed thus to the Fourth Article:

Obj. 1. It would seem that the precepts of the Decalogue are unsuitably distinguished from one another. For worship is a virtue distinct from faith. Now the precepts are about acts of virtue. But that which is said at the beginning of the Decalogue, "Thou shalt not have strange gods before Me," belongs to faith, and that which is added, "Thou shalt not make . . . any graven thing," etc., belongs to worship. Therefore, these are not one precept, as Augustine asserts,[19] but two.

Obj. 2. Further, the affirmative precepts in the Law are distinct from the negative precepts, e.g., "Honor thy father and thy mother" and "Thou shalt not kill." But this, "I am the Lord thy God," is affirmative, and that which follows, "Thou shalt not have strange gods before Me," is negative. Therefore, these are two precepts and do not, as Augustine says, make one.

Obj. 3. Further, the Apostle says: "I had not known concupiscence if the Law did not say: 'Thou shalt not covet.' "[20] Hence it seems that this precept, "Thou shalt not covet," is one precept and, therefore, should not be divided into two.

On the contrary stands the authority of Augustine, who, in commenting on Exodus, distinguishes three precepts as referring to God and seven as referring to our neighbor.[21]

I answer that The precepts of the Decalogue are differently divided by different authorities. For Hesychius, commenting on Lev. 26:26, "Ten women shall bake your bread in one oven," says that the precept of the Sabbath-day observance is not one of the ten precepts because its observance in the letter is not binding for all time.[22] But he distinguishes four precepts pertaining to God: the first being "I am the Lord thy God"; the second, "Thou shalt not have strange gods before Me" (thus also Jerome distinguishes these two precepts in his commentary on Hos. 10:10, "On your two iniquities"[23]); the third precept according to him is "Thou shalt not make to thyself any graven thing"; and the fourth, "Thou shalt not take the name of the Lord thy God in vain." He states that there are six precepts pertaining to our neighbor: the first, "Honor thy father and thy mother"; the second, "Thou shalt not kill"; the third, "Thou shalt not commit adultery"; the fourth, "Thou shalt not steal"; the fifth, "Thou shalt not bear false witness"; the sixth, "Thou shalt not covet."

But, in the first place, it seems unbecoming for the precept of the Sabbath-day observance to be put among the precepts of the Decalogue if it nowise belonged to the Decalogue. Secondly, because, since it is written: "No man can serve two masters,"[24] the two statements, "I am the Lord thy God" and "Thou shalt not have strange gods before Me," seem to be of the same nature and to form one precept. Hence Origen, who also distinguishes four precepts as referring to God, unites these two under one precept and reckons in the second place, "Thou shalt not make . . . any graven thing"; as third, "Thou shalt not take the name of the Lord thy God in vain"; and as fourth, "Remember that thou keep holy the Sabbath day."[25] The other six he reckons in the same way as Hesychius.

Since, however, the making of graven things or the likeness

of anything is not forbidden except as to the point of their being worshiped as gods—for God commanded an image of the Seraphim to be made and placed in the tabernacle, as related in Ex.[26] Augustine more fittingly unites these two, "Thou shalt not have strange gods before Me" and "Thou shalt not make . . . any graven thing," into one precept. Likewise, to covet another's wife for the purpose of carnal knowledge belongs to the concupiscence of the flesh, whereas, to covet other things, which are desired for the purpose of possession, belongs to the concupiscence of the eyes; wherefore Augustine reckons as distinct precepts that which forbids the coveting of another's goods and that which prohibits the coveting of another's wife. Thus he distinguishes three precepts as referring to God and seven as referring to our neighbor. And this is better.

Reply Obj. 1. Worship is merely a declaration of faith; wherefore the precepts about worship should not be reckoned as distinct from those about faith. Nevertheless, precepts should be given about worship rather than about faith because the precept about faith is presupposed to the precepts of the Decalogue, as is also the precept of charity. For just as the first general principles of the natural law are self-evident to a subject having natural reason and need no promulgation, so also to believe in God is a first and self-evident principle to a subject possessed of faith; "for he that comes to God must believe that He is."[27] Hence, it needs no other promulgation than the infusion of faith.

Reply Obj. 2. The affirmative precepts are distinct from the negative when one is not comprised in the other; thus that man should honor his parents does not include that he should not kill another man, nor does the latter include the former. But when an affirmative precept is included in a negative or vice versa, we do not find that two distinct precepts are given; thus there is not one precept saying that "Thou shalt not steal" and another binding one to keep another's property intact or to give it back to its owner. In the same way, there are not different precepts about believing in God and about not believing in strange gods.

Reply Obj. 3. All covetousness has one common note, and, therefore, the Apostle speaks of the commandment about covetousness as though it were one. But because there are various special kinds of covetousness, therefore Augustine distinguishes different prohibitions against coveting; for covetousness differs specifically in respect of the diversity of actions or things coveted, as the Philosopher says.[28]

FIFTH ARTICLE
Are the Precepts of the Decalogue Suitably Set Forth?

We proceed thus to the Fifth Article:

Obj. 1. It would seem that the precepts of the Decalogue are unsuitably set forth because sin, as stated by Ambrose, is "a transgression of the divine law and a disobedience to the commandments of heaven."[29] But sins are distinguished according as man sins against God or his neighbor or himself. Since, then, the Decalogue does not include any precepts directing man in his relations to himself but only such as direct him in his relations to God and his neighbor, it seems that the precepts of the Decalogue are insufficiently enumerated.

Obj. 2. Further, just as the Sabbath-day observance pertained to the worship of God, so also did the observance of other solemnities and the offering of sacrifices. But the Decalogue contains a precept about the Sabbath-day observance. Therefore, it should contain others also pertaining to the other solemnities and to the sacrificial rite.

Obj. 3. Further, as sins against God include the sin of perjury, so also do they include blasphemy or other ways of lying against the teaching of God. But there is a precept forbidding perjury, "Thou shalt not take the name of the Lord thy God in vain."[30] Therefore, there should be also a precept of the Decalogue forbidding blasphemy and false doctrine.

Obj. 4. Further, just as man has a natural affection for his parents, so has he also for his children. Moreover, the commandment of charity extends to all our neighbors. Now the precepts of the Decalogue are ordained unto charity, according to 1 Tim.: "The end of the commandment is charity."[31] Therefore, as there is a precept referring to parents, so should there have been some precepts referring to children and other neighbors.

Obj. 5. Further, in every kind of sin, it is possible to sin in desire or in deed. But in some kinds of sin, namely in theft and adultery, the prohibition of sins of deed, when it is said, "Thou shalt not commit adultery," "Thou shalt not steal," is distinct from the prohibition of the sin of desire, when it is said, "Thou shalt not covet they neighbor's goods" and "Thou shalt not covet thy neighbor's wife." Therefore, the same should have been done in regard to the sins of homicide and false witness.

Obj. 6. Further, just as sin happens through disorder of the concupiscible faculty, so does it arise through disorder of the irascible faculty. But some precepts forbid inordinate concupiscence, when it is said, "Thou shalt not covet." Therefore, the Decalogue should have included some precepts forbidding the disorders of the irascible faculty. Therefore, it seems that the ten precepts of the Decalogue are unfittingly enumerated.

On the contrary, It is written: "He showed you His covenant, which He commanded you to do, and the ten words that He wrote in two tables of stone."[32]

I answer that, As stated above, just as the precepts of human law direct man in his relations to the human community, so the precepts of the divine law direct man in his relations to a community or commonwealth of men under God.[33] Now, in order that any man may dwell aright in a community, two things are required: the first is that he behave well to the head of the community; the other is that he behave well to those who are his fellows and partners in the community. It is, therefore, necessary that the divine law should contain in the first place precepts ordering man in his relations to God, and in the second place, other precepts ordering man in his relations to other men who are his neighbors and live with him under God.

Now, man owes three things to the head of the community: first, fidelity; secondly, reverence; thirdly, service. Fidelity to his master consists in his not giving sovereign honor to another, and this is the sense of the First Commandment, in the words "Thou shalt not have strange gods." Reverence to his master requires that he should do nothing injurious to him, and this is conveyed by the Second Commandment, "Thou shalt not take the name of the Lord thy God in vain." Service is due to the master in return for the benefits which his subjects receive from him, and to this belongs the Third Commandment of the sanctification of the Sabbath in memory of the creation of all things.

To his neighbors, a man behaves himself well both in particular and in general. In particular, as to those to whom he is indebted, by paying his debts, and in this sense is to be taken the commandment about honoring one's parents. In general, as to all men, by doing harm to none either by deed or by word or by desire. By deed, harm is done to one's neighbor—sometimes in his person, i.e., as to his personal existence, and this is prohibited by the words, "Thou shalt not kill"; sometimes in a person united to him, as to the propagation of offspring, and this is prohibited by the words, "Thou shalt not commit adultery"; sometimes in his possessions, which are directed to both the aforesaid, and with regard to this, it is said, "Thou shalt not steal." Harm done by word is forbidden when it is said, "Thou shalt not bear false witness against thy neighbor"; harm by desire is forbidden in the words, "Thou shalt not covet."

The three precepts that direct man in his behavior towards God may also be differentiated in this same way. For the first refers to deeds, wherefore it is said, "Thou shalt not make . . . a graven thing"; the second to words, wherefore it is said, "Thou shalt not take the name of the Lord thy God in vain"; the third to desires because the sanctification of the Sabbath, as the subject of a moral precept, requires repose of the heart in God. Or, according to Augustine: by the First Commandment, we reverence the unity of the First Principle; by the Second, the divine truth; by the Third, His goodness, whereby we are sanctified, and wherein we rest as in our last end.[34]

Reply Obj. 1. This objection may be answered in two ways. First, because the precepts of the Decalogue can be reduced to the precepts of charity. Now there was need for man to receive a precept about loving God and his neighbor because, in this respect, the natural law had become obscured on account of sin, but not about the duty of loving oneself because, in this respect, the natural law retained its vigor; or, again, because love of oneself is contained in the love of God and of one's neighbor, since true self-love consists in directing oneself to God. And for this reason the Decalogue includes those precepts only which refer to our neighbor and to God.

Secondly, it may be answered that the precepts of the Decalogue are those which the people received from God immediately; wherefore it is written: "He wrote in the tables, according as He had written before, the ten words which the Lord spoke to you."[35] Hence, the precepts of the Decalogue need to be such as the people can understand at once. Now, a precept implies the notion of duty. But it is easy for a man, especially for a believer, to understand that, of necessity, he owes certain duties to God and to his neighbor. But that, in matters which regard himself and not another, man has, of necessity, certain duties to himself is not so evident; for, at the first glance, it seems that everyone is free in matters that concern himself. And, therefore, the precepts which prohibit disorders of a man with regard to himself reach the people through the instruction of men who are versed in such matters, and, consequently, they are not contained in the Decalogue.

Reply Obj. 2. All the solemnities of the Old Law were instituted in celebration of some divine favor, either in memory of past favors or in sign of some favor to come; in like manner, all the sacrifices were offered up with the same purpose. Now, of all the divine favors to be commemorated, the chief was that of the Creation, which was called to mind by the sanctification of the Sabbath; wherefore the reason for this precept is given in Ex.: "In six days the Lord made heaven and earth,"[36] etc. And of all future blessings, the chief and final was the repose of the mind in God, either, in the present life, by grace or, in the future life, by glory, which repose was also foreshadowed in the Sabbath-day observance; wherefore it is written: "If you turn away your foot from the Sabbath, from doing your own will in My holy day, and call the Sabbath delightful and the holy of the Lord glorious,"[37] because these favors first and chiefly are borne in mind by men, especially by the faithful. But other solemnities were celebrated on account of certain particular favors temporal and transitory, such as the celebration of the Passover in memory of the past favor of the delivery from Egypt and as a sign of the future Passion of Christ, which, though temporal and transitory, brought us to the repose of the spiritual Sabbath.

Consequently, the Sabbath alone and none of the other solemnities and sacrifices is mentioned in the precepts of the Decalogue.

Reply Obj. 3. As the Apostle says, "men swear by one greater than themselves, and an oath of confirmation is the end of all their controversy."[38] Hence, since oaths are common to all, inordinate swearing is the matter of a special prohibition by a precept of the Decalogue. The sin of false teaching, by contrast, pertains only to a few, and so it is not fitting that the precepts of the Decalogue mention it. According to one interpretation, however, the words, "Thou shalt not take the name of the Lord thy God in vain," are a prohibition of false doctrine, for one gloss expounds them thus: "Thou shalt not say that Christ is a creature."[39]

Reply Obj. 4. Natural reason immediately dictates to a man that he should not do harm to anyone, and, therefore, the precepts that forbid the doing of harm are binding on all men. But natural reason does not immediately dictate that a man should do something for another, unless he happen to be indebted to someone. Now a son's debt to his father is so evident that it cannot be denied by turning away from it, since the father is the principle of generation and being and also of upbringing and teaching. Wherefore the Decalogue does not prescribe deeds of kindness or service to be done to anyone except to one's parents. On the other hand, parents do not seem to be indebted to their children for any favors received, but rather the reverse is the case. Again, a child is a part of his father, and "parents love their children as being a part of themselves," as the Philosopher states.[40] Hence, just as the precepts of the Decalogue contain no ordinance as to man's behavior towards himself, so, for the same reason, it includes no precepts about loving one's children.

Reply Obj. 5. The pleasure of adultery and the usefulness of wealth, insofar as they have the character of pleasurable or useful good, are, of themselves, objects of appetite, and for this reason, they needed to be forbidden not only in the deed but also in the desire. But murder and falsehood are of themselves objects of repulsion (since it is natural for man to love his neighbor and the truth) and are desired only for the sake of something else. Consequently, with regard to sins of murder and false witness, it was necessary to proscribe, not sins of desire, but only sins of deed.

Reply Obj. 6. As stated above,[41] all the passions of the irascible faculty arise from the passions of the concupiscible faculty. Hence, as the precepts of the Decalogue are, as it were, the first elements of the Law, there was no need for mention of the irascible passions but only of the concupiscible passions.

SIXTH ARTICLE

Are the Ten Precepts of the Decalogue Set in Proper Order?

We proceed thus to the Sixth Article:

Obj. 1. It would seem that the ten precepts of the Decalogue are not set in proper order because love of one's neighbor is seemingly previous to love of God, since our neighbor is better known to us than God is; according to 1 Jn.: "He that loves not his brother, whom he sees, how can he love God, Whom he sees not?"[42] But the first three precepts belong to the love of God, while the other seven pertain to the love of our neighbor. Therefore, the precepts of the Decalogue are not set in proper order.

Obj. 2. Further, acts of virtue are prescribed by the affirmative precepts, and acts of vice are forbidden by the negative precepts. But according to Boethius in his *Commentary on the Categories,* vices should be uprooted before virtues are sown.[43] Therefore, among the precepts concerning our neighbor, the negative precepts should have preceded the affirmative.

Obj. 3. Further, the precepts of the Law are about men's actions. But actions of desire precede actions of word or outward deed. Therefore, the precepts about not coveting, which regard our desires are unsuitably placed last in order.

On the contrary, The Apostle says: "The things that are of God are well ordered."[44] But the precepts of the Decalogue were given immediately by God, as stated above.[45] Therefore, they are arranged in becoming order.

I answer that, As stated above, the precepts of the Decalogue are such as the mind of man is ready to grasp at once.[46] Now it is evident that a thing is so much the more easily grasped by the reason as its contrary is more grievous and repugnant to reason. Moreover, it is clear, since the order of reason begins with the end, that for a man to be inordinately disposed towards his end is supremely contrary to reason. Now the end of human life and society is God. Consequently, it was necessary for the precepts of the Decalogue, first of all, to direct man to God, since the contrary to this is most grievous. Thus also in an army, which is ordained to the commander as to its end, it is requisite first that the soldier should be subject to the commander, and the opposite of this is most grievous, and secondly it is requisite that he should be in co-ordination with the other soldiers.

Now among those things whereby we are ordained to God, the first is that man should be subjected to Him faithfully, by having nothing in common with His enemies; the second is that he should show Him reverence; the third that he should offer Him service. Thus, in an army, it is a greater sin for a soldier to act treacherously and make a compact with the foe than to be insolent to his commander, and this last is more grievous than if he be found wanting in some point of service to him.

As to the precepts that direct man in his behavior towards his neighbor, it is evident that it is more repugnant to reason and a more grievous sin if man does not observe the due order as to those persons to whom he is most indebted. Consequently, among those precepts that direct man in his relations to his neighbor, the first place is given to that one which regards his parents. Among the other precepts, we again find the order to be according to the gravity of sin. For it is more grave and more repugnant to reason to sin by deed than by word, and by word than by desire. And among sins of deed, murder, which destroys life in one already living, is more grievous than adultery, which casts doubt concerning prospective life, and adultery is more grave than theft, which regards external goods.

Reply Obj. 1. Although our neighbor is better known than God by way of the senses, nevertheless, the love of God is the reason for the love of our neighbor, as shall be declared later on.[47] Hence the precepts ordaining man to God demanded precedence of the others.

Reply Obj. 2. Just as God is the universal principle of being in respect of all things, so is a father a principle of being in respect of his son. Therefore, the precept regarding parents was fittingly placed after the precepts regarding God. This argument holds in respect of affirmative and negative precepts about the same kind of deed, although even then it is not altogether cogent. For although, in the order of execution, vices should be uprooted before virtues are sown, according to Ps. 33:15: "Turn away from evil and do good," and Is. 1:16, 17: "Cease to do perversely, learn to do well," yet in the order of knowledge, virtue precedes vice because "the crooked line is known by the straight,"[48] and "by the law is the knowledge of sin."[49] Wherefore the affirmative precept demanded the first place. However, this is not the reason for the order but that which is given above: because, in the precepts regarding God, which belong to the first table, an affirmative precept is placed last, since its transgression implies a less grievous sin.

Reply Obj. 3. Although sin of desire stands first in the order of execution, yet its prohibition holds a later position in the order of reason.

SEVENTH ARTICLE
Are the Precepts of the Decalogue Suitably Formulated?

We proceed thus to the Seventh Article:

Obj. 1. It would seem that the precepts of the Decalogue are unsuitably formulated because the affirmative precepts direct man to acts of virtue, while the negative precepts withdraw him from acts of vice. But, in every matter, there are virtues and vices opposed to one another. Therefore, in whatever matter there is an ordinance of a precept of the Decalogue, there should have been an affirmative and a negative precept. Therefore, it was unfitting that affirmative precepts should be framed in some matters, and negative precepts in others.

Obj. 2. Further, Isidore says that every law is based on reason.[50] But all the precepts of the Decalogue belong to the divine law. Therefore, the reason should have been pointed out in each precept and not only in the first and third.

Obj. 3. Further, by observing the precepts, man deserves to be rewarded by God. But the divine promises concern the rewards of the precepts. Therefore, the promise should have been included in each precept and not only in the second and fourth.

Obj. 4. Further, the Old Law is called "the law of fear," insofar as it induced men to observe the precepts by means of the threat of punishments. But all the precepts of the Decalogue belong to the Old Law. Therefore, a threat of punishment should have been included in each and not only in the first and second.

Obj. 5. Further, all the commandments of God should be retained in the memory, for it is written: "Write them in the tables of your heart."[51] Therefore, it was not fitting that mention of the memory should be made in the third commandment only. Consequently, it seems that the precepts of the Decalogue are unsuitably formulated.

On the contrary, It is written that "God made all things in measure, number, and weight."[52] Much more, therefore, did He observe a suitable manner in formulating His Law.

I answer that The highest wisdom is contained in the precepts of the divine law; wherefore it is written: "This is your wisdom and understanding in the sight of nations."[53] Now it belongs to wisdom to arrange all things in due manner and order. Therefore, it must be evident that the precepts of the Law are suitably set forth.

Reply Obj. 1. Affirmation of one thing always leads to the denial of its opposite, but the denial of one opposite does not always lead to the affirmation of the other. For it follows that, if a thing is white, it is not black, but it does not follow that, if it is not black, it is white, because negation extends further than affirmation. And hence, too, that one ought not to do harm to another, which pertains to the negative precepts, extends to more persons, as a primary dictate of reason, than that one ought to do someone a service or kindness. Nevertheless, it is a primary dictate of reason that man is a debtor in the point of rendering a service or kindness to those from whom he has received kindness if he has not yet repaid the debt. Now there are two whose favors no man can sufficiently repay, viz., God and man's father, as stated in *Eth.* VIII.[54] Therefore, it is that there are only two affirmative precepts: one about the honor due to parents, the other about the celebration of the Sabbath in memory of the divine favor.

Reply Obj. 2. The reasons for the purely moral precepts are manifest; hence there was no need to add the reason. But some of the precepts include ceremonial matter or a determination of a general moral precept; thus the first precept includes the determination, "Thou shalt not make a graven thing," and in the third precept, the Sabbath day is fixed. Consequently, there was need to state the reason in each case.

Reply Obj. 3. Generally speaking, men direct their actions to some point of utility. Consequently, in those precepts in which it seemed that there would be no useful result, or that some utility might be hindered, it was necessary to add a promise of reward. And since parents are already on the way to depart from us, no benefit is expected from them; wherefore a promise of reward is added to the precept about honoring one's parents. The same applies to the precept forbidding idolatry since thereby it seemed that men were hindered from receiving the apparent benefit which they think they can get by entering into a compact with the demons.

Reply Obj. 4. Punishments are necessary against those who are prone to evil, as stated in *Ethics* X.[55] Wherefore, a threat of punishment is only affixed to those precepts of the law which forbade evils to which men were prone. Now, men were prone to idolatry by reason of the general custom of the nations. Likewise, men are prone to perjury on account of the frequent use of oaths. Hence it is that a threat is affixed to the first two precepts.

Reply Obj. 5. The commandment about the Sabbath was made in memory of a past blessing. Wherefore special mention of the memory is made therein. Or, again, the commandment about the Sabbath has a determination affixed to it that does not belong to the natural law; wherefore this precept needed a special admonition.

EIGHTH ARTICLE
Are the Precepts of the Decalogue Dispensable?

We proceed thus to the Eighth Article:

Obj. 1. It would seem that the precepts of the Decalogue are dispensable. For the precepts of the Decalogue belong to the natural law. But the natural law fails in some cases and is

changeable, like human nature, as the Philosopher says.[56]
Now, the failure of law to apply in certain particular cases is
a reason for dispensation, as stated above.[57] Therefore, a dispensation can be granted in the precepts of the Decalogue.

Obj. 2. Further, man stands in the same relation to human
law as God does to divine law. But man can dispense from
the precepts of a law made by man. Therefore, since the
precepts of the Decalogue are ordained by God, it seems that
God can dispense from them. Now, our prelates are God's
vicegerents on earth; for the Apostle says: "For what I have
pardoned, if I have pardoned anything, for your sakes have I
done it in the person of Christ."[58] Therefore, prelates can
dispense from the precepts of the Decalogue.

Obj. 3. Further, among the precepts of the Decalogue is one
forbidding murder. But it seems that a dispensation is given
by men in this precept, for instance, when, according to the
prescription of human law, such as evildoers or enemies are
lawfully slain. Therefore, the precepts of the Decalogue are
dispensable.

Obj. 4. Further, the observance of the Sabbath is ordained
by a precept of the Decalogue. But a dispensation was granted in this precept, for it is written: "And they determined in
that day, saying: 'Whosoever shall come up to fight against us
on the Sabbath day, we will fight against him.' "[59] Therefore,
the precepts of the Decalogue are dispensable.

On the contrary are the words of Is. 24:5, where some are
reproved because "they have changed the ordinance, they
have broken the everlasting covenant," which seemingly apply principally to the precepts of the Decalogue. Therefore,
the precepts of the Decalogue cannot be changed by dispensation.

I answer that, As stated above,[60] precepts admit of dispensation when there occurs a particular case in which, if the
letter of the law be observed, the intention of the lawgiver is
frustrated. Now, the intention of every lawgiver is directed
first and chiefly to the common good; secondly, to the order
of justice and virtue, whereby the common good is preserved
and attained. If, therefore, there be any precepts which contain the very preservation of the common good or the very
order of justice and virtue, such precepts contain the intention of the lawgiver and, therefore, are indispensable. For
instance, if in some community a law were enacted such as

this, that no man should work for the destruction of the commonwealth or betray the political community to its enemies, or that no man should do anything unjust or evil, such precepts would not admit of dispensation. But if other precepts were enacted, subordinate to the above, and determining certain special modes of procedure, these latter precepts would admit of dispensation insofar as the omission of these precepts in certain cases would not be prejudicial to the former precepts which contain the intention of the lawgiver. For instance, if, for the safeguarding of the commonwealth, it were enacted in some city that, from each ward, some men should keep watch as sentries in case of siege, some might be dispensed from this on account of some greater utility.

Now, the precepts of the Decalogue contain the very intention of the lawgiver, who is God. For the precepts of the first table, which direct us to God, contain the very order to the common and final good, which is God, while the precepts of the second table contain the order of justice to be observed among men, that nothing undue be done to anyone, and that each one be given his due; for it is in this sense that we are to take the precepts of the Decalogue. Consequently, the precepts of the Decalogue admit of no dispensation whatever.

Reply Obj. 1. The Philosopher is not speaking of the naturally just, which contains the very order of justice, for it is a never-failing principle that "justice should be preserved." But he is speaking in reference to certain fixed modes of observing justice which fail to apply in certain cases.

Reply Obj. 2. As the Apostle says, God "continues faithful, He cannot deny Himself."[61] But He would deny Himself if He were to do away with the very order of His own justice, since He is justice itself. Wherefore, God cannot dispense a man so that it be lawful for him not to direct himself to God or not to be subject to His justice even in those matters in which men are directed to one another.

Reply Obj. 3. The slaying of a man is forbidden in the Decalogue insofar as it bears the character of something undue; for, in this sense, the precept contains the very essence of justice. Human law cannot make it lawful for a man to be slain unduly. But it is not undue for evil-doers or foes of the common weal to be slain; hence this is not contrary to the precept of the Decalogue, and such a killing is no murder as forbidden by that precept, as Augustine observes.[62] In like manner, when a man's property is taken from him, if it be due that he should lose it, this is not theft or robbery as forbidden by the Decalogue.

Consequently, when the children of Israel, by God's command, took away the spoils of the Egyptians, this was not theft since it was due to them by the sentence of God. Likewise, when Abraham consented to slay his son, he did not consent to murder because his son was due to be slain by the command of God, Who is Lord of life and death; for He it is Who inflicts the punishment of death on all men, both godly and ungodly, on account of the sin of our first parent, and if a man be the executor of that sentence by divine authority, he will be no murderer any more than God would be. Again, Hosea, by taking unto himself a fornicating wife or an adulterous woman [sic], was not guilty either of adultery or of fornication, because he took unto himself one who was his by command of God, Who is the Author of the institution of marriage.

Accordingly, therefore, the precepts of the Decalogue, as to the essence of justice which they contain, are unchangeable, but as to any determination by application to individual actions—for instance, that this or that be murder, theft, or adultery, or not—in this point, they admit of change; sometimes by divine authority alone, namely, in such matters as are exclusively of divine institution, as marriage and the like; sometimes also by human authority, namely, in such matters as are subject to human jurisdiction, for, in this respect, men stand in the place of God, and yet not in all respects.

Reply Obj. 4. This determination was an interpretation rather than a dispensation. For a man is not taken to break the Sabbath if he does something necessary for human welfare, as Our Lord proves.[63]

NINTH ARTICLE
Does the Mode of Virtue Fall under the Precept of the Law?

We proceed thus to the Ninth Article:

Obj. 1. It would seem that the mode of virtue falls under the precept of the law. For the mode of virtue is that deeds of justice should be done justly, that deeds of fortitude should be done bravely, and in like manner as to the other virtues. But it is commanded that "you shall follow justly after that which is just."[64] Therefore, the mode of virtue falls under the precept.

Obj. 2. Further, that which belongs to the intention of the lawgiver comes chiefly under the precept. But the intention of the lawgiver is directed chiefly to make men virtuous, as stated in *Ethics* II, 1,[65] and it belongs to a virtuous man to act virtuously. Therefore, the mode of virtue falls under the precept.

Obj. 3. Further, the mode of virtue seems to consist properly in working willingly and with pleasure. But this falls under a precept of the divine law, for it is written: "Serve the Lord with gladness"[66] and "not with sadness or necessity, for God loves a cheerful giver";[67] whereupon the gloss says: "Whatever you do, do gladly, and then you will do it well, whereas if you do it sorrowfully, it is done in you, not by you."[68] Therefore, the mode of virtue falls under the precept of the law.

On the contrary, No man can act as a virtuous man acts unless he has the habit of virtue, as the Philosopher explains.[69] Now, whoever transgresses a precept of the law deserves to be punished. Hence, it would follow that a man who has not the habit of virtue would deserve to be punished, whatever he does. But this is contrary to the intention of the law, which aims at leading man to virtue by habituating him to good works. Therefore, the mode of virtue does not fall under the precept.

I answer that, As stated above, a precept of law has compulsory power.[70] Hence, that on which the compulsion of the law is brought to bear falls directly under the precept of the law. Now the law compels through fear of punishment, as stated in *Ethics* X,[71] because that properly falls under the precept of the law for which the penalty of the law is inflicted. But divine law and human law are differently situated as to the appointment of penalties since the penalty of the law is inflicted only for those things which come under the judgment of the lawgiver, for the law punishes in accordance with the verdict given. Now man, the framer of human law, is competent to judge only of outward acts because "man sees those things that appear," according to 1 Kings;[72] while God alone, the framer of the divine law, is competent to judge of the inward movements of wills, according to Ps. 7:10: "The searcher of hearts and loins is God."

Accordingly, therefore, we must say that the mode of virtue is in some sort regarded both by human and by divine law; in some respect, it is regarded by the divine but not by the human law, and in another way, it is regarded neither by the human nor by the divine law. Now the mode of virtue consists in three things, as the Philosopher states in *Ethics* II, 3.[73] The first is that man should act knowingly, and this is subject to the judgment of both divine and human law because what a man does in ignorance he does accidentally. Hence, according to both human and divine law, certain things are judged in respect of ignorance to be punishable or pardonable.

The second point is that a man should act deliberately, i.e., from choice, choosing that particular action for its own sake; wherein a twofold internal movement is implied, of volition and of intention, about which we have spoken above,[74] and concerning these two, divine law alone and not human law is competent to judge. For human law does not punish the man who wishes to slay but slays not, whereas the divine law does, according to Mt.: "Whosoever is angry with his brother, shall be in danger of the judgment."[75]

The third point is that he should act from a firm and immovable principle, which firmness belongs properly to a habit and implies that the action proceeds from a rooted habit. In this respect, the mode of virtue does not fall under the precept either of divine or of human law, since neither by man nor by God is he punished as breaking the law who gives due honor to his parents and yet has not the habit of filial piety.

Reply Obj. 1. The mode of doing acts of justice, which falls under the precept, is that they be done in accordance with right, but not that they be done from the habit of justice.

Reply Obj. 2. The intention of the lawgiver is twofold. His aim, in the first place, is to lead men to something by the precepts of the law, and this is virtue. Secondly, his intention is brought to bear on the matter itself of the precept, and this is something leading or disposing to virtue, viz., an act of virtue. For the end of the precept and the matter of the precept are not the same, just as neither in other things is the end the same as that which conduces to the end.

Reply Obj. 3. That works of virtue should be done without sadness falls under the precept of the divine law, for whoever works with sadness works unwillingly. But to work with pleasure, i.e., joyfully or cheerfully, in one respect falls under the precept, viz., insofar as pleasure ensues from the love of God and one's neighbor (which love falls under the precept), and love causes pleasure, and in another respect does not fall under the precept, insofar as pleasure ensues from a habit; for "pleasure taken in a work proves the existence of a habit," as stated in *Ethics* II.[76] For an act may give pleasure either on account of its end or through its proceeding from a becoming habit.

TENTH ARTICLE
Does the Mode of Charity Fall under the Precept of the Divine Law?

We proceed thus to the Tenth Article:

Obj. 1. It would seem that the mode of charity falls under the precept of the divine law. For it is written: "If you wish to enter into life, keep the commandments";[77] whence it seems to follow that the observance of the commandments suffices for entrance into life. But good works do not suffice for entrance into life except they be done from charity; for it is written: "If I should distribute all my goods to feed the poor, and if I should deliver my body to be burned and have not charity, it profits me nothing."[78] Therefore, the mode of charity is included in the commandment.

Obj. 2. Further, the mode of charity consists properly speaking in doing all things for God. But this falls under the precept, for the Apostle says: "Do all to the glory of God."[79] Therefore, the mode of charity falls under the precept.

Obj. 3. Further, if the mode of charity does not fall under the precept, it follows that one can fulfill the precepts of the law without having charity. Now what can be done without charity can be done without grace, which is always united with charity. Therefore, one can fulfill the precepts of the law without grace. But this is the error of Pelagius, as Augustine declares.[80] Therefore, the mode of charity is included in the commandment.

On the contrary, Whoever breaks a commandment sins mortally. If, therefore, the mode of charity falls under the precept, it follows that whoever acts otherwise than from charity sins mortally. But whoever has not charity acts otherwise than from charity. Therefore, it follows that whoever has not charity sins mortally in whatever he does, however good this may be in itself, which is unfitting.

I answer that Opinions have been contrary on this question. For some have said absolutely that the mode of charity comes under the precept, and yet that it is possible for one not having charity to fulfill this precept, because he can dispose himself to receive charity from God. Nor (say they) does it follow that a man not having charity sins mortally whenever he does something good of its kind, because it is an affirmative precept that binds one to act from charity and is binding not for all time but only for such time as one is in a state of charity. On the other hand, some have said that the mode of charity is altogether outside the precept.

Both these opinions are true up to a certain point because the act of charity can be considered in two ways. First, as an act by itself, and thus it falls under the precept of the law which specially prescribes it, viz., "Thou shalt love the Lord thy God"[81] and "Thou shalt love thy neighbor."[82] In this sense, the first opinion is true because it is not impossible to observe this precept which regards the act of charity, since man can dispose himself to possess charity, and when he possesses it, he can use it. Secondly, the act of charity can be considered as being the mode of the acts of the other virtues, i.e., inasmuch as the acts of the other virtues are ordained to charity, which is "the end of the command" as stated in 1 Tim.,[83] for it has been said above that the intention of the end is a formal mode of the act ordained to that end.[84] In this sense, the second opinion is true in saying that the mode of charity does not fall under the precept, that is to say, that this commandment, "Honor thy father," does not mean that a man must honor his father from charity, but merely that he must honor him. Wherefore he that honors his father, yet has not charity, does not break this precept, although he does break the precept concerning the act of charity, for which reason he deserves to be punished.

Reply Obj. 1. Our Lord did not say, "If you wish to enter into life, keep one commandment," but "keep" all "the commandments," among which is included the commandment concerning the love of God and our neighbor.

Reply Obj. 2. The precept of charity contains the injunction that God should be loved from our whole heart, which means that all things would be referred to God. Consequently, man cannot fulfill the precept of charity unless he also refer all things to God. Wherefore he that honors his father and mother is bound to honor them from charity, not in virtue of the precept, "Honor thy father and mother," but in virtue of the precept, "Thou shalt love the Lord thy God with thy whole heart." And though these are two affirmative precepts not binding for all times, they can be binding, each one at a different time, so that it may happen that a man fulfills the precept of honoring his father and mother without at the same time breaking the precept concerning the omission of the mode of charity.

Reply Obj. 3. Man cannot fulfill all the precepts of the law unless he fulfill the precept of charity, which is impossible without grace. Consequently, it is not possible, as Pelagius maintained, for man to fulfill the law without grace.

ELEVENTH ARTICLE

Is It Right to Distinguish Other Moral Precepts of the Law besides the Decalogue?

We proceed thus to the Eleventh Article:

Obj. 1. It would seem that it is wrong to distinguish other moral precepts of the law besides the Decalogue because, as Our Lord declared, "on these two commandments" of charity "depends the whole law and the prophets."[85] But these two commandments are explained by the Ten Commandments of the Decalogue. Therefore, there is no need for other moral precepts.

Obj. 2. Further, the moral precepts are distinct from the judicial and ceremonial precepts, as stated above.[86] But the determinations of the general moral precepts belong to the

judicial and ceremonial precepts, and the general moral precepts are contained in the Decalogue or are even presupposed
to the Decalogue, as stated above.[87] Therefore, it was unsuit-
able to lay down other moral precepts besides the Decalogue.

Obj. 3. Further, the moral precepts are about the acts of all
the virtues, as stated above.[88] Therefore, as the Law contains
besides the Decalogue moral precepts pertaining to religion,
liberality, mercy, and chastity, so there should have been added some precepts pertaining to the other virtues, for instance, fortitude, sobriety, and so forth. And yet such is not
the case. It is, therefore, unbecoming to distinguish other
moral precepts in the Law besides those of the Decalogue.

On the contrary, It is written: "The law of the Lord is
unspotted, converting souls."[89] But man is preserved from
the stain of sin, and his soul is converted to God, by other
moral precepts besides those of the Decalogue. Therefore, it
was right for the Law to include other moral precepts.

I answer that, As is evident from what has been stated, the
judicial and ceremonial precepts derive their force from their
institution alone, since, before they were instituted, it
seemed of no consequence whether things were done in this
or that way.[90] But the moral precepts derive their efficacy
from the very dictate of natural reason, even if they were
never included in the Law. Now of these there are three
grades. For some are most certain and so evident as to need
no promulgaton, such as the commandments of the love of
God and our neighbor and others like these, as stated
above,[91] which are, as it were, the ends of the commandments; wherefore no man can have an erroneous judgment
about them. Some precepts are more detailed, the reason of
which even an uneducated man can easily grasp, and yet they
need to be promulgated because human judgment, in a few
instances, happens to be led astray concerning them; these
are the precepts of the Decalogue. Again, there are some
precepts the reason of which is not so evident to everyone
but only to the wise; these are moral precepts added to the
Decalogue and given to the people by God through Moses
and Aaron.

But since the things that are evident are the principles
whereby we know those that are not evident, these other
moral precepts added to the Decalogue are reducible to the

precepts of the Decalogue as so many corollaries. Thus the First Commandment of the Decalogue forbids the worship of strange gods, and to this are added other precepts forbidding things relating to the worship of idols; thus it is written: "Neither let there be found among you anyone that shall purify his son or daughter, making them to pass through the fire; . . . neither let there be any wizard or charmer or anyone that consults pythonic spirits or fortune-tellers or that seeks the truth from the dead."[92] The Second Commandment forbids perjury. To this is added the prohibition of blasphemy[93] and the prohibition of false doctrine.[94] To the Third Commandment are added all the ceremonial precepts. To the Fourth Commandment prescribing the honor due to parents is added the precept about honoring the aged, according to Lev. 19:32: "Rise up before the hoary head and honor the person of the aged man," and likewise all precepts prescribing the reverence to be observed towards our betters or kindliness towards our equals or inferiors. To the Fifth Commandment, which forbids murder, is added the prohibition of hatred and of any kind of violence inflicted on our neighbor, according to Lev. 19:16: "You shall not stand against the blood of your neighbor"; likewise the prohibition against hating one's brother (ibid., v. 17): "You shall not hate your brother in your heart." To the Sixth Commandment, which forbids adultery, is added the prohibition about whoredom, according to Dt. 23:17: "There shall be no whore among the daughters of Israel nor whoremonger among the sons of Israel," and the prohibition against unnatural sins, according to Lev. 18:22, 23: "You shall not lie with mankind; . . . you shall not copulate with any beast." To the Seventh Commandment, which prohibits theft, is added the precept forbidding the taking of interest, according to Dt. 23:19: "You shall not lend to your brother money at interest," and the prohibition against fraud, according to Dt. 25:13: "You shall not have diverse weights in your bag," and universally all prohibitions relating to peculations and larceny. To the Eighth Commandment forbidding false testimony is added the prohibition against false judgment, according to Ex. 23:2: "Neither shall you yield in judgment to the opinion of the most part to stray from the truth," and the prohibition against lying (ibid., v. 7): "You shall flee lying," and the prohibition against detraction, according to Lev. 19:16: "You shall not be a detractor nor a whisperer among the people." To the other two Commandments, no further precepts are added because thereby are forbidden all kinds of evil desires.

Reply Obj. 1. The precepts of the Decalogue are ordained to the love of God and our neighbor as pertaining to our duty towards them, but the other precepts are so ordained as pertaining thereto less evidently.

Reply Obj. 2. It is in virtue of their institution that the ceremonial and judicial precepts are determinations of the precepts of the Decalogue, not by reason of a natural instinct, as in the case of the superadded moral precepts.

Reply Obj. 3. The precepts of a law are ordained for the common good, as stated above.[95] And since those virtues which direct our conduct towards others pertain directly to the common good, as also does the virtue of chastity insofar as the generative act conduces to the common good of the species; hence precepts bearing directly on these virtues are given both in the Decalogue and in addition thereto. As to the act of fortitude, there are the precepts to be given by the commanders in a war which is undertaken for the common good, as is clear from Dt. 20:3, where the priest is commanded [to speak thus]: "Be not afraid, do not go back." In like manner, the prohibition of acts of gluttony is left to paternal admonition, since they are contrary to the good of the household; hence it is said in the person of parents: "He slights hearing our admonitions, he gives himself to reveling and to debauchery and banquetings."[96]

TWELFTH ARTICLE

Did the Moral Precepts of the Old Law Justify Man?

We proceed thus to the Twelfth Article:

Obj. 1. It would seem that the moral precepts of the Old Law justified man, because the Apostle says: "For not the hearers of the Law are justified before God, but the doers of the Law shall be justified."[97] But the doers of the Law are those who fulfill the precepts of the Law. Therefore, the fulfilling of the precepts of the Law was a cause of justification.

Obj. 2. Further, it is written: "Keep My laws and My judgments, which, if a man do, he shall live in them."[98] But the spiritual life of man is through justice. Therefore, the fulfilling of the precepts of the Law was a cause of justification.

Obj. 3. Further, the divine law is more efficacious than human law. But human law justifies man, since there is a kind of justice consisting in fulfilling the precepts of law. Therefore, the precepts of the law justified man.

On the contrary, The Apostle says: "The letter kills,"[99] which, according to Augustine,[100] refers even to the moral precepts. Therefore, the moral precepts did not cause justice.

I answer that, Just as "healthy" is said properly and first of that which is possessed of health and secondarily of that which is a sign or a safeguard of health, so justification means first and properly the causing of justice, while secondarily and improperly, as it were, it may denote a sign of justice or a disposition thereto. If justice be taken in these two ways, it is evident that it was conferred by the precepts of the Law insofar, to wit, as they disposed men to the justifying grace of Christ, which they also signified, because, as Augustine says, "even the life of that people foretold and foreshadowed Christ."[101]

But if we speak of justification properly so called, then we must notice that it can be considered as in the habit or as in the act, so that, accordingly, justification may be taken in two ways: first, according as man is made just by becoming possessed of the habit of justice; secondly, according as he does works of justice, so that, in this sense, justification is nothing else than the execution of justice. Now justice, like the other virtues, may denote either the acquired or the infused virtue, as is clear from what has been stated.[102] The acquired virtue is caused by works, but the infused virtue is caused by God Himself through His grace. The latter is true justice, of which we are speaking now, and in this respect of which a man is said to be just before God, according to Rom.:[103] "If Abraham were justified by works, he has whereof to glory, but not before God." Hence this justice could not be caused by the moral precepts, which are about human actions; wherefore the moral precepts could not justify man by causing justice.

If, on the other hand, by justification we understand the execution of justice, thus all the precepts of the Law justified man, but in various ways. Because the ceremonial precepts taken as a whole contained something just in itself insofar as they aimed at offering worship to God, whereas, taken individually, they contained that which is just, not in itself but by being a determination of the divine law. Hence, it is said of these precepts that they did not justify man save through the devotion and obedience of those who complied with them. On the other hand, the moral and judicial precepts, either in general or also in particular, contained that which is just in itself, but the moral precepts contained that which is just in itself according to that general justice which is "every virtue" according to *Ethics* V,[104] whereas the judicial precepts belonged to special justice, which is about contracts connected with the human mode of life between one man and another.

Reply Obj. 1. The Apostle takes justification for the execution of justice.

Reply Obj. 2. The man who fulfilled the precepts of the Law is said to live in them because he did not incur the penalty of death, which the Law inflicted on its transgressors; in this sense the Apostle quotes this passage.[105]

Reply Obj. 3. The precepts of human law justify man by acquired justice; it is not about this that we are inquiring now but only about that justice which is before God.

ST I–II

Question 105
Of the Reason for the Judicial Precepts

[In Four Articles, of Which Article One Is Included]

FIRST ARTICLE

Did the Old Law Enjoin Fitting Precepts Concerning Rulers?

We proceed thus to the First Article:

Obj. 1. It would seem that the Old Law made unfitting precepts concerning rulers, because, as the Philosopher says, "the ordering of the people depends mostly on the chief ruler."[1] But the Law contains no precept relating to the institution of the chief ruler, and yet we find therein prescriptions concerning the inferior rulers: firstly, "Provide out of all the people wise men,"[2] etc.; again, "Gather to Me seventy men of the ancients of Israel";[3] and again, "Let Me have from among you wise and understanding men,"[4] etc. Therefore, the Law provided insufficiently in regard to the rulers of the people.

Obj. 2. Further, "The best gives of the best," as Plato states.[5] Now the best ordering of a political community or of any nation is to be ruled by a king because this kind of government approaches nearest in resemblance to the divine government, whereby God rules the world from the beginning. Therefore, the Law should have set a king over the people, and they should not have been allowed a choice in the matter, as indeed they were allowed: "When you . . . shall say: 'I will set a king over me . . . ', you shall set him,"[6] etc.

Obj. 3. Further, according to Mt.: "Every kingdom divided against itself shall be made desolate"[7]—a saying which was verified in the Jewish people, whose destruction was brought about by the division of the kingdom. But the Law should aim chiefly at things pertaining to the general well-being of the people. Therefore, it should have forbidden the kingdom to be divided under two kings, nor should this have been introduced even by divine authority, as we read of its being introduced by the authority of the prophet Ahijah the Shilonite.[8]

Obj. 4. Further, just as priests are instituted for the benefit of the people in things concerning God, as stated in Heb.,[9] so are rulers set up for the benefit of the people in human affairs. But certain things were allotted as a means of livelihood for the priests and Levites of the Law, such as the tithes and first-fruits and many like things. Therefore, in like manner, certain things should have been determined for the livelihood of the rulers of the people, the more that they were forbidden to accept presents, as is clearly stated in Ex.: "You shall not take bribes, which even blind the wise and pervert the words of the just."[10]

Obj. 5. Further, as a kingdom is the best form of government, so is tyranny the most corrupt. But when the Lord appointed the king, He established a tyrannical law, for it is written: "This will be the right of the king that shall reign over you: He will take your sons,"[11] etc. Therefore, the Law made unfitting provision with regard to the institution of rulers.

On the contrary, The people of Israel is commended for the beauty of its order: "How beautiful are your tabernacles, O Jacob, and your tents, O Israel."[12] But the beautiful ordering of a people depends on the right establishment of its rulers. Therefore, the Law made right provision for the people with regard to its rulers.

I answer that Two points are to be observed concerning the right ordering of rulers in a political community or nation. One is that all should take some share in the government, for this form of constitution ensures peace among the people, and all love and defend it, as stated in *Politics* II.[13] The other point to be observed is in respect of the kinds of government or the different ways in which the constitutions are established. For, whereas these differ in kind, as the Philosopher states,[14] nevertheless, the first place is held by the kingdom, where the power of government is vested in one according to his virtue, and aristocracy, which signifies government by the best, where the government is vested in a few according to their virtue. Accordingly, the best form of government is in a political community or kingdom wherein one is given the power to preside over all according to his virtue, while under him are others having governing powers according to their virtue, and yet a government of this kind is shared by all, both because all are eligible to govern, and because the rulers are chosen by all. For this is the best form of polity, being partly kingdom since there is one at the head of all, partly aristocracy insofar as a number of persons are set in authority, partly democracy, i.e., government by the people, insofar as the rulers can be chosen from the people, and the people have the right to choose their rulers.

Such was the form of government established by the divine law. For Moses and his successors governed the people in such a way that each of them was ruler over all, so that there was a kind of kingdom. Moreover, seventy-two men were chosen who were elders in virtue; for it is written: "I took out of your tribes men wise and honorable and appointed them rulers,"[15] so that there was an element of aristocracy.

But it was a democratic government insofar as the rulers were chosen from all the people; for it is written: "Provide out of all the people wise men,"[16] etc.; and, again, insofar as they were chosen by the people; wherefore it is written: "Let me have from among you wise men,"[17] etc. Consequently, it is evident that the ordering of the rulers which the Law provided was the best.

Reply Obj. 1. This people was governed under the special care of God; wherefore it is written: "The Lord your God has chosen you to be His peculiar people,"[18] and this is why the Lord reserved to Himself the institution of the chief ruler. For this, too, did Moses pray: "May the Lord the God of the spirits of all the flesh provide a man that may be over this multitude."[19] Thus, by God's orders, Joshua was set at the head to succeed Moses, and we read about each of the judges who succeeded Joshua that God "raised . . . up a savior" for the people, and that "the spirit of the Lord was" in them.[20] Hence the Lord did not leave the choice of a king to the people but reserved this to Himself, as appears from Dt.: "You shall set up him whom the Lord your God shall choose."[21]

Reply Obj. 2. A kingdom is the best form of government of the people so long as it is not corrupt. But since the power granted to a king is so great, it easily degenerates into tyranny unless he to whom this power is given be a very virtuous man; for it is only the virtuous man that conducts himself well in the midst of prosperity, as the Philosopher observes.[22] Now, perfect virtue is to be found in few, and especially were the Jews inclined to cruelty and avarice, which vices above all turn men into tyrants. Hence, from the very first, the Lord did not set up the kingly authority with full powers but gave them judges and governors to rule them. But afterwards, when the people asked Him to do so, being indignant with them, so to speak, He granted them a king, as is clear from His words to Samuel: "They have not rejected you but Me, that I should not reign over them."[23]

Nevertheless, as regards the appointment of a king, He did establish the manner of election from the very beginning,[24] and then He determined two points: first, that, in choosing a king, they should wait for the Lord's decision, and that they should not make a man of another nation king, because such kings are wont to take little interest in the people they are set over and consequently to have no care for their welfare; secondly, He prescribed how the king, after his appointment, should behave in regard to himself, namely, that he should not accumulate chariots and horses or wives or immense wealth because, through craving for such things, princes become tyrants and forsake justice. He also appointed the manner in which they were to conduct themselves toward God, namely, that they should continually read and ponder on God's Law and should ever fear and obey God. Moreover, He decided how they should behave toward their subjects, namely, that they should not proudly despise them or ill-treat them, and that they should not depart from the paths of justice.

Reply Obj. 3. The division of the kingdom and a number of kings was rather a punishment inflicted on that people for their many dissensions, especially against the just rule of David, than a benefit conferred on them for their profit. Hence it is written: "I will give you a king in My wrath,"[25] and: "They have reigned, but not by Me; they have been princes, and I knew not."[26]

Reply Obj. 4. The priestly office was bequeathed by succession from father to son, and this in order that it might be held in greater respect if not any man from the people could become a priest, since honor was given to them out of reverence for the divine worship. Hence it was necessary to put aside certain things for them both as to tithes and as to first-fruits, and, again, as to oblations and sacrifices, that they might be afforded a means of livelihood. On the other hand, the rulers, as stated above, were chosen from the whole people, wherefore they had their own possessions from which to derive a living; and so much the more since the Lord forbade even a king to have superabundant wealth or to make too much show of magnificence, both because he could scarcely avoid the excesses of pride and tyranny arising from such things, and because, if the rulers were not very rich, and if their office involved much work and anxiety, it would not tempt the ambition of the common people and would not become an occasion of sedition.

Reply Obj. 5. That right was not given to the king by divine institution; rather was it foretold that kings would usurp that right by framing unjust laws and by degenerating into tyrants who preyed on their subjects. This is clear from the context that follows: "And you shall be his slaves," which is significative of tyranny since a tyrant rules his subjects as though they were his slaves. Hence Samuel spoke these words to deter them from asking for a king, since the narrative continues: "But the people would not hear the voice of Samuel." It may happen, however, that even a good king, without being a tyrant, may take away the sons and make them tribunes and centurions and may take many things from his subjects in order to secure the common weal.

Notes to Chapter 2
ST I–II, Q. 90, AA. 1–4

1. Q. 114.

2. Rom. 7:23; "the Apostle" refers to St. Paul.

3. I–II, Q. 57.

4. I–II, Q. 9, A. 1.

5. *Digest* I, 4, 1. K I, 35a.

6. I–II, Q. 17, A. 1.

7. I–II, Q. 1, A. 1, *ad* 3.

8. *Phys.* II, 9. 200a22.

9. I–II, Q. 13, A. 3; Q. 76, A. 1.

10. *Eth.* VII, 3. 1147a24.

11. I–II, Q. 17, A. 1.

12. *Etym.* II, 10. PL 82, 130; V, 3. PL 82, 199.

13. *Etym.* V, 21. PL 82, 203.

14. A. 1.

15. I–II, Q. 2, A. 7; Q. 3, A. 1.

16. *Eth.* V, 1. 1129b17.

17. 1252a5.

18. Rom. 2:14.

19. *Eth.* II, 1. 1103b3.

20. *Etym.* V, 10. PL 82, 200.

21. A. 1, *ad* 1.

22. *Eth.* X, 9. 1180a20.

23. I–II, Q. 92, A. 2, *ad* 3; II–II, Q. 64, A. 3.

24. 1252a5.

25. *Codex Justinianus* I, 1, 14, 7. K I, 68a.

26. A. 1.

27. *Etym.* II, 10. PL 82, 130.

ST I–II, Q. 91, AA. 1–6

1. *De lib. arb.* I, 6. PL 32, 1229.

2. I–II, Q. 90, A. 1, *ad.* 2; AA. 3, 4.

3. I, Q. 22, AA. 1, 2.

4. *De lib. arb.* I, 6. PL 32, 1229.

5. I–II, Q. 90, A. 2.

6. *Glossa ordin.* PL 114, 476.

7. I–II, Q. 90, A. 1, *ad* 1.

8. A. 1.

9. Ps. 4:6.

10. I–II, Q. 10, A. 1.

11. I–II, Q. 90, A. 1.

12. A. 2.

13. *De lib. arb.* I, 6. PL 32, 1229.

14. I–II, Q. 90, A. 1.

15. 1053a31.

16. *De lib. arb.* I, 6. PL 32, 1229.

17. I–II, Q. 90, A. 1.

18. I–II, Q. 90, AA. 2, 3, 4.

19. Cicero, *Rhetor.* II, 53.

20. A. 2.

21. A. 1.

22. Sir. 15:14.

23. I–II, Q. 14, A. 1.

24. A. 3.

25. Ps. 118:33.

26. I–II, Q. 5, A. 5.

27. *De lib. arb.* I, 5. PL 32, 1228.

28. Heb. 7:12.

29. Q. 30, A. 3.

30. Gal. 3:24, 25.

31. I–II, Q. 90, A. 2.

32. Ex. 3:8, 17.

33. Mt. 4:17.

34. *Contra Faust.* IV, 2. PL 42, 217.

35. A. 4.

36. Peter Lombard, *Sent.* III, dist. 40, 1.

37. *Contra Adimant.* 17. PL 42, 159; the "little difference" refers to the fact that the Latin word for fear *(timor)* has one more letter than the Latin word for love *(amor)*.

38. As Aquinas explains in the article, concupiscence is the inclination to sensuality antecedant and contrary to dictates of reason—a consequence of Adam's Fall. The Latin word *"fomes,"* translated here as "concupiscence," literally means "tinderwood."

39. *Etym.* V, 3. PL 82, 199.

40. I–II, Q. 90, A. 2.

41. Rom. 7:23.

42. A. 2; Q. 90, A. 1, *ad* 1.

ST I–II, Q. 92, AA. 1–2

1. *Digest* I, 3, 7. K I, 34a.

2. 1106a15.

3. I–II, Q. 55, A. 4.

4. I–II, Q. 90, A. 2.

5. *Pol.* III, 11. 1282b12.

6. *Eth.* II, 1. 1103b3.

7. I–II, Q. 90, A. 1, *ad* 2; AA. 3, 4.

8. *Pol.* I, 5. 1260a20.

9. I–II, Q. 63, A. 2.

10. *Eth.* II, 5. 1103b3.

11. I–II, Q. 63, A. 1.

12. *Conf.* III, 8. PL 32, 689.

13. *Pol.* III, 2. 1277a20.

14. *Digest* I, 3, 1. K I, 33b.

15. A. 1.

16. Ibid.

17. *Contra duas epist. Pelag.* II, 9. PL 44, 586.

18. *Etym.* V, 19. PL 82, 202.

19. I–II, Q. 90, AA. 1, 2; Q. 91, A. 4.

20. I–II, Q. 18, A. 8.

21. *Eth.* V, 1. 1129b19.

22. I Cor. 7:12.

ST I–II, Q. 93, AA. 1–6

1. *Quaest.* I, 46. PL 40, 30.

2. I–II, Q. 90, A. 4.

3. I, Q. 34, A. 1.

4. *De vera relig.* 30. PL 34, 147.

5. *De lib. arb.* I, 6. PL 32, 1229.

6. I–II, Q. 90.

7. I, Q. 14, A. 8.

8. I, Q. 103, A. 5.

9. I, Q. 15, A. 2.

10. I–II, Q. 90, A. 2.

11. *De Trin.* XV, 14. PL 42, 1076.

12. I, Q. 16, A. 1.

13. 1 Cor. 2:11.

14. *De lib. arb.* I, 6. PL 32, 1229.

15. *De vera relig.* 31. PL 34, 148.

16. I, 3. 1094b27.

17. *De lib. arb.* I, 6. PL 32, 1229.

18. *De vera relig.* 31. PL 34, 147.

19. *Eth.* I, 3. 1094b27.

20. I–II, Q. 91, A. 6.

21. Rom. 8:7.

22. A. 2, *Obj.* 2.

23. *De lib. arb.* I, 5. PL 32, 1228.

24. A. 1.

25. Pr. 8:15.

26. A. 1.

27. I–II, Q. 90, AA. 1, 2.

28. *De lib. arb,* I, 6. PL 32, 1229.

29. I–II, Q. 91, A. 6.

30. 13:1.

31. 15:28, 24.

32. I–II, Q. 92, A. 2.

33. A. 1.

34. *De vera relig.* 31. PL 34, 147.

35. This *"reply"* is really a development of the statement beginning *"On the contrary"* in the body of the article.

36. *Metaph.* V, 4. 1015b10.

37. I–II, Q. 90, A. 4.

38. 1102b25.

39. A. 1.

40. Pr. 8:29.

41. I–II, Q. 1, A. 2.

42. I, Q. 22, A. 2.

43. A. 1.

44. Gal. 5:18.

45. 8:14.

46. Rom. 8:7.

47. *De lib. arb.* I, 6. PL 32, 1229.

48. *City of God* XIX, 12. PL 41, 640.

49. A. 5.

50. A. 2.

51. *Eth.* II, 1. 1103a25.

52. *De lib. arb.* I, 15. PL 32, 1238.

53. *De catech. rud.* 18. PL 40, 333.

54. *Glossa*, on Gal. 5. PL 192, 158.

55. A. 4, *ad* 2.

56. 2 Cor. 3:17.

57. I–II, Q. 85, A. 2.

ST I–II, Q. 94, AA. 1–6

1. *Eth.* II, 5. 1105b20.

2. Cf. *In Hexaem.*, hom. 7. PG 29, 158.

3. I, Q. 79, A. 12.

4. A. 6.

5. *De bono conjug.* 21. PL 40, 390.

6. I–II, Q. 90, A. 1, *ad* 2.

7. I–II, Q. 92, A. 2.

8. I–II, Q. 90, A. 1.

9. I–II, Q. 91, A. 3.

10. *De hebdom.* PL 64, 1311.

11. 3. 1005b29–34.

12. *Digest* I, 1, 1. K I, 29a.

13. I–II, Q. 90, A. 2.

14. *De fide orth.* III, 14. PG 94, 1045.

15. A. 2.

16. *De fide orth.* II, 30. PG 94, 976.

17. *Decretum* I, 1, 1. RF I, 1.

18. Rom. 10:16.

19. 3. 1129b12.

20. AA. 2, 3.

21. *Etym.* V, 4. PL 82, 199.

22. AA. 2, 3.

23. 1. 184a16.

24. *De bello Gal.* VI, 23.

25. *Glossa ordin.* PL 109, 876.

26. Gen. 22:2.

27. Ex. 12:25.

28. Hos. 1:2.

29. *Etym.* V, 4. PL 82, 199.

30. *Decretum* I, 1, 5. RF I, 7.

31. A. 4.

32. A. 4.

33. 2:6.

34. I, Q. 105, A. 6, *ad* 1.

35. *Glossa.* PL 191, 1345.

36. *Conf.* II, 4. PL 32, 678.

37. AA. 4, 5.

38. I–II, Q. 77, A. 2.

39. Rom. 1:24.

ST I–II, Q. 95, AA. 1–4

1. I–II, Q. 92, A. 1.

2. *Eth.* V, 4. 1132a22.

3. I–II, Q. 90, AA. 1, 2.

4. *Etym.* V, 20. PL 82, 202.

5. I–II, Q. 63, A. 1; Q. 94, A. 3.

6. *Pol.* I, 13. 1253a31.

7. *Rhet.* I, 7. 1354a31.

8. *Eth.* V, 7. 1134b20.

9. *Etym.* V, 4. PL 82, 199.

10. *Eth.* V, 7. 1134b18.

11. I–II, Q. 94, A. 4.

12. *Eth.* V, 7. 1134b19.

13. *Digest* I, 3, 20. K I, 34a.

14. Cicero, *Rhetor.* II, 53.

15. *De lib. arb.* I, 5. PL 32, 1227.

16. I–II, Q. 91, A. 2, *ad* 2.

17. *Eth.* VI, 11. 1143b11.

18. *Etym.* V, 21. PL 82, 203.

19. *Etym.* V, 3. PL 82, 199.

20. Cicero, *De offic.* I, 7.

21. *Etym.* II, 10. PL 82, 131.

22. 200a10; b5.

23. A. 2; Q. 93, A. 3.

24. *Digest* I, 3, 25. K I, 34b.

25. I–II, Q. 90, A. 2.

26. *Etym.* V, 6. PL 82, 200; *Etym.* V, 4. PL 82, 199.

27. *Etym.* V, 9. PL 82, 200.

28. A. 2.

29. Ibid.

30. 1253a2.

31. I–II, Q. 90, A. 3.

32. *Pol.* III, 5. 1279a32; b4.

33. I.e., monarchy, aristocracy, oligarchy, and democracy.

34. *Etym.* V, 10. PL 82, 200.

ST I–II, Q. 96, AA. 1–6

1. *Eth.* V, 7. 1134b23.

2. I–II, Q. 90, AA. 1, 2.

3. Ibid.

4. 1. 1053al.

5. *Digest* I, 3, 3. K I, 34a; I. 3, 4. K I, 34a.

6. *Etym.* V, 21. PL 82, 203.

7. *City of God* XXII, 6. PL 41, 759.

8. *Eth.* V, 7. 1134b20.

9. *Metaph.* X, 1. 1052b18.

10. I–II, Q. 92, A. 2, *Obj. 2.*

11. *Eth.* I, 3. 1094b13.

12. *Etym.* V, 20. PL 82, 202.

13. I–II, Q. 95, A. 2.

14. I, 5. PL 32, 1228.

15. I–II, Q. 90, AA. 1, 2.

16. 1. 1053a24.

17. *Etym.* V, 21. PL 82, 203.

18. Pr. 30:33.

19. Mt. 9:17.

20. *De lib. arb.* I, 5. PL 32, 1228.

21. A. 2.

22. I–II, Q. 90, A. 2.

23. *Eth.* V, 1. 1129b19.

24. I–II, Q. 54, A. 2; Q. 60, A. 1; Q. 62, A. 2.

25. I–II, Q. 90, A. 2.

26. 1 Pet. 2:19.

27. *De lib. arb.* I, 5. PL 32, 1227.

28. Rom. 13:1, 2.

29. 1 Tim. 1:9.

30. *Decretum* XIX, 2, 2. RF I, 840.

31. Rom. 8:14.

32. *Digest* I, 3, 31. K I, 34b.

33. Rom. 13:1.

34. I–II, Q. 90, AA. 1, 2; A. 3, *ad* 2.

35. Rom. 2:14, 15.

36. 2:13.

37. *Glossa.* PL 191, 486.

38. *Decretals* I, 2, 6. RF II, 8.

39. Decius Ausonius, *Sententiae*, Pittacus, vers. 5. PL 19, 876.

40. Mt. 23:3, 4.

41. *De vera relig.* 31. PL 34, 148.

42. Pr. 8:15.

43. *De Trin.* IV, 14. PL 10, 107.

44. A. 4.

45. *Digest* I, 3, 25. K I, 34b.

ST I–II, Q. 97, AA. 1–4

1. I–II, Q. 95, A. 2.

2. *Eth.* V, 5. 1133a25.

3. I–II, Q. 90, AA. 1, 2.

4. I–II, Q. 95, A. 2.

5. *De lib. arb.* I, 6. PL 32, 1229.

6. I–II, Q. 91, A. 3.

7. *De lib arb.* I, 6. PL 32, 1229.

8. I–II, Q. 91, A. 2.

9. 1103a16.

10. *Decretum* I, 12, 5. RF I, 28.

11. A. 1.

12. *Digest* I, 4, 2. K I, 35a.

13. *Pol.* II, 5. 1269a20.

14. I–II, Q. 93, A. 3; Q. 95, A. 2.

15. *Epist.* 36, ad Casulanum I. PL 33, 136.

16. *Synon.* II, 16. PL 83, 863.

17. I–II, Q. 96, A. 6.

18. Cf. I–II, Q. 95, A. 3.

19. *Etym.* V, 21. PL 82, 203.

20. *Eth.* I, 2. 1094b10.

21. Dt. 1:17.

22. *Etym.* V, 3. PL 82, 199.

23. 1 Cor. 9:17.

24. I–II, Q. 96, A. 6.

25. Lk. 12:42.

ST I–II, Q. 100, AA. 1–12

1. Sir. 17:9.

2. Gal. 5:6.

3. Rom. 2:14.

4. I–II, Q. 94, AA. 2, 4.

5. Ex. 20:12, 13, 15; Dt. 5:16, 17, 19.

6. Lev. 19:32.

7. Ex. 20:4; Dt. 5:8, 11.

8. *Etym.* V, 21. PL 82, 203.

9. *Eth.* V, 1. 1130a4.

10. *De paradiso* 8. PL 14, 309.

11. I–II, Q. 90, A. 2.

12. *Pol.* IV, 1. 1289a11, a22.

13. *Eth.* V, 1. 1129b23.

14. *Eth.* V, 11. 1138b5.

15. 22:37, 39.

16. Ex. 20:8; Dt. 5:12.

17. PL 114, 90.

18. Aquinas does not here qualify "self-evident," as he did in the body of the article.

19. *Quaest. in Heptat.* II, Q. 71, super Ex. 20:3. PL 34, 621.

20. Rom. 7:7.

21. Loc. cit. in n. 19. Aquinas follows the Vulgate numbering and division of the Commandments; in the King James numbering and division, four Commandments refer to God, and six to neighbor.

22. *In Lev.* VII. PG 93, 1150.

23. *In Osee* III. PL 25, 908.

24. Mt. 6:24.

25. *Hom. in Exod.*, hom. 8. PG 12, 351.

26. 25:18.

27. Heb. 11:6.

28. *Eth.* X, 5. 1175b28.

29. *De paradiso* 8. PL 14, 309.

30. Ex. 20:7.

31. 1:5.

32. Dt. 4:13.

33. A. 2.

34. *In Ps.*, on Ps. 32:2. PL 36, 281.

35. Dt. 10:4.

36. 20:11.

37. Is. 58:13.

38. Heb. 6:16.

39. *Glossa ordin.* PL 113, 458.

40. *Eth.* VIII, 12. 1161b19.

41. I–II, Q. 25, A. 1.

42. 4:20.

43. *Commentary on the Categories* IV *(De oppositis).* PL 64, 277.

44. Rom. 13:1.

45. A. 3.

46. A. 3 and A. 5, *ad* 1.

47. II–II, Q. 25, A. 1; Q. 26, A. 2.

48. Aristotle, *De anima* I, 5. 411a5.

49. Rom. 3:20.

50. *Etym.* II, 10. PL 82, 130.

51. Pr. 3:3.

52. Wis. 11:21.

53. Dt. 4:6.

54. 14. 1163b15.

55. 9. 1180a4.

56. *Eth.* V, 7. 1134b29.

57. I–II, Q. 96, A. 6; Q. 97, A. 4.

58. 2 Cor. 2:10.

59. 1 Macc. 2:41.

60. I–II, Q. 96, A. 6; Q. 97, A. 4.

61. 2 Tim. 2:13.

62. *De lib. arb.* I, 4. PL 32, 1226.

63. Mt. 12:3.

64. Dt. 16:20.

65. 1103b3.

66. Ps. 99:2.

67. 2 Cor. 9:7.

68. *Glossa.* PL 192, 63.

69. *Eth.* II, 4. 1105a17; V, 8. 1135b24.

70. I–II, Q. 90, A. 3, *ad* 2.

71. 9. 1179b11.

72. 16:7.

73. 1104b3.

74. I–II, QQ. 8, 12.

75. 5:22.

76. 3. 1104b3.

77. Mt. 19:17.

78. 1 Cor. 13:3.

79. 1 Cor. 10:31.

80. *De haeres.* 88. PL 42, 47.

81. Dt. 6:5.

82. Lev. 19:18.

83. 1:5.

84. I–II, Q. 12, A. 4.

85. Mt. 22:40.

86. I–II, Q. 99, AA. 3, 4.

87. A. 3.

88. A. 2.

89. Ps. 18:8.

90. I–II, Q. 99, AA. 3, 4.

91. A. 3.

92. Dt. 18:10, 11.

93. Lev. 24:15.

94. Dt. 13.

95. I–II, Q. 90, A. 2.

96. Dt. 21:20.

97. Rom. 2:13.

98. Lev. 18:5.

99. 2 Cor. 3:6.

100. *De spiritu et littera* 14. PL 44, 215.

101. *Contra Faust.* XXII, 24. PL 42, 417.

102. I–II, Q. 63, A. 4.

103. 4:2.

104. 1. 1129b30.

105. Gal. 3:12.

ST I–II, Q. 105, A. 1.

1. *Pol.* III, 4. 1278b8.

2. Ex. 18:21.

3. Num. 11:16.

4. Dt. 1:13.

5. Plato, *Timaeus.* 29A, 29E.

6. Dt. 17:14, 15.

7. 12:25.

8. 1 Kings 11:29.

9. 5:1.

10. 23:8.

11. 1 Sam. 8:11.

12. Num. 24:5.

13. 9. 1270b17.

14. *Pol.* III, 5. 1279a32, b4.

15. Dt. 1:15.

16. Ex. 18:21.

17. Dt. 1:13.

18. Dt. 7:6.

19. Num. 27:16.

20. Judges 3:9, 10, 15.

21. 17:15.

22. *Eth.* IV, 3. 1124a30.

23. 1 Sam. 8:7.

24. Dt. 17:14.

25. Hos. 13:11.

26. Ibid., 8:4.

3

Justice

ST II–II

Question 57
Of Right

[In Four Articles]

After considering prudence we must in due sequence consider justice, the consideration of which will be fourfold: (1) of justice; (2) of its parts; (3) of the corresponding gift; (4) of the precepts relating to justice.

Four points will have to be considered about justice: (1) right;[1] (2) justice itself; (3) injustice; (4) judgment.

Under the first head, there are four points of inquiry: (1) Whether right is the object of justice? (2) Whether right is fittingly divided into natural and positive right? (3) Whether the right common among nations is the same as natural right? (4) Whether right of dominion and paternal right are distinct species?

FIRST ARTICLE
Is Right the Object of Justice?

We proceed thus to the First Article:

Objection 1. It would seem that right is not the object of justice. For the jurist Celsus says that "right is the art of goodness and equality."[2] Now, art is not the object of justice but is by itself an intellectual virtue. Therefore, right is not the object of justice.

Obj. 2. Further, "Law," according to Isidore, "is a kind of right."[3] Now, law is the object, not of justice, but of prudence; wherefore the Philosopher reckons legislative as one of the parts of prudence.[4] Therefore, right is not the object of justice.

Obj. 3. Further, justice, before all, subjects man to God, for Augustine says that "justice is love serving God alone and consequently governing aright all things subject to man."[5]

136

Now right *(jus)* does not pertain to divine things but only to human affairs, for Isidore says that *"fas* is the divine law, and *jus* the human law."[6] Therefore right is not the object of justice.

On the contrary, Isidore says that *"jus* (right) is so called because it is just."[7] Now, the just is the object of justice, for the Philosopher declares that "all are agreed in giving the name of justice to the habit which makes men capable of doing just actions."[8]

I answer that It is proper to justice, as compared with the other virtues,[9] to direct man in his relations with others, because it denotes a kind of equality, as its very name implies; indeed we are wont to say that things are adjusted when they are made equal, for equality is in reference of one thing to some other. On the other hand, the other virtues perfect man in those matters only which befit him in relation to himself. Accordingly, that which is right in the works of the other virtues, and to which the intention of the virtue tends as to its proper object, depends on its relation to the agent only, whereas the right in a work of justice, besides its relation to the agent, is set up by its relation to others. Because a man's work is said to be just when it is related to some other by way of some kind of equality, for instance, the payment of the wage due for a service rendered. And so a thing is said to be just, as having the rectitude of justice, when it is the term of an act of justice, without taking into account the way in which it is done by the agent; whereas in the other virtues nothing is declared to be right unless it is done in a certain way by the agent. For this reason, justice has its own special proper object over and above the other virtues, and this object is called the just, which is the same as right. Hence it is evident that right is the object of justice.

Reply Obj. 1. It is usual for words to be distorted from their original signification so as to mean something else; thus the word medicine was first employed to signify a remedy used for curing a sick person, and then it was drawn to signify the art by which this is done. In like manner, the word *jus* (right) was first of all used to denote the just thing itself, but afterwards it was transferred to designate the art whereby it is known what is just, and further to denote the place where justice is administered, thus a man is said to appear *in jure*,[10] and yet, further, we say even that a man who has the office of exercising justice administers the *jus* even if his sentence be unjust.

Reply Obj. 2. Just as there pre-exists in the mind of the craftsman an expression of the things to be made externally by his craft, which expression is called the rule of his craft, so too there pre-exists in the mind an expression of the particular just work which the reason determines, and which is a kind of rule of prudence. If this rule be expressed in writing, it is called a law, which according to Isidore is a "written decree";[11] and so law is not the same as right but an expression of right.

Reply Obj. 3. Since justice implies equality, and since we cannot offer God an equal return, it follows that we cannot make Him a perfectly just repayment. For this reason, the Divine law is not properly called "*jus*" but "*fas*," because, to wit, God is satisfied if we accomplish what we can. Nevertheless, justice tends to make man repay God as much as he can, by subjecting his mind to Him entirely.

SECOND ARTICLE
Is Right Fittingly Divided into Natural Right and Positive Right?

We proceed thus to the Second Article:

Obj. 1. It would seem that right is not fittingly divided into natural right and positive right. For that which is natural is unchangeable and is the same for all. Now, nothing of the kind is to be found in human affairs, since all the rules of human right fail in certain cases, nor do they obtain force everywhere. Therefore, there is no such thing as natural right.

Obj. 2. Further a thing is called positive when it proceeds from the human will. But a thing is not just simply because it proceeds from the human will, else a man's will could not be unjust. Since then the just and the right are the same, it seems that there is no positive right.

Obj. 3. Further, divine right is not natural right, since it transcends human nature. In like manner, neither is it positive right, since it is based, not on human, but on divine authority. Therefore, right is unfittingly divided into natural and positive.

On the contrary, The Philosopher says that "political justice is partly natural and partly legal," i.e., established by law.[12]

I answer that, As stated above, the right or the just is a work that is adjusted to another person according to some kind of equality.[13] Now, a thing can be adjusted to a man in two ways: first, by its very nature, as when a man gives so much that he may receive equal value in return, and this is called natural right. In another way, a thing is adjusted or commensurated to another person by agreement, or by common consent, when, to wit, a man deems himself satisfied if he receive so much. This can be done in two ways: first, by private agreement, as that which is confirmed by an agreement between private individuals; secondly, by public agreement, as when the whole community agrees that something should be deemed as though it were adjusted and commensurated to another person, or when this is decreed by the ruler who is placed over the people and acts in its stead, and this is called positive right.

Reply Obj. 1. That which is natural to one whose nature is unchangeable must needs be such always and everywhere. But man's nature is changeable, wherefore that which is natural to man may sometimes fail. Thus the restitution of a deposit to the depositor is in accordance with natural equality, and if human nature were always right, this would always have to be observed, but since it happens sometimes that man's will is unrighteous, there are cases in which a deposit should not be restored, lest a man of unrighteous will make evil use of the thing deposited, as when a madman or an enemy of the common weal demands the return of his weapons.

Reply Obj. 2. The human will can, by common agreement, make a thing to be just provided it be not, of itself, contrary to natural justice, and it is in such matters that positive right has its place. Hence the Philosopher says that "in the case of the legal just, it does not matter in the first instance whether it takes one form or another; it only matters when once it is laid down."[14] If, however, a thing is, of itself, contrary to natural right, the human will cannot make it just, for instance, by decreeing that it is lawful to steal or to commit adultery. Hence, it is written, "Woe to them that make wicked laws."[15]

Reply Obj. 3. The divine right is that which is promulgated by God. Such things are partly those that are naturally just, yet their justice is hidden to man, and partly are those made just by God's decree. Hence, also, divine right may be divided in respect of these two things, even as human right is. For the divine law commands certain things because they are good and forbids others because they are evil, while others are good because they are prescribed, and others evil because they are forbidden.

THIRD ARTICLE

Is Right Common among Nations the Same As Natural Right?

We proceed thus to the Third Article:

Obj. 1. It would seem that right common among nations is the same as natural right. For all men do not agree save in that which is natural to them. Now, all men agree in right common among nations, since the Jurist says that "right common among nations is that which is in use among all nations."[16] Therefore, right common among nations is natural right.

Obj. 2. Further, slavery[17] among men is natural, for some are naturally slaves according to the Philosopher.[18] Now, "slavery belongs to right common among nations," as Isidore states.[19] Therefore, right common among nations is natural right.

Obj. 3. Further, right as stated above is divided into natural and positive.[20] Now, right common among nations is not a positive right, since all nations never agreed to decree anything by common agreement. Therefore, right common among nations is natural right.

On the contrary, Isidore says that "right is either natural or civil or common among nations,"[21] and consequently right common among nations is distinct from natural right.

I answer that, As stated above, natural right or just is that which by its very nature is adjusted to or commensurate with another person.[22] Now this may happen in two ways: first, according as it is considered absolutely; thus a male by its very nature is commensurate with the female to beget off-spring by her, and a parent is commensurate with the off-spring to nourish it. Secondly, a thing is naturally commensurate with another person, not according as it is considered absolutely, but according to something resultant from it, for instance, the possession of property. For if a particular piece of land be considered absolutely, it contains no reason why it should belong to one man more than to another, but if it be considered in respect of its adaptability to cultivation and the unmolested use of the land, it has a certain commensuration to be the property of one and not of another man, as the Philosopher shows.[23]

Now, it belongs not only to man but also to other animals to apprehend a thing absolutely; wherefore the right which we call natural is common to us and other animals according to the first kind of commensuration. But right common among nations falls short of natural right in this sense, as the Jurist says, because "the latter is common to all animals, while the former is common to men only."[24] On the other hand, to consider a thing by comparing it with what results from it is proper to reason; wherefore this same is natural to man in respect to natural reason which dictates it. Hence the jurist Gaius says, "Whatever natural reason decrees among all men is observed by all equally and is called right common among nations."[25] This suffices for the *Reply* to the *First Objection.*

Reply Obj. 2. Considered absolutely, the fact that this particular man should be a slave rather than another man is based not on natural reason but on some resultant utility, in that it is useful to this man to be ruled by a wiser man, and to the latter to be helped by the former, as the Philosopher states.[26] Wherefore, servitude which belongs to right common among nations is natural in the second way but not in the first.

Reply Obj. 3. Since natural reason dictates matters which are according to right common among nations, as implying a proximate equality, it follows that they need no special institution, for they are instituted by natural reason itself, as stated by the authority quoted above.[27]

FOURTH ARTICLE

Should Paternal Right and Right of Dominion Be Distinguished as Special Species?

We proceed thus to the Fourth Article:

Obj. 1. It would seem that paternal right and right of dominion should not be distinguished as special species. For it belongs to justice to render to each one what is his, as Ambrose states.[28] Now, right is the object of justice, as stated above.[29] Therefore, right belongs to each one equally, and we ought not to distinguish the rights of fathers and masters as distinct species.

Obj. 2. Further, the law is an expression of what is just, as stated above.[30] Now, a law looks to the common good of a city or kingdom, as stated above,[31] but not to the private good of an individual or even of one household. Therefore, there is no need for a special right of dominion or paternal right, since the master and the father pertain to a household, as stated in *Pol.* I, 2.[32]

Obj. 3. Further, there are many other differences of degrees among men, for instance, some are soldiers, some are priests, some are princes. Therefore, some special kind of right should be allotted to them.

On the contrary, The Philosopher distinguishes right of dominion, paternal right, and so on.[33]

I answer that Right or just depends on commensuration with another person. Now, another has a twofold signification. First, it may denote something that is other simply, as that which is altogether distinct; as, for example, two men neither of whom is subject to the other and both of whom are subjects of the ruler of the political community, and between these, according to the Philosopher, there is the just simply.[34] Secondly, a thing is said to be other from something else, not simply but as belonging in some way to that something else; in this way, as regards human affairs, a son belongs to his father, since he is part of him somewhat, as stated in *Eth.* VIII, 12,[35] and a slave belongs to his master, because he is his instrument, as stated in *Pol.* I, 2.[36] Hence, a father is not compared to his son as to another simply, and so between

them there is not the just simply but a kind of just, called
paternal. In like manner, neither is there the just simply between master and slave but that which is called dominative.
A wife, though she is something belonging to the husband,
since she stands related to him as to her own body, as the
Apostle declares,[37] is nevertheless more distinct from her
husband than a son from his father, or a slave from his master, for she is received into a kind of social life, that of
matrimony; wherefore, according to the Philosopher,[38] there
is more scope for right between husband and wife than between father and son or master and slave, because, as husband and wife have an immediate relation to the community
of the household, as stated in *Pol.* I, 2, 5,[39] it follows that
between them there is domestic right rather than civic right.

Reply Obj. 1. It belongs to justice to render to each one his
right, the distinction between individuals being presupposed;
for if a man gives himself his due, this is not strictly called
just. And since what belongs to the son is his father's, and
what belongs to the slave is his master's, it follows that,
properly speaking, there is not justice of father to son, or of
master to slave.

Reply Obj. 2. A son, as such, belongs to his father, and a
slave, as such, belongs to his master; yet each, considered as a
man, is something having separate existence and distinct
from others. Hence, in so far as each of them is a man, there
is justice towards them in a way, and for this reason too there
are certain laws regulating the relations of a father to his son
and of a master to his slave, but in so far as each is something
belonging to another, the perfect idea of right or just is wanting to them.

Reply Obj. 3. All other differences between one person and
another in a political community have an immediate relation
to the common order of the polity and to its ruler; wherefore
there is justice respecting them in the perfect sense of justice.
This right however is distinguished according to various offices; hence, when we speak of military, or magisterial, or
priestly right, it is not as though such rights fell short of the
simply right, as when we speak of paternal right or right of
dominion, but for the reason that something proper is due to
each class of person in respect of his particular office.

Question 58
Of Justice

[In Twelve Articles]

We must now consider justice. Under this head there are twelve points of inquiry: (1) What is justice? (2) Whether justice is always towards another? (3) Whether it is a virtue? (4) Whether it is in the will as its subject? (5) Whether it is a general virtue? (6) Whether, as a general virtue, it is essentially the same as every virtue? (7) Whether there is a particular justice? (8) Whether particular justice has a matter of its own? (9) Whether it is about passions or about operations only? (10) Whether the mean of justice is an objective mean? (11) Whether the act of justice is to render to everyone his own? (12) Whether justice is the chief of the moral virtues?

FIRST ARTICLE

Is Justice Fittingly Defined as Being the Perpetual and Constant Will to Render to Each One His Right?

We proceed thus to the First Article:

Obj. 1. It would seem that lawyers have unfittingly defined justice as being "the perpetual and constant will to render to each one his right."[1] For, according to the Philosopher, justice is a habit which makes a man "capable of doing what is just and of being just in action and in intention."[2] Now, "will" denotes a power or also an act. Therefore, justice is unfittingly defined as being a will.

Obj. 2. Further, rectitude of the will is not the will; else if the will were its own rectitude, it would follow that no will is unrighteous. Yet, according to Anselm, justice is rectitude. Therefore, justice is not the will.[3]

Obj. 3. Further, no will is perpetual save God's. If, therefore, justice is a perpetual will, in God alone will there be justice.

Obj. 4. Further, whatever is perpetual is constant, since it is unchangeable. Therefore, it is needless in defining justice to say that it is both perpetual and constant.

Obj. 5. Further, it belongs to the ruler to give each one his right. Therefore, if justice gives each one his right, it follows that it is in none but the ruler, which is absurd.

Obj. 6. Further, Augustine says that "justice is love serving God alone."[4] Therefore, it does not render to each one what is his.

I answer that The aforesaid definition of justice is fitting if understood aright. For, since every virtue is a habit, that is, the principle of a good act, a virtue must needs be defined by means of the good act bearing on the matter proper to that virtue. Now, the proper matter of justice consists of those things that belong to our intercourse with other men, as shall be shown further on.[5] Hence the act of justice in relation to its proper matter and object is indicated in the words, "Rendering to each one his right," since, as Isidore says, "a man is said to be just because he respects the right [jus] of others."[6]

Now, in order that an act bearing upon any matter whatever be virtuous, it should be voluntary, stable, and firm, because the Philosopher says that, in order for an act to be virtuous, it needs first of all to be done knowingly; secondly, to be done by choice and for a due end; thirdly, to be done resolutely.[7] Now the first of these is included in the second, since "what is done through ignorance is involuntary."[8] Hence the definition of justice mentions first the will, in order to show that the act of justice must be voluntary, and mention is made afterwards of its constancy and perpetuity in order to indicate the firmness of the act.

Accordingly, this is a complete definition of justice, save that the act is mentioned instead of the habit, which takes its species from that act, because habit implies relation to act. And if anyone would reduce it to the proper form of a definition, he might say that "justice is a habit whereby a man renders to each one his due by a constant and perpetual will"; this is about the same definition as that given by the Philosopher, who says that "justice is a habit whereby a man is said to be capable of doing just actions in accordance with his choice."[9]

Reply Obj. 1. "Will" here denotes the act, not the power, and it is customary among writers to define habits by their acts; thus Augustine says that "faith is to believe what one sees not."[10]

Reply Obj. 2. Justice is the same as rectitude, not essentially but causally, for it is a habit which rectifies the deed and the will.

Reply Obj. 3. The will may be called perpetual in two ways. First, on the part of the will's act which endures forever, and thus God's will alone is perpetual. Secondly, on the part of the subject, because, to wit, a man wills to do a certain thing always, and this is a necessary condition of justice. For it does not satisfy the conditions of justice that one wish to observe justice in some particular matter for the time being, because one could scarcely find a man·willing to act unjustly in every case, and it is requisite that one should have the will to observe justice at all times and in all cases.

Reply Obj. 4. Since perpetual does not imply perpetuity of the act of the will, it is not superfluous to add constant, for, while the perpetual will denotes the purpose of observing justice always, constant signifies a firm perseverance in this purpose.

Reply Obj. 5. A judge renders to each one what belongs to him by way of command and direction, because a judge is the "personification of justice, and the ruler is its guardian."[11] On the other hand, the subjects render to each one what belongs to him by way of execution.

Reply Obj. 6. Just as love of God includes love of our neighbor, as stated above,[12] so too the service of God includes rendering to each one his due.

SECOND ARTICLE

Is Justice Always towards Another?

We proceed thus to the Second Article:

Obj. 1. It would seem that justice is not always towards another. For the Apostle says that "the justice of God is by faith in Jesus Christ."[13] Now, faith does not concern the dealings of one man with another. Neither, therefore, does justice.

Obj. 2. Further, according to Augustine, "It belongs to justice that man should direct to the service of God his authority over the things that are subject to him."[14] Now the sensitive appetite is subject to man, according to Gen. 4:7, where it is written: "The lust thereof," viz., of sin, "shall be under you, and you shall have dominion over it." Therefore, it belongs to justice to have dominion over one's own appetite, so that justice is towards oneself.

Obj. 3. Further, the justice of God is eternal. But nothing else is co-eternal with God. Therefore, justice is not essentially towards another.

Obj. 4. Further, man's dealings with himself need to be rectified no less than his dealings with another. Now, man's dealings are rectified by justice, according to Pr. 11:5, "The justice of the upright shall make his way prosperous." Therefore, justice is about our dealings, not only with others but also with ourselves.

On the contrary, Tully says that "the object of justice is to keep men together in society and mutual intercourse."[15] Now this implies relationship of one man to another. Therefore, justice is concerned only about our dealings with others.

I answer that, As stated above,[16] since justice by its name implies equality, it denotes essentially relation to another, for a thing is equal, not to itself, but to another. And, inasmuch as it belongs to justice to rectify human acts, as stated above,[17] this otherness which justice demands must needs be between beings capable of action. Now, actions belong to ultimate objects of attribution and wholes and, properly speaking, not to parts and forms or powers, for we do not say properly that the hand strikes, but a man with his hand, nor that heat makes a thing hot, but fire by heat, although such expressions may be employed metaphorically. Hence justice, properly speaking, demands a distinction of ultimate objects of attribution and consequently is only in one man towards another. Nevertheless, in one and the same man we may speak metaphorically of his various principles of action, such as reason and the irascible and the concupiscible appetites, as though they were so many agents, so that metaphorically in one and the same man there is said to be justice insofar as the reason commands the irascible and concupiscible, and these obey reason, and in general insofar as to each part of man is ascribed what is becoming to it. Hence the Philosopher calls this "metaphorical justice."[18]

Reply Obj. 1. The justice which faith works in us is that

whereby the ungodly is justified; it consists in the due co-ordination of the parts of the soul, as stated above where we were treating of the justification of the ungodly.[19] Now, this belongs to metaphorical justice, which may be found even in a man who lives all by himself.

This suffices for the *Reply* to the *Second Objection*.

Reply Obj. 3. God's justice is from eternity in respect to the eternal will and purpose (and it is chiefly in this that justice consists), although it is not eternal as regards its effect, since nothing is co-eternal with God.

Reply Obj. 4. Man's dealings with himself are sufficiently rectified by the rectification of the passions by the other moral virtues. But his dealings with others need a special rectification, not only in relation to the agent by whom they are directed but also in relation to the person to whom they are directed. Hence about such dealings there is a special virtue, and this is justice.

THIRD ARTICLE
Is Justice a Virtue?

We proceed thus to the Third Article:

Obj. 1. It would seem that justice is not a virtue. For it is written "When you shall have done all these things that are commanded you, say: We are unprofitable servants; we have done that which we ought to do."[20] Now, it is not unprofit-able to do a virtuous deed, for Ambrose says: "We look to a profit that is estimated not by pecuniary gain but by the acquisition of godliness."[21] Therefore, to do what one ought to do is not a virtuous deed. And yet it is an act of justice. Therefore, justice is not a virtue.

Obj. 2. Further, that which is done of necessity is not meri-torious. But to render to a man what belongs to him, as justice requires, is of necessity. Therefore, it is not meritori-ous. Yet it is by virtuous actions that we gain merit. There-fore, justice is not a virtue.

Obj. 3. Further, every moral virtue is about matters of ac-tion. Now, those things which are wrought externally are not things concerning behavior but concerning the production of things, according to the Philosopher.[22] Therefore, since it be-longs to justice to produce externally a deed that is just in itself, it seems that justice is not a moral virtue.

On the contrary, Gregory says that "the entire structure of good works is built on four virtues,"[23] viz., temperance, prudence, fortitude, and justice.

I answer that A human virtue is one which renders a human act and man himself good, and this can be applied to justice. For a man's act is made good through attaining the rule of reason, which is the rule whereby human acts are regulated. Hence, since justice regulates human operations, it is evident that it renders man's operations good, and, as Tully declares, "good men are so called chiefly from their justice";[24] wherefore, as he says again, "The luster of virtue appears above all in justice."[25]

Reply Obj. 1. When a man does what he ought, he brings no gain to the person to whom he does what he ought but only abstains from doing him a harm. He does, however, profit himself insofar as he does what he ought spontaneously and readily, and this is to act virtuously. Hence it is written that divine wisdom "teaches temperance, and prudence, and justice, and fortitude, which are such things as men," i.e., virtuous men, "can have nothing more profitable in life."[26]

Reply Obj. 2. Necessity is twofold. One arises from constraint, and this removes merit, since it runs counter to the will. The other arises from the obligation of a command, or from the necessity of obtaining an end, when, to wit, a man is unable to achieve the end of virtue without doing some particular thing. The latter necessity does not remove merit, insofar as a man does voluntarily that which is necessary in this way. It does, however, exclude the credit of supererogation,[27] according to 1 Cor. 9:16, "If I preach the Gospel, it is no glory to me, for a necessity lies upon me."

Reply Obj. 3. Justice is concerned about external things, not by making them, which pertains to art, but by using them in our dealings with other men.

FOURTH ARTICLE
Is Justice in the Will as Its Subject?

We proceed thus to the Fourth Article:

Obj. 1. It would seem that justice is not in the will as its subject. For justice is sometimes called truth. But truth is not in the will but in the intellect. Therefore, justice is not in the will as its subject.

Obj. 2. Further, justice is about our dealings with others. Now, it belongs to the reason to direct one thing in relation to another. Therefore, justice is not in the will as its subject but in the reason.

Obj. 3. Further, justice is not an intellectual virtue, since it is not directed to knowledge; wherefore it follows that it is a moral virtue. Now, the subject of moral virtue is the faculty which is rational by participation, viz., the irascible and the concupiscible, as the Philosopher declares.[28] Therefore, justice is not in the will as its subject but in the irascible and concupiscible appetites.

On the contrary, Anselm says that "justice is rectitude of evil observed for its own sake."[29]

I answer that, The subject of a virtue is the power whose act that virtue aims at rectifying. Now, justice does not aim at directing an act of the cognitive power, for we are not said to be just through knowing something aright. Hence the subject of justice is not the intellect or reason, which is a cognitive power. But, since we are said to be just through doing something aright, and because the proximate principle of action is the appetitive power, justice must needs be in some appetitive power as its subject.

Now the appetite is twofold, namely, the will which is in the reason, and the sensitive appetite which follows on sensitive apprehension and is divided into the irascible and the concupiscible, as stated in the First Part.[30] Again, the act of rendering his due to each man cannot proceed from the sensitive appetite, because sensitive apprehension does not go so far as to be able to consider the relation of one thing to another, but this is proper to reason. Therefore, justice cannot be in the irascible or concupiscible appetites as its subject but only in the will; hence the Philosopher defines justice by an act of the will,[31] as may be seen above.[32]

Reply Obj. 1. Since the will is the rational appetite, when the rectitude of the reason which is called truth is imprinted on the will on account of its nighness to reason, this imprint retains the name of truth; hence it is that justice sometimes goes by the name of truth.

Reply Obj. 2. The will is borne towards its object consequent to the apprehension of reason; wherefore, since reason directs one thing in relation to another, the will can will one thing in relation to another, and this belongs to justice.

Reply Obj. 3. Not only the irascible and concupiscible appetites are rational by participation, but the "entire appetitive" faculty, as stated in *Eth.* I, 13,[33] because all appetite is subject to reason. Now, the will is contained in the appetitive faculty; wherefore it can be the subject of moral virtue.

FIFTH ARTICLE
Is Justice a General Virtue?

We proceed thus to the Fifth Article:

Obj. 1. It would seem that justice is not a general virtue. For justice is specified with the other virtues, according to Wis. 8:7, "She teaches temperance and prudence and justice and fortitude." Now, the general is not specified or reckoned together with the species contained under the same general. Therefore, justice is not a general virtue.

Obj. 2. Further, as justice is accounted a cardinal virtue, so are temperance and fortitude. Now, neither temperance nor fortitude is reckoned to be a general virtue. Therefore, neither should justice in any way be reckoned a general virtue.

Obj. 3. Further, justice is always towards others, as stated above.[34] But a sin committed against one's neighbor cannot be a general sin because it is distinguished from sin committed against oneself. Therefore, neither is justice a general virtue.

On the contrary, The Philosopher says that "justice is every virtue."[35]

I answer that Justice, as stated above, directs man in his relations with other men.[36] Now, this may happen in two ways: first, as regards his relation with individuals; secondly, as regards his relations with others in general, insofar as a man who serves a community serves all those who are included in that community. Accordingly, justice in its proper acceptation can be directed to another in both these senses. Now, it is evident that all who are included in a community stand in relation to that community as parts to a whole, while a part, as such, belongs to a whole, so that whatever is the good of a part can be directed to the good of the whole. It follows, therefore, that the good of any virtue, whether such virtue direct man in relation to himself or in relation to certain other individual persons, is referable to the common good, to which justice directs, so that all acts of virtue can pertain to justice insofar as it directs man to the common good. It is in this sense that justice is called a general virtue. And since it belongs to the law to direct to the common good, as stated above,[37] it follows that the justice which is in this way styled general is called legal justice, because thereby man is in harmony with the law which directs the acts of all the virtues to the common good.

Reply Obj. 1. Justice is specified or enumerated with the other virtues not as a general but as a special virtue, as we shall state further on.[38]

Reply Obj. 2. Temperance and fortitude are in the sensitive appetite, viz., in the concupiscible and irascible. Now, these powers are appetitive of certain particular goods, even as the senses are cognitive of particulars. On the other hand, justice is in the intellective appetite as its subject, which can have the universal good as its object, knowledge whereof belongs to the intellect. Hence justice can be a general virtue rather than temperance or fortitude.

Reply Obj. 3. Things referable to oneself are referable to another, especially in regard to the common good. Wherefore legal justice, in so far as it directs to the common good, may be called a general virtue. In like manner, injustice may be called a general sin; hence it is written that all "sin is iniquity."[39]

SIXTH ARTICLE

Is Justice, as a General Virtue, Essentially the Same As All Virtue?

We proceed thus to the Sixth Article:

Obj. 1. It would seem that justice, as a general virtue, is essentially the same as all virtue. For the Philosopher says that virtue and legal justice "are the same as all virtue but differ in their mode of being."[40] Now, things that differ merely in their mode of being or logically do not differ essentially.

Therefore, justice is essentially the same as every virtue.

Obj. 2. Further, every virtue that is not essentially the same as all virtue is a part of virtue. Now, the aforesaid justice, according to the Philosopher, "is not a part but the whole of virtue."[41] Therefore, the aforesaid justice is essentially the same as all virtue.

Obj. 3. Further, a virtue is not essentially changed by the fact that the virtue directs its act to some higher end, as the habit of temperance remains essentially the same even though its act be directed to the divine good. Now, it belongs to legal justice that the acts of all the virtues are directed to a higher end, namely, the common good of the multitude, which trandscends the good of one single individual. Therefore, it seems that legal justice is essentially all virtue.

Obj. 4. Further, every good of a part can be directed to the good of the whole, so that, if it be not thus directed, it would seem without use or purpose. But that which is in accordance with virtue cannot be so directed. Therefore, it seems that there can be no act of any virtue that does not belong to general justice, which directs to the common good, and so it seems that general justice is essentially the same as all virtue.

On the contrary, The Philosopher says that "many are able to be virtuous in matters affecting themselves but are unable to be virtuous in matters relating to others,"[42] and that "the virtue of the good man is not strictly the same as the virtue of the good citizen."[43] Now, the virtue of a good citizen is general justice, whereby a man is directed to the common good. Therefore, general justice is not the same as virtue in general, and it is possible to have one without the other.

I answer that A thing is said to be general in two ways. First, by predication; thus animal is general in relation to man and horse and the like, and in this sense that which is general must be essentially the same as the things in relation to which it is general, for the reason that the genus belongs to the essence of the species and forms part of its definition. Secondly, a thing is said to be general according to its efficacy; thus a universal cause is general in relation to all its effects, the sun, for instance, in relation to all bodies that are illumined or transmuted by its power, and in this sense there is no need for that which is general to be essentially the same as those things in relation to which it is general, since cause and effect are not essentially the same. Now, it is in the latter sense that, according to what has been said,[44] legal justice is said to be a general virtue, inasmuch, to wit, as it directs the acts of the other virtues to its own end, and this is to move all the other virtues by its command; for just as charity may be called a general virtue insofar as it directs the acts of all the virtues to the divine good, so too is legal justice insofar as it directs the acts of all the virtues to the common good. Accordingly, just as charity, which regards the divine good as its proper object, is a special virtue in respect to its essence, so too legal justice is a special virtue in respect to its essence, insofar as it regards the common good as its proper object. And thus it is in the ruler principally and by way of a master-craft, while it is secondarily and quasi-ministratively in his subjects.

However, the name of legal justice can be given to every virtue insofar as every virtue is directed to the common good by the aforesaid legal justice, which, though special essentially, is nevertheless general according to its efficacy. Speaking in this way, legal justice is essentially the same as all virtue but differs therefrom logically, and it is in this sense that the Philosopher speaks.

Wherefore the *Replies* to the *First* and *Second Objections* are manifest.

Reply Obj. 3. This argument again takes legal justice for the virtue commanded by legal justice.

Reply Obj. 4. Every virtue, strictly speaking, directs its act to that virtue's proper end; that it should happen to be directed to a further end either always or sometimes does not belong to that virtue considered strictly, for it needs some higher virtue to direct it to that end. Consequently, there must be one supreme virtue essentially distinct from every other virtue, which directs all the virtues to the common good, and this virtue is legal justice.

SEVENTH ARTICLE

Is There a Particular besides a General Justice?

We proceed thus to the Seventh Article:

Obj. 1. It would seem that there is not a particular besides a general justice. For there is nothing superfluous in the virtues, as neither is there in nature. Now, general justice directs man sufficiently in all his relations with other men. Therefore, there is no need for a particular justice.

Obj. 2. Further, the species of a virtue does not vary according to one and many. But legal justice directs one man to another in matters relating to the multitude, as shown above.[45] Therefore, there is not another species of justice directing one man to another in matters relating to the individual.

Obj. 3. Further, between the individual and the general public stands the household community. Consequently, if in addition to general justice there is a particular justice corresponding to the individual, for the same reason there should be a domestic justice directing man to the common good of a household, and yet this is not the case. Therefore, neither should there be a particular besides a legal justice.

On the contrary, Chrysostom, in his commentary on Mt. 5:6, "Blessed are they that hunger and thirst after justice," says, "By justice He signifies either the general virtue, or the particular virtue which is opposed to covetousness."[46]

I answer that, As stated above, legal justice is not essentially the same as every virtue.[47] Besides legal justice, which directs man immediately to the common good, there is a need for other virtues to direct him immediately in matters relating to particular goods, and these virtues may be relative to himself or to another individual person. Accordingly, just as, in addition to legal justice, there is a need for particular virtues to direct man in relation to himself, such as temperance and fortitude, so too, besides legal justice, there is need for particular justice to direct man in his relations to other individuals.

Reply Obj. 1. Legal justice does indeed direct man sufficiently in his relations towards others. As regards the common good, it does so immediately, but as to the good of the individual, it does so mediately. Wherefore there is need for particular justice to direct a man immediately to the good of another individual.

Reply Obj. 2. The common good of the realm and the particular good of the individual differ not only in respect to the many and the few but also with respect to a formal difference. For the concept of the common good differs from the concept of the individual good, even as the concept of whole differs from that of part. Wherefore the Philosopher says that "they are wrong who maintain that the political community and the home and the like differ only as many and few and not specifically."[48]

Reply Obj. 3. The household community, according to the Philosopher, differs in respect of a threefold fellowship,[49] namely, of husband and wife, father and son, master and slave, in each of which one person is, as it were, part of the other. Wherefore, between such persons, there is not justice simply but a species of justice, viz., domestic justice, as stated in *Eth.* V, 6.[50]

EIGHTH ARTICLE
Has Particular Justice a Special Matter?

We proceed thus to the Eighth Article:

Obj. 1. It would seem that particular justice has no special matter. Because a gloss on Gen. 2:14, "The fourth river is Euphrates," says, "Euphrates signifies fruitful, nor is it stated through what country it flows, because justice pertains to all the parts of the soul."[51] Now, this would not be the case if justice had a special matter, since every special matter belongs to a special power. Therefore, particular justice has no special matter.

Obj. 2. Further, Augustine says that "the soul has four virtues whereby, in this life, it lives spiritually, viz., temperance, prudence, fortitude, and justice, and he says that the fourth is justice, which pervades all the virtues."[52] Therefore, particular justice, which is one of the four cardinal virtues, has no special matter.

Obj. 3. Further, justice directs man sufficiently in matters relating to others. Now, a man can be directed to others in all matters relating to this life. Therefore, the matter of justice is general and not special.

On the contrary, The Philosopher reckons particular justice to be specially about those things which belong to social life.[53]

I answer that Whatever can be rectified by reason is the matter of moral virtue, for this is defined in reference to right reason, according to the Philosopher.[54] Now, reason can rectify not only the internal passions of the soul but also external actions and those external things of which man can make use. And yet it is in respect to external actions and external things by means of which men can communicate with one another that the relation of one man to another is to be considered, whereas it is in respect of internal passions that we consider man's rectitude in himself. Consequently, since justice is directed to others, it is not about the entire matter of moral virtue but only about external actions and things, under a certain special aspect of the object, insofar as one man is related to another through them.

Reply Obj. 1. It is true that justice belongs essentially to one part of the soul, where it resides as in its subject, and this is the will, which moves by its command all the other parts of the soul; accordingly, justice belongs to all the parts of the soul, not directly but by a kind of diffusion.

Reply Obj. 2. As stated above, the cardinal virtues may be taken in two ways: first, as special virtues, each having a determinate matter; secondly, as certain general modes of virtue.[55] In this latter sense, Augustine speaks in the passage quoted. For he says that "prudence is knowledge of what we should seek and avoid; temperance is the curb on the lust for fleeting pleasures; fortitude is strength of mind in bearing with passing trials; justice is the love of God and our neighbor which pervades the other virtues, that is to say, is the common principle of the entire order between one man and another."[56]

Reply Obj. 3. A man's internal passions, which are a part of moral matter, are not in themselves directed to another man, which direction belongs to the specific nature of justice; yet their effects, i.e. external actions, are capable of being directed to another man. Consequently, it does not follow that the matter of justice is general.

NINTH ARTICLE
Is Justice about the Passions?

We proceed thus to the Ninth Article:

Obj. 1. It would seem that justice is about the passions. For the Philosopher says that "moral virtue is about pleasure and pain."[57] Now, pleasure, or delight, and pain are passions, as stated above when we were treating of the passions.[58] Therefore, justice, being a moral virtue, is about the passions.

Obj. 2. Further, justice is the means of rectifying a man's operations in relation to another man. Now, such like operations cannot be rectified unless the passions be rectified, because it is owing to disorder of the passions that there is disorder in the aforesaid operations; thus sexual lust leads to adultery, and over-much love of money leads to theft. Therefore, justice must needs be about the passions.

Obj. 3. Further, even as particular justice is towards another person, so is legal justice. Now, legal justice is about the passions, else it would not extend to all the virtues, some of which are evidently about the passions. Therefore, justice is about the passions.

On the contrary, The Philosopher says that justice is about operations.[59]

I answer that The true answer to this question may be gathered from a twofold source. First, from the subject of justice, i.e., from the will, whose movements or acts are not passions, as stated above,[60] for it is only the sensitive appetite whose movements are called passions. Hence justice is not about the passions, as are temperance and fortitude, which are about the irascible and concupiscible appetite. Secondly, on the part of the matter, because justice is about a man's relations with another, and we are not directed immediately to another by the internal passions. Therefore, justice is not about the passions.

Reply Obj. 1. Not every moral virtue is about pleasure and pain as its proper matter, since fortitude is about fear and daring, but every moral virtue is directed to pleasure and pain, as to ends to be acquired. For, as the Philosopher says, "pleasure and pain are the principal end in respect of which we say that this is an evil, and that a good,"[61] and in this way too they belong to justice, since "a man is not just unless he rejoice in just actions."[62]

Reply Obj. 2. External operations are means, as it were, between external things, which are their matter, and internal passions, which are their origin. Now, it happens sometimes that there is one of these without there being a defect in the other. Thus, a man may steal another's property, not through the desire to have the thing but through the will to hurt the man; or, vice versa, a man may covet another's property without wishing to steal it. Accordingly, the directing of operations, insofar as they tend towards external things, belongs to justice, but insofar as they arise from the passions, it belongs to the other moral virtues, which are about the passions. Hence, justice hinders theft of another's property insofar as stealing is contrary to the equality that should be maintained in external things, while liberality hinders it as resulting from an immoderate desire for wealth. Since, however, external operations take their species, not from the internal passions but from external things as being their objects, it follows that external operations are essentially the matter of justice rather than of the other moral virtues.

Reply Obj. 3. The common good is the end of each individual member of a community, just as the good of the whole is the end of each part. On the other hand, the good of one individual is not the end of another individual; wherefore legal justice, which is directed to the common good, is more capable of extending to the internal passions, whereby man is disposed in some way or other in himself, than is particular justice, which is directed to the good of another individual, although legal justice extends chiefly to other virtues in the point of their external operations, insofar, to wit, as "the law commands us to perform the actions of a courageous person, . . . the actions of a temperate person, . . . and the actions of a gentle person."[63]

TENTH ARTICLE
Is the Mean of Justice an Objective Mean?

We proceed thus to the Tenth Article:

Obj. 1. It seems that the mean of justice is not the mean of some object. For the concept of a genus is preserved in all its species. But moral virtue is defined in the *Ethics* as "a willed habit which observes a mean determined in relation to us by reason."[64] Therefore, just so, there is in justice a rational mean, not an objective one.

Obj. 2. Further, in things that are good simply, there is neither excess nor defect, and consequently neither is there a mean, as is clearly the case with the virtues according to *Eth.* II, 6.[65] Now, justice is about things that are good simply, as stated in *Eth.* V.[66] Therefore, in justice there is not an objective mean.

Obj. 3. Further, the reason why the other virtues are said to observe the rational and not an objective mean is because, in their case, the mean varies according to different persons, since what is too much for one is too little for another.[67] Now, this is also the case in justice, for one who strikes a prince does not receive the same punishment as one who strikes a private individual. Therefore, just so, justice does not possess an objective mean but a rational one.[68]

On the contrary, The Philosopher says that the mean of justice is to be taken according to arithmetical proportion, which is an objective mean.

I answer that, As stated above,[69] the other moral virtues are chiefly concerned with the passions, the regulation of which is gauged entirely by the measure of the very man who is the subject of those passions, insofar as his anger and desire are as much as they ought to be in various circumstances. Hence, the mean in such like virtues is measured not by the proportion of one thing to another but merely by comparison with the virtuous man himself, so that with them the mean is only that which is fixed by reason in our regard.

On the other hand, the matter of justice is external operation, insofar as an operation or the thing used in that operation is duly proportionate to another person; wherefore the mean of justice consists in a certain proportion of equality between the external thing and the external person. Now, equality is the real mean between greater and less, as stated in *Metaph.* IX;[70] wherefore justice observes the mean objectively.

Reply Obj. 1. This objective mean is also the rational mean; wherefore justice satisfies the conditions of a moral virtue.

Reply Obj. 2. We may speak in two ways of a thing being good simply. First, a thing may be good in every way; thus the virtues are good, and there is neither mean nor extremes in things that are simply good in this sense. Secondly, a thing is said to be simply good through being good absolutely, i.e., in its nature, although it may become evil through being abused. Such are riches and honors, and in the like it is possible to find excess, deficiency, and mean as regards men, who can use them well or ill, and it is in this sense that justice is about things that are good simply.

Reply Obj. 3. The injury inflicted bears a different proportion to a ruler from that which it bears to a private person; wherefore each injury needs to be equalized by punishment in a different way, and this implies an objective and not merely a rational diversity.

ELEVENTH ARTICLE
Is the Act of Justice to Render to Each One His Own?

We proceed thus to the Eleventh Article:

Obj. 1. It would seem that the act of justice is not to render to each one his own. For Augustine ascribes to justice the act of succoring the needy.[71] Now, in succoring the needy, we give them what is not theirs but ours. Therefore, the act of justice does not consist in rendering to each one his own.

Obj. 2. Further, Tully says that "beneficence, which we may call kindness or liberality, belongs to justice."[72] Now, it pertains to liberality to give to another of one's own, not of what is his. Therefore, the act of justice does not consist in rendering to each one his own.

Obj. 3. Further, it belongs to justice not only to distribute things duly but also to repress injurious actions, such as murder, adultery, and so forth. But the rendering to each one of what is his seems to belong solely to the distribution of things. Therefore, the act of justice is not sufficiently described by saying that it consists in rendering to each one his own.

On the contrary, Ambrose says, "It is justice that renders to each one what is his and claims not another's property; it disregards its own profit in order to preserve the common equity."[73]

I answer that, As stated above, the matter of justice is an external operation, insofar as either it or the thing we use by it is made proportionate to some other person to whom we are related by justice.[74] Now, each man's own is that which is due to him according to equality of proportion. Therefore, the proper act of justice is nothing else than to render to each one his own.

Reply Obj. 1. Since justice is a cardinal virtue, other secondary virtues, such as mercy, liberality, and the like, are connected with it, as we shall state further on.[75] Wherefore, to succor the needy, which belongs to mercy or pity, and to be liberally beneficent, which pertains to liberality, are by a kind of reduction ascribed to justice as to their principal virtue.

This suffices for the *Reply* to the *Second Objection.*

Reply Obj. 3. As the Philosopher states, in matters of justice, the name of profit is extended to whatever is excessive, and whatever is deficient is called loss.[76] The reason for this is that justice is first of all and more commonly exercised in voluntary interchanges of things, such as buying and selling, wherein those expressions are properly employed, and yet they are transferred to all other matters of justice. The same applies to the rendering to each one of what is his own.

TWELFTH ARTICLE

Does Justice Stand Foremost among All Moral Virtues?

We proceed thus to the Twelfth Article:

Obj. 1. It would seem that justice does not stand foremost among all moral virtues because it belongs to justice to render to each one what is his, whereas it belongs to liberality to give of one's own, and the latter is more virtuous. Therefore, liberality is a greater virtue than justice.

Obj. 2. Further, nothing is adorned by a less excellent thing than itself. Now, magnanimity is the ornament both of justice and of all the virtues, according to *Eth.* IV, 3.[77] Therefore, magnanimity is more excellent than justice.

Obj. 3. Further, virtue is about that which is difficult and good, as stated in *Eth.* II, 3.[78] But fortitude is about more difficult things than justice is, since it is about dangers of death, according to *Eth.* III, 6.[79] Therefore, fortitude is more excellent than justice.

On the contrary, Tully says, "Justice is the most resplendent of the virtues and gives its name to a good man."[80]

I answer that, If we speak of legal justice, it is evident that it stands foremost among all the moral virtues, forasmuch as the common good transcends the individual good of one person. In this sense, the Philosopher declares "the most excellent of the virtues would seem to be justice, and more glorious than either the evening or the morning star."[81] But, even if we speak of particular justice, it excels the other moral virtues for two reasons. The first reason may be taken from the subject, because justice is in the more excellent part of the soul, viz., the rational appetite or will, whereas the other moral virtues are in the sensitive appetite, whereunto appertain the passions which are the matter of the other moral virtues. The second reason is taken from the object, because the other virtues are commendable in respect of the sole good of the virtuous person himself, whereas justice is praiseworthy in respect to the virtuous person being well disposed towards another, so that justice is somewhat the good of another person, as stated in *Eth.* V, 1.[82] (Hence the Philosopher says, "The greatest virtues must needs be those which are most profitable to other persons because virtue is a faculty of doing good to others. For this reason the greatest honors are accorded the brave and the just, since bravery is useful to others in warfare, and justice is useful to others both in warfare and in time of peace."[83])

Reply Obj. 1. Although the liberal man gives of his own, yet he does so insofar as he takes into consideration the good of his own virtue, while the just man gives to another what is his through consideration of the common good. Moreover, justice is observed towards all, whereas liberality cannot extend to all. Again, liberality which gives of a man's own is based on justice, whereby one renders to each man what is his.

Reply Obj. 2. When magnanimity is added to justice, it increases the latter's goodness; and yet without justice it would not even be a virtue.

Reply Obj. 3. Although fortitude is about the most difficult things, it is not about the best, for it is only useful in warfare, whereas justice is useful both in war and in peace, as stated above.

ST II–II

Question 61
Of Commutative and Distributive Justice

*[In Four Articles, of Which
the Fourth Is Omitted]*

FIRST ARTICLE

Are Two Species of Justice Suitably Assigned,
Viz., Commutative and Distributive?

We proceed thus to the First Article:

Obj. 1. It would seem that the two species of justice are unsuitably assigned, viz., distributive and commutative. That which is hurtful to the many cannot be a species of justice, since justice is directed to the common good. Now it is hurtful to the common good of the many if the goods of the community are distributed among many, both because the goods of the community would be exhausted, and because the morals of men would be corrupted. For Tully says, "He who receives becomes worse and the more ready to expect that he will receive again."[1] Therefore, distribution does not belong to any species of justice.

Obj. 2. Further, the act of justice is to render to each one what is his own, as stated above.[2] But when things are distributed, a man does not receive what was his but becomes possessed of something which belonged to the community. Therefore, this does not pertain to justice.

Obj. 3. Further, justice is not only in the ruler but also in the subject, as stated above.[3] But it belongs exclusively to the ruler to distribute. Therefore, distribution does not always belong to justice.

Obj. 4. Further, "Distributive justice regards common goods."[4] Now, matters regarding the community pertain to legal justice. Therefore, distributive justice is a species, not of particular, but of legal justice.

Obj. 5. Further, unity or multitude does not change the species of a virtue. Now, commutative justice consists in rendering something to one person, while distributive justice consists in giving something to many. Therefore, they are not different species of justice.

On the contrary, The Philosopher assigns two parts to justice and says that "one directs distributions, the other exchanges."[5]

I answer that, As stated above,[6] particular justice is directed to the private individual, who is compared to the community as a part to the whole. Now, a twofold order may be considered in relation to a part. In the first place, there is the order of one part to another, to which corresponds the order of one private individual to another. This order is directed by commutative justice, which is concerned about the mutual dealings between two persons. In the second place, there is the order of the whole towards the parts, to which corresponds the order of that which belongs to the community in relation to each single person. This order is directed by distributive justice, which distributes common goods proportionately. Hence, there are two species of justice, distributive and commutative.

Reply Obj. 1. Just as a private individual is praised for moderation in his bounty and blamed for excess therein, so too ought moderation to be observed in the distribution of common goods, wherein distributive justice directs.

Reply Obj. 2. Even as part and whole are somewhat the same, so too that which pertains to the whole pertains somewhat to the part also, so that when the goods of the community are distributed among a number of individuals, each one receives that which, in a way, is his own.

Reply Obj. 3. The act of distributing the goods of the community belongs to none but those who exercise authority over those goods, and yet distributive justice is also in the subjects to whom those goods are distributed insofar as they are contented by a just distribution. Moreover, distribution of common goods is sometimes made, not of the goods of the civic order but of those of one family, and such distribution can be made by authority of a private individual.

Reply Obj. 4. Movement takes its species from the end to which it is directed. Hence it belongs to legal justice to direct to the common good those matters which concern private individuals, whereas, on the contrary, it belongs to particular justice to direct the common good to particular individuals by way of distribution.

Reply Obj. 5. Distributive and commutative justice differ not only in respect of unity and multitude but also in respect to different kinds of debt because common property is due to an individual in one way, and his personal property in another way.

SECOND ARTICLE

Is the Mean to Be Observed in the Same Way in Distributive As in Commutative Justice?

We proceed thus to the Second Article:

Obj. 1. It would seem that the mean in distributive justice is to be observed in the same way as in commutative justice. For each of these is a kind of particular justice, as stated above.[7] Now, the mean is taken in the same way in all the parts of temperance or fortitude. Therefore, the mean should also be observed in the same way in both distributive and commutative justice.

Obj. 2. Further, the form of a moral virtue consists in observing the mean which is determined in accordance with reason. Since, then, one virtue has one form, it seems that the mean for both should be the same.

Obj. 3. Further, in order to observe the mean in distributive justice, we have to consider the various deserts of persons. Now, a person's deserts are considered also in commutative justice, for instance, in punishments; thus a man who strikes a ruler is punished more than one who strikes a private individual. Therefore, the mean is observed in the same way in both kinds of justice.

On the contrary, The Philosopher says that the mean in distributive justice is observed according to "geometrical proportion," whereas in commutative justice it follows "arithmetical proportion."[8]

I answer that, As stated above, in distributive justice something is given to a private individual, insofar as what belongs to the whole is due to the part, and in a quantity that is proportionate to the importance of the position of that part in respect of the whole.[9] Consequently, in distributive justice a person receives all the more of the common goods according as he holds a more prominent position in the community. This prominence in an aristocratic community is gauged according to virtue, in an oligarchy according to wealth, in a democracy according to liberty, and in various ways according to various forms of community. Hence, in distributive justice the mean is observed, not according to equality between thing and thing but according to proportion between things and persons, in such a way that even as one person surpasses another, so also that which is given to one person surpasses that which is allotted to another. Hence the Philosopher says that the mean in the latter case follows "geometrical proportion," wherein equality depends not on quantity but on proportion.[10] For example, we say that six is to four as three is to two because in either case the proportion equals one and a half, since the greater number is the sum of the lesser plus its half, whereas the equality of excess is not one of quantity because six exceeds four by two, while three exceeds two by one.

On the other hand, in exchanges, something is paid to an individual on account of something of his that has been received, as may be seen chiefly in selling and buying, where the notion of commutation is found primarily. Hence it is necessary to equalize thing with thing, so that the one person should pay back to the other just so much as he has become richer out of that which belonged to the other. The result of this will be equality according to the "arithmetical mean," which is gauged according to equal excess in quantity. Thus five is the mean between six and four, since it exceeds the latter and is exceeded by the former, by one. Accordingly, if, at the start, both persons have five, and one of them receives one out of the other's belongings, the one that is the receiver will have six, and the other will be left with four, and so there will be justice if both be brought back to the mean, one being taken from him that has six and given to him that has four, for then both will have five, which is the mean.

Reply Obj. 1. In the other moral virtues, the rational, not the objective mean, is to be followed, but justice follows the objective mean; wherefore the mean in justice depends on the diversity of things.

Reply Obj. 2. Equality is the general form of justice, wherein distributive and commutative justice agree, but in one we find equality of geometrical proportion, whereas in the other we find equality of arithmetical proportion.

Reply Obj. 3. In actions and passions, a person's station affects the quantity of a thing, for it is a greater injury to strike a ruler than a private person. Hence, in distributive justice a person's station is considered in itself, whereas in commutative justice it is considered insofar as it causes a diversity of things.

THIRD ARTICLE

Is There a Different Matter for Both Kinds of Justice?

We proceed thus to the Third Article:

Obj. 1. It would seem that there is not a different matter for both kinds of justice. Diversity of matter causes diversity of virtue, as in the case of fortitude and temperance. Therefore, if distributive and commutative justice have different matters, it would seem that they are not comprised under the same virtue, viz., justice.

Obj. 2. Further, the distribution that has to do with distributive justice is one of "wealth or of honors or of whatever can be distributed among the members of the community,"[11] which very things are the subject matter of exchanges between one person and another, and this belongs to commutative justice. Therefore, the matters of distributive and commutative justice are not distinct.

Obj. 3. Further, if the matter of distributive justice differs from that of commutative justice for the reason that they differ specifically, where there is no specific difference there ought to be no diversity of matter. Now, the Philosopher reckons commutative justice as one species, and yet this has many kinds of matter.[12] Therefore, the matter of these species of justice is, seemingly, not of many kinds.

On the contrary, It is stated in *Eth.* V, 2 that "one kind of justice directs distributions, and another exchanges."[13]

I answer that, As stated above, justice is about certain external operations, namely distribution and exchange.[14] These consist in the use of certain externals, whether things, persons, or even works: of things, as when one man takes from or restores to another that which is his; of persons, as when a man does an injury to the very person of another, for instance, by striking or insulting him, or even when showing respect for him; and of works, as when a man justly exacts a work of another or does a work for him. Accordingly, if we take for the matter of each kind of justice the things themselves of which the operations are the use, the matter of distributive and commutative justice is the same, since things can be distributed out of the common property to individuals and be the subject of exchange between one person and another, and also there is a certain distribution of and payment for laborious works.

If, however, we take for the matter of both kinds of justice the principal actions themselves whereby we make use of persons, things, and works, there is then a difference of matter between them. For distributive justice directs distributions, while commutative justice directs exchanges that can take place between two persons. Of these, some are involuntary, some voluntary. They are involuntary when anyone uses another man's possessions, person, or work against his will, and this may be done secretly by fraud or openly by violence. In either case, the offense may be committed against the other man's possession, his proper person, or a person connected with him. If the offense is against his possession, and this be taken secretly, it is called theft; if openly, it is called robbery. If it be against another man's proper person, it may affect either the very substance of his person or his dignity. If it be against the substance of his person, a man is injured secretly if he is treacherously slain, struck, or poisoned; he is injured openly if he is publicly slain, imprisoned, struck, or maimed. If it be against his personal dignity, a man is injured secretly by false witness, detractions, and so forth, whereby he is deprived of his good name; he is injured openly by being accused in a court of law or by public insult. If it be against a person connected with him, a man is injured in the person of his wife, secretly for the most part, by adultery, and in the person of his slave[15] if the latter be induced to leave his master; these things can also be done openly. The same applies to other persons connected with him, and whatever injury may be committed against the principal may be committed against them also. Adultery, however, and inducing a slave to leave his master are properly injuries against the person; yet the latter, since a slave is a kind of possession of his master, is referred to theft.

Voluntary exchanges are when a man voluntarily transfers what belongs to him to another person. And if he transfers it simply, so that the recipient incurs no debt, as in the case of gifts, it is an act not of justice but of liberality. A voluntary transfer belongs to justice insofar as it includes the notion of debt, and this may occur in many ways. First, when one man simply transfers his property to another in exchange for another thing, as happens in selling and buying. Secondly, when a man transfers his property to another, that the latter may have the use of it with the obligation of returning it to its owner. If he grant the use of a thing gratuitously, it is called usufruct in things that bear fruit, or simply borrowing on loan in things that bear no fruit, such as money, pottery, etc., but if not even the use is granted gratis, it is called letting or hiring. Thirdly, a man transfers his property with the intention of recovering it, not for the purpose of its use but that it may be kept safe, as in a deposit, or under some obligation, as when a man pledges his property, or when one man stands security for another. In all these actions, whether voluntary or involuntary, the mean is taken in the same way according to the equality of repayment. Hence all these actions belong to the one same species of justice, namely, commutative justice. And this suffices for the *Replies* to the *Objections.*

Notes to Chapter 3
ST II–II, Q. 57, AA. 1–4

1. *See* Glossary, s.v. "right."

2. *Digest* I, 1, 1. K I, 29a.

3. *Etym.* V, 2. PL 82, 199.

4. Aristotle, *Eth.* VI, 8. 1141b25.

5. *De mor. Ecc.* I, 15. PL 32, 1322.

6. *Etym.* V, 2. PL 82, 198.

7. *Etym.* V, 3. PL 82, 199.

8. *Eth.* V, 1. 1129a7.

9. *See* Glossary, s.v. "virtue." For contrasting interpretations of the relationship of the position of St. Thomas on virtues to that of Aristotle, see Harry Jaffa, *Thomism and Aristotelianism* (Chicago: University of Chicago Press, 1952), and Robert Sokolowski, *The God of Faith and Reason* (Notre Dame, Ind.: University of Notre Dame Press, 1982).

10. Places where justice is administered.

11. *Etym.* V, 3. PL 82, 199.

12. *Eth.* V, 7. 1134b18.

13. A. 1.

14. *Eth.* V, 7. 1134b20.

15. Is. 10:1.

16. *Digest* I, 1, 1. K I, 29a.

17. *See* Glossary, s.v. "slavery."

18. *Politics* I, 2. 1254a15.

19. *Etym.* V, 6. PL 82, 199.

20. A. 2.

21. *Etym.* V, 6. PL 82, 199.

22. A. 2.

23. *Politics* II, 2. 1263a21.

24. *Digest* I, 1, 1. K I, 29a.

25. *Digest*, I, 1, 9. K I, 29b.

26. *Politics* I, 6. 1255b5.

27. *Digest*, I, 1, 9. K I, 29b.

28. *De officiis* I, 24. PL 16, 62.

29. A. 1.

30. A. 1, *ad* 2.

31. I–II, Q. 90, A. 2.

32. 1253b5.

33. *Eth.* V, 6. 1134b8.

34. *Eth.* V, 5. 1134a26.

35. *Eth.* VIII, 12. 1161b18.

36. *Politics* I, 2. 1253b32, 1254a14.

37. Eph. 5:28.

38. *Eth.* V, 6. 1134b15.

39. 1253b6 and 1259a39.

ST II–II, Q. 58, AA. 1–12

1. *Digest* I, 1, 10. K I, 23b. *Institutes* I, 1, 1. K I, 1a.

2. *Eth.* V, 1. 1129a7.

3. *Dialogus de veritate* 12. PL 158, 480.

4. *De mor. Ecc.* I, 15. PL 32, 1322.

5. A. 2.

6. *Etym.* X. PL 82, 380.

7. *Eth.* II, 4. 1105a31.

8. *Eth.* III, 1. 1109b35.

9. *Eth.* V, 5. 1134a1.

10. *In Joan.* 40, on 8:32. PL 35, 1690.

11. *Eth.* V, 4. 1132a21 and 6. 1134a1.

12. II–II, Q. 25, A. 1.

13. Rom. 3:22.

14. *De mor. Ecc.* I, 15. PL 32, 1322.

15. Cicero, *De offic.* I, 7.

16. II–II, Q. 57, A. 1.

17. Ibid. and I–II, Q. 113, A. 1.

18. *Eth.* V, 11. 1138b6.

19. I–II, Q. 113, A. 1.

20. Lk. 17:10.

21. *De officiis* II, 6. PL 16, 116.

22. *Metaphysics* VIII, 8. 1050a30.

23. *Moral.* (in Job) II, 49. PL 75, 592.

24. *De offic.* I, 7.

25. Ibid.

26. Wis. 8:7.

27. Supererogation: good deeds performed above the demands of moral obligation.

28. *Eth.* I, 13. 1102b30.

29. *De verit.* 12. PL 158, 482.

30. Q. 81, A. 2.

31. *Eth.* V, 1. 1129a9.

32. A. 1.

33. 1102b30.

34. A. 2.

35. *Eth.* V, 1. 1130a9.

36. A. 2.

37. I–II, Q. 90, A. 2.

38. AA. 7, 12.

39. 1 Jn. 3:4.

40. *Eth.* V, 1. 1130a12.

41. *Eth.* V, 1. 1130a9.

42. Eth. V, 1. 1129b33.

43. *Politics* III, 2. 1277a22.

44. A. 5.

45. AA. 5, 6.

46. *In Matt. hom.*, hom. 15. PG 57, 227.

47. A. 6.

48. *Politics* I, 1. 1252a7.

49. *Politics* I, 2. 1253b6.

50. 1134b8.

51. St. Augustine, *De Genesi contra Manichaeos* II, 10. PL 34, 204.

52. *Quaest.* I, 61. PL 40, 51.

53. *Eth.* V, 2. 1130b31.

54. *Eth.* II, 6. 1107a1.

55. I–II, Q. 61, AA. 3, 4.

56. *Quaest.* I, 61. PL 40, 51.

57. *Eth.* II, 3. 1104b8.

58. ST I–II, Q. 23.

59. *Eth.* V, 1. 1129a3.

60. I–II, Q. 22, A. 3; Q. 59, A. 4.

61. *Eth.* VII, 11. 1152b2.

62. *Eth.* I, 8. 1099a18.

63. *Eth.* V, 1. 1129b19.

64. *Eth.* II, 6. 1106b36.

65. 1107a22.

66. *Eth.* V, 1. 1129b5.

67. *Eth.* II, 6. 1106a36.

68. *Eth.* V, 4. 1132a1.

69. A. 9; I–II, Q. 59, A. 4.

70. IX, 5. 1056a22.

71. *De Trin.* XIV, 9. PL 42, 1046.

72. *De offic.* I, 7.

73. *De officiis* I, 24. PL 16, 62.

74. AA. 8, 10.

75. Q. 80, A. 1.

76. *Eth.* V, 1. 1130a3.

77. *Eth.* IV, 3. 1124a1.

78. 1105a9.

79. 1115a24.

80. *De offic.* I, 7.

81. *Eth.* V, 1. 1129b27.

82. 1130a3.

83. *Rhet.* I, 9. 1366b3.

ST II–II, Q. 61, AA. 1–3

1. *De offic.* II, 15.

2. II–II, Q. 58, A. 2.

3. II–II, Q. 58, A. 6.

4. *Eth.* V, 4. 1131b27.

5. *Eth.* V, 2. 1130b31.

6. II–II, Q. 58, AA. 7, 8.

7. A. 1.

8. *Eth.* V, 3 and 4. 1131a29 and b32.

9. A. 1.

10. *Eth.* V, 3. 1131a29 and 1131b32.

11. *Eth.* V, 2. 1130b31.

12. *Eth.* V, 2. 1131a1.

13. 1130b31.

14. II–II, Q. 57, AA. 8, 10.

15. *See* Glossary, s.v. "slavery."

4

Property

ST II–II

Question 66
Of Theft and Robbery

[In Nine Articles]

We must now consider the sins opposed to justice whereby a man injures his neighbor in his belongings: namely theft and robbery.

Under this head there are nine points of inquiry: (1) Whether it is natural to man to possess external things? (2) Whether it is lawful for a man to possess something as his own? (3) Whether theft is the secret taking of another's property? (4) Whether robbery is a species of sin distinct from theft? (5) Whether every theft is a sin? (6) Whether theft is a mortal sin? (7) Whether it is lawful to thieve in a case of necessity? (8) Whether every robbery is a mortal sin? (9) Whether robbery is a more grievous sin than theft?

FIRST ARTICLE

Is It Natural for Man to Possess External Things?

We proceed thus to the First Article:

Objection 1. It would seem that it is not natural for man to possess external things. For no man should ascribe to himself that which is God's. Now, the dominion over all creatures is proper to God, according to Ps. 23:1, "The earth is the Lord's," etc. Therefore, it is not natural for man to possess external things.

Obj. 2. Further, Basil, in expounding the words of the rich man, "I will gather together all my crops and my possessions,"[1] says, "Tell me: Which are yours? Where did you take them from and bring them into being?"[2] Now, whatever man possesses naturally, he can fittingly call his own. Therefore, man does not naturally possess external things.

Obj. 3. Further, according to Ambrose, "dominion denotes power."[3] But man has no power over external things, since he can work no change in their nature. Therefore, the possession of external things is not natural to man.

On the contrary, It is written: "You have subjected all things under his feet."[4]

I answer that External things can be considered in two ways. First, as regards their nature, and this is not subject to the power of man but only to the power of God, Whose mere will all things obey. Secondly, as regards their use, and in this way man has a natural dominion over external things because, by his reason and will, he is able to use them for his own profit, as they were made on his account, for the imperfect is always for the sake of the perfect, as stated above.[5] It is by this argument that the Philosopher proves that the possession of external things is natural to man.[6] Moreover, this natural dominion of man over other creatures, which is competent to man in respect to his reason, wherein God's image resides, is shown forth in man's creation by the words: "Let us make man to Our image and likeness, and let him have dominion over the fishes of the sea," etc.[7]

Reply Obj. 1. God has sovereign dominion over all things, and He, according to His providence, directed certain things to the sustenance of man's body. For this reason, man has a natural dominion over things as regards the power to make use of them.

Reply Obj. 2. The rich man is reproved for deeming external things to belong to him principally, as though he had not received them from another, namely, from God.

Reply Obj. 3. This argument considers the dominion over external things as regards their nature. Such a dominion belongs to God alone, as stated above.

SECOND ARTICLE

Is It Lawful for a Man to Possess a Thing as His Own?

We proceed thus to the Second Article:

Obj. 1. It would seem unlawful for a man to possess a thing as his own. For whatever is contrary to the natural law is unlawful. Now, according to the natural law, all things are common property, and the possession of property is contrary to this community of goods. Therefore, it is unlawful for any man to appropriate any external thing to himself.

Obj. 2. Further, Basil in expounding the words of the rich man quoted above,[8] says, "The rich who deem as their own property the common goods they have seized upon are like to those who by going beforehand to the play prevent others from coming, and appropriate to themselves what is intended for common use."[9] Now, it would be unlawful to prevent others from obtaining possession of common goods. Therefore, it is unlawful to appropriate to oneself what belongs to the community.

Obj. 3. Further, Abrose says, and his words are quoted in the *Decretum,* "Let no man call his own that which is common property,"[10] and by common he means external things, as is clear from the context. Therefore, it seems unlawful for a man to appropriate an external thing to himself.

On the contrary, Augustine says, "The 'Apostolics' are those who with extreme arrogance have given themselves that name, because they admit into their communion only persons who are not married or possess nothing of their own, such as both the monks and clerics who in considerable number are to be found in the Catholic Church."[11] Now, the reason these people are heretics is that, severing themselves from the Church, they think that those who enjoy the use of the above things, which they themselves lack, have no hope of salvation. Therefore, it is erroneous to maintain that it is unlawful for a man to possess property.

I answer that Two things are competent to man in respect of exterior things. One is the power to procure and dispense them, and in this regard it is lawful for man to possess property. Moreover, this is necessary to human life for three reasons. First, because every man is more careful to procure what is for himself alone than that which is common to many or to all, since each one would shirk the labor and leave to another that which concerns the community, as happens where there is a great number of servants. Secondly, because human affairs are conducted in more orderly fashion if each man is charged with taking care of some particular thing himself, whereas there would be confusion if everyone had to look after any one thing indeterminately. Thirdly, because a more peaceful state is ensured to man if each one is contented with his own. Hence it is to be observed that quarrels arise more frequently where there is no division of the things possessed.

The second thing that is competent to man with regard to external things is their use. In this respect man ought to possess external things, not as his own, but as common, so that, to wit, he is ready to communicate them to others in their need. Hence the Apostle says, "Charge the rich of this world . . . to give easily, to share," etc.[12]

Reply Obj. 1. Community of goods is ascribed to the natural law, not because the natural law dictates that all things should be possessed in common, and that nothing should be possessed as one's own, but because there is division of possessions, not according to the natural law, but rather according to human agreement, which belongs to positive law, as stated above.[13] Hence, the ownership of possessions is not contrary to the natural law but an addition thereto devised by human reason.

Reply Obj. 2. A man would not act unlawfully if by going beforehand to the play he prepared the way for others, but he acts unlawfully if by doing so he hinders others from going. In like manner, a rich man does not act unlawfully if he anticipates someone in taking possession of something which at first was common property and gives others a share, but he sins if he excludes others indiscriminately from using it. Hence Basil says, "Why are you rich while another is poor, unless it be that you may have the merit of a good stewardship, and he the reward of patience?"[14]

Reply Obj. 3. When Ambrose says: "Let no man call his own that which is common," he is speaking of ownership as regards use; wherefore he adds: "He who spends too much is a robber."[15]

THIRD ARTICLE

Does the Essence of Theft Consist in Taking Another's Property Secretly?

We proceed thus to the Third Article:

Obj. 1. It would seem that it is not essential to theft to take another's thing secretly. For that which diminishes a sin does not, apparently, belong to the essence of a sin. Now, to sin secretly tends to diminish a sin, just as, on the contrary, it is written as indicating an aggravating circumstance of the sin of some: "They have proclaimed abroad their sin as Sodom did, and they have not hidden it."[16] Therefore, it is not essential to theft that it should consist in taking another's property secretly.

Obj. 2. Further, Ambrose says, and his words are embodied in the *Decretum,* "It is no less a crime to take from him that has than to refuse to succor the needy when you can and are well off."[17] Therefore, just as theft consists in taking another's property, so does it consist in keeping it back.

Obj. 3. Further, a man may take by stealth from another even that which is his own, for instance, a thing that he has deposited with another or that has been taken away from him unjustly. Therefore, it is not essential to theft that it should consist in taking another's property secretly.

On the contrary, Isidore says, "*Fur* [thief] is derived from *furvus* and so from *fuscus* [dark], because he takes advantage of the night."[18]

I answer that Three things combine together to constitute theft. The first belongs to theft as being contrary to justice, which gives to each one that which is his, so that it belongs to theft to take possession of what is another's. The second thing belongs to theft as distinct from those sins which are committed against the person, such as murder and adultery, and in this respect it belongs to theft to be about a thing possessed, for if a man takes what is another's, not as a possession but as a part (for instance, if he amputates a limb), or as a person connected with him (for instance, if he carry off his daughter or his wife), it is not, strictly speaking, a case of theft. The third difference is that which completes the nature of theft and consists in a thing being taken secretly, and in this respect it belongs properly to theft that it consists in taking another's property secretly.

Reply Obj. 1. Secrecy is sometimes a cause of sin, as when a man employs secrecy in order to commit a sin, for instance, in fraud and guile. In this way, it does not diminish sin but constitutes a species of sin, and thus it is in theft. In another way, secrecy is merely a circumstance of sin, and thus it diminishes sin, both because it is a sign of shame, and because it removes scandal.

Reply Obj. 2. To keep back what is due to another inflicts the same kind of injury as taking a thing unjustly; wherefore an unjust detention is included in an unjust taking.

Reply Obj. 3. Nothing prevents that which belongs to one person simply from belonging to another in some respect; thus a deposit belongs simply to the depositor, but, with regard to its custody, it is the depositary's, and the thing stolen is the thief's, not simply but as regards its custody.

FOURTH ARTICLE
Are Theft and Robbery Sins of Different Species?

We proceed thus to the Fourth Article:

Obj. 1. It would seem that theft and robbery are not sins of different species. For theft and robbery differ as secret and manifest, because theft is taking something secretly, while robbery is to take something violently and openly. Now, in the other kinds of sins, the secret and the manifest do not differ specifically. Therefore, theft and robbery are not different species of sin.

Obj. 2. Further, moral actions take their species from the end, as stated above.[19] Now, theft and robbery are directed to the same end, viz., the possession of another's property. Therefore, they do not differ specifically.

Obj. 3. Further, just as a thing is taken by force for the sake of possession, so is a woman taken by force for pleasure; wherefore Isidore says, "He who commits a rape is called a corrupter, and the victim of the rape is said to be corrupted."[20] Now, it is a case of rape whether the woman be carried off publicly or secretly. Therefore, the thing appropriated is said to be taken by force whether it be done secretly or publicly. Therefore, theft and robbery do not differ.

On the contrary, The Philosopher distinguishes theft from robbery and states that theft is done in secret, but that robbery is done openly.[21]

I answer that Theft and robbery are vices contrary to justice, inasmuch as one man does another an injustice. Now, "no man suffers an injustice willingly," as stated in *Eth.* V, 9.[22] Wherefore theft and robbery derive their sinful nature through the taking being involuntary on the part of the person from whom something is taken. Now, the involuntary is twofold, namely, through violence and through ignorance, as stated in *Eth*. III, 1.[23] Therefore, the sinful aspect of robbery differs from that of theft, and consequently they differ specifically.

Reply Obj. 1. In the other kinds of sin, the sinful nature is not derived from something involuntary, as in the sins opposed to justice, and so, where there is a different kind of involuntary, there is a different species of sin.

Reply Obj. 2. The remote end of robbery and theft is the same. But this is not enough for identity of species, because there is a difference of proximate ends, since the robber wishes to take a thing by his own power, but the thief by cunning.

Reply Obj. 3. The robbery of a woman cannot be secret on the part of the woman who is taken; wherefore, even if it be secret as regards the others from whom she is taken, the nature of robbery remains on the part of the woman to whom violence is done.

FIFTH ARTICLE
Is Theft Always a Sin?

We proceed thus to the Fifth Article:

Obj. 1. It would seem that theft is not always a sin. For no sin is commanded by God, since it is written, "He has commanded no man to do wickedly."[24] Yet we find that God commanded theft, for it is written, "And the children of Israel did as the Lord had commanded Moses, . . . and they stripped the Egyptians."[25] Therefore, theft is not always a sin.

Obj. 2. Further, if a man finds a thing that is not his and takes it, he seems to commit a theft, for he takes another's property. Yet this seems lawful according to natural equity, as the jurists hold.[26] Therefore, it seems that theft is not always a sin.

Obj. 3. Further, he that takes what is his own does not seem to sin, because he does not act against justice, since he does not destroy its equality. Yet a man commits a theft even if he secretly takes his own property that is detained by or in the safekeeping of another. Therefore, it seems that theft is not always a sin.

On the contrary, It is written, "Thou shalt not steal."[27]

I answer that, If anyone consider what is meant by theft, he will find that it is sinful on two counts. First, because of its opposition to justice, which gives to each one what is his, so that for this reason theft is contrary to justice, through being a taking of what belongs to another. Secondly, because of the guile or fraud committed by the thief, by laying hands on another's property secretly and cunningly. Wherefore, it is evident that every theft is a sin.

Reply Obj. 1. It is no theft for a man to take another's property either secretly or openly by order of a judge who has commanded him to do so, because it becomes his due by the very fact that it is adjudicated to him by the sentence of the court. Hence still less was it a theft for the Israelites to take away the spoils of the Egyptians at the command of the Lord, Who ordered this to be done on account of the ill-treatment accorded to them by the Egyptians without any cause; wherefore it is written significantly: "The just took the spoils of the wicked."[28]

Reply Obj. 2. With regard to a found treasure, a distinction must be made. For some there are that were never in anyone's possession, for instance, precious stones and jewels found on the sea-shore, and such the finder is allowed to keep.[29] The same applies to treasure hidden underground long since and belonging to no man, except that, according to civil law, the finder is bound to give half to the owner of the land if the treasure found be in the land of another person.[30] Hence, in the parable of the gospel, it is said of the finder of the treasure hidden in a field that he bought the field, as though he purposed thus to acquire the right of possessing the whole treasure.[31] On the other hand, the treasure found may be nearly in someone's possession, and then, if anyone take it with the intention, not of keeping it but of returning it to the owner, who does not look upon such things as unappropriated, he is not guilty of theft. In like manner, if the thing found appears to be unappropriated, and if the finder believes it to be so, although he keep it, he does not commit a theft.[32] In any other case, the sin of theft is committed;[33] wherefore Augustine says in a homily, "If you have found a thing and not returned it, you have stolen it."[34]

Reply Obj. 3. He who by stealth takes his own property, which is deposited with another man, burdens the depositary,

who is bound either to restitution or to prove himself innocent. Hence he is clearly guilty of sin and is bound to ease the
depositary of his burden. On the other hand, he who by
stealth takes his own property, if this be unjustly detained by
another, sins indeed, yet not because he burdens the retainer,
and so he is not bound to restitution or compensation, but he
sins against general justice by disregarding the order of justice and usurping judgment concerning his own property.
Hence he must make satisfaction to God and endeavor to
allay whatever scandal he may have given his neighbor by
acting this way.

SIXTH ARTICLE
Is Theft a Mortal Sin?

We proceed thus to the Sixth Article:

Obj. 1. It would seem that theft is not a mortal sin. For it is
written: "The fault is not so great when a man has stolen."[35]
But every mortal sin is a great fault. Therefore, theft is not a
mortal sin.

Obj. 2. Further, mortal sin deserves to be punished with
death. But in the Law, theft is punished not by death but by
indemnity, according to Ex. 22:1, "If any man steal an ox or a
sheep, . . . he shall restore five oxen for one ox, and four
sheep for one sheep." Therefore, theft is not a mortal sin.

Obj. 3. Further, theft can be committed in small even as in
great things. But it seems unreasonable for a man to be punished with eternal death for the theft of a small thing, such as
a needle or a quill. Therefore, theft is not a mortal sin.

On the contrary, No man is condemned by the divine judgment save for a mortal sin. Yet a man is condemned for theft,
according to Zech. 5:3, "This is the curse that goes forth over
the face of the earth; for every thief shall be judged as is there
written." Therefore, theft is a mortal sin.

I answer that, As stated above, a mortal sin is one that is
contrary to charity as the spiritual life of the soul.[36] Now,
charity consists principally in the love of God, and secondarily in the love of our neighbor, which is shown in our wishing
and doing him well. But theft is a means of doing harm to
our neighbor in his belongings, and if men were to steal from
one another habitually, human society would be undone.

Therefore, theft, as being opposed to charity, is a mortal sin.

Reply Obj. 1. The statement that theft is not a great fault is in view of two cases. First, when a person is led to thieve through necessity. This necessity diminishes or entirely removes sin, as we shall show further on.[37] Hence, the text continues: "For he steals to fill his hungry soul."[38] Secondly, theft is stated not to be a great fault in comparison with the guilt of adultery, which is punished with death. Hence the text goes on to say of the thief that "if he be taken, he shall restore sevenfold, . . . but he that is an adulterer . . . shall destroy his own soul."[39]

Reply Obj. 2. The punishments of this life are medicinal rather than retributive. For retribution is reserved to the divine judgment which is pronounced against sinners "according to truth."[40] Wherefore, according to the judgment of the present life, the death punishment is inflicted, not for every mortal sin but only for such as inflict an irreparable harm, or, again, for such as contain some horrible deformity. Hence, according to the present judgment, the pain of death is not inflicted for theft which does not inflict an irreparable harm, except when it is aggravated by some grave circumstance, as in the case of sacrilege, which is the theft of a sacred thing, of peculation, which is theft of common property, as Augustine states,[41] and of kidnapping, which is stealing a man, for which the pain of death is inflicted.[42]

Reply Obj. 3. Reason accounts as nothing that which is little, so that a man does not consider himself injured in very little matters, and the person who takes such things can presume that this is not against the will of the owner. And if a person take such like very little things, he may be proportionately excused from mortal sin. Yet if his intention is to steal from and injure his neighbor, there may be a mortal sin even in these very little things, even as there may be through consent in a mere thought.

SEVENTH ARTICLE
Is It Lawful to Steal through Stress of Need?

We proceed thus to the Seventh Article:

Obj. 1. It would seem unlawful to steal through stress of need. For penance is not imposed except on one who has sinned. Now, it is stated: "If anyone, through stress of hunger or nakedness, steal food, clothing, or beast, he shall do penance for three weeks."[43] Therefore, it is not lawful to steal through stress of need.

Obj. 2. Further, the Philosopher says that "there are some actions whose very name implies wickedness," and among these he reckons theft.[44] Now, that which is wicked in itself may not be done for a good end. Therefore, a man cannot lawfully steal in order to remedy a need.

Obj. 3. Further, a man should love his neighbor as himself. Now, according to Augustine, it is unlawful to steal in order to succor one's neighbor by giving him an alms.[45] Therefore, neither is it lawful to steal in order to remedy one's own needs.

On the contrary, In cases of need, all things are common property, so that there would seem to be no sin in taking another's property, for need has made it common.

I answer that Things which are of human right cannot derogate from natural right or divine right. Now, according to the natural order established by divine Providence, inferior things are ordained to supply the needs of men. Wherefore the division and appropriation of things which are based on human law do not preclude the fact that man's needs have to be remedied by means of these very things. Hence, whatever goods some have in superabundance are due, by natural law, to the sustenance of the poor. For this reason, Ambrose says, and his words are embodied in the *Decretum,* "It is the hungry man's bread that you withhold, the naked man's cloak that you store away; the money that you bury in the earth is the price of the poor man's ransom and freedom."[46]

Since, however, there are many who are in need, and it is impossible for all to be succored by means of the same thing, each one is entrusted with the stewardship of his own things, so that out of them he may come to the aid of those who are in need. Nevertheless, if the need be so manifest and urgent that it is evident that the present need must be remedied by whatever means be at hand (for instance, when a person is in some imminent danger, and there is no other possible remedy), then it is lawful for a man to succor his own need by means of another's property, by taking it either openly or secretly, nor is this properly speaking theft or robbery.

Reply Obj. 1. This decretal considers cases where there is no urgent need.

Reply Obj. 2. It is not theft, properly speaking, to take secretly and use another's property in a case of extreme need because that which a man takes for the support of his life becomes his own property by reason of that need.

Reply Obj. 3. In a case of a like need, a man may also take secretly another's property in order to succor his neighbor in need.

EIGHTH ARTICLE
May Robbery Be Committed without Sin?

We proceed thus to the Eighth Article:

Obj. 1. It would seem that robbery may be committed without sin. For spoils are taken by violence, and this seems to belong to the essence of robbery, according to what has been said.[47] Now, it is lawful to take spoils from the enemy, for Ambrose says, "When the conqueror has taken possession of the spoils, military discipline demands that all should be reserved for the ruler,"[48] in order, to wit, that he may distribute them. Therefore, in certain cases, robbery is lawful.

Obj. 2. Further, it is lawful to take from a man what is not his. Now, the things which unbelievers have are not theirs, for Augustine says, "You falsely call things your own, for you do not possess them justly, and according to the laws of earthly kings you are commanded to forfeit them."[49] Therefore, it seems that one may lawfully rob unbelievers.

Obj. 3. Further, earthly rulers violently extort many things from their subjects, and this seems to savor of robbery. Now, it would seem a grievous matter to say that they sin in acting thus, for in that case nearly every ruler would be damned. Therefore, in some cases, robbery is lawful.

On the contrary, Whatever is taken lawfully may be offered to God in sacrifice and oblation. Now, this cannot be done with the proceeds of robbery, according to Is. 61:8, "I am the Lord that loves judgment, and hates robbery in a holocaust." Therefore, it is not lawful to take anything by robbery.

I answer that Robbery implies a certain violence and coer-

cion employed in taking unjustly from a man that which is
his. Now, in human society, no man can exercise coercion
except through public authority, and, consequently, if a private individual not having public authority takes another's
property by violence, he acts unlawfully and commits a robbery, as burglars do. As regards rulers, the public power is
entrusted to them that they may be the guardians of justice.
Hence it is unlawful for them to use violence or coercion,
save within the bounds of justice, either by fighting against
the enemy or against citizens, by punishing evil-doers, and
whatever is taken by violence of this kind is not the spoils of
robbery, since it is not contrary to justice. On the other hand,
to take other people's property violently and against justice
in the exercise of public authority is to act unlawfully and to
be guilty of robbery, and whoever does so is bound to restitution.

Reply Obj. 1. A distinction must be made in the matter of
spoils. For if they who take spoils from the enemy are waging
a just war, such things as they seize in the war become their
own property. This is no robbery, and so they are not bound
to restitution. Nevertheless, even they who are engaged in a
just war may sin in taking spoils through cupidity arising
from an evil intention, if, to wit, they chiefly fight not for
justice but for spoil. For Augustine says that "it is a sin to
fight for booty."[50] If, however, those who take the spoil are
waging an unjust war, they are guilty of robbery and are
bound to restitution.

Reply Obj. 2. Unbelievers possess their goods unjustly insofar as they are ordered by the laws of earthly rulers to
forfeit those goods. Hence these may be taken violently from
them, not by private but by public authority.

Reply Obj. 3. It is no robbery if rulers exact from their
subjects that which is due to them for safeguarding the common good, even if they use violence in so doing, but if they
extort something unduly by means of violence, it is robbery,
even highway robbery. Hence Augustine says, "If justice be
disregarded, what are kingdoms but mighty robberies?—
since what are robberies but little kingdoms?[51] And it is written: "Her princes in the midst of her, are like wolves ravening
the prey."[52] Wherefore they are bound to restitution, just as
robbers are, and by so much do they sin more grievously than

robbers, as their actions are fraught with greater and more universal danger to public justice, whose wardens they are.

NINTH ARTICLE
Is Theft a More Grievous Sin than Robbery?

We proceed thus to the Ninth Article:

Obj. 1. It would seem that theft is a more grievous sin than robbery. For theft adds fraud and guile to the taking of another's property, and these things are not found in robbery. Now, fraud and guile are sinful in themselves, as stated above.[53] Therefore, theft is a more grievous sin than robbery.

Obj. 2. Further, shame is fear about a wicked deed, as stated in *Eth.* IV, 9.[54] Now, men are more ashamed of theft than of robbery. Therefore, theft is more wicked than robbery.

Obj. 3. Further, the more persons a sin injures, the more grievous it would seem to be. Now, the great and the lowly may be injured by theft, whereas only the weak can be injured by robbery, since it is possible to use violence towards them. Therefore, the sin of theft seems to be more grievous than the sin of robbery.

On the contrary, According to the laws, robbery is more severely punished than theft.

I answer that Robbery and theft are sinful, as stated above, on account of the involuntariness on the part of the person from whom something is taken,[55] but in theft the involuntariness is due to ignorance, whereas in robbery it is due to violence. Now, a thing is more involuntary through violence than through ignorance, because violence is more directly opposed to the will than ignorance. Therefore, robbery is a more grievous sin than theft. There is also another reason, since robbery not only inflicts a loss on a person in his things but also conduces to the ignominy and injury of his person, and this is of graver import than fraud or guile, which belong to theft. Hence the *Reply* to the *First Objection* is evident.

Reply Obj. 2. Men who adhere to sensible things think more of external strength, which is evidenced in robbery, than of internal virtue, which is forfeit through sin; wherefore they are less ashamed of robbery than of theft.

Reply Obj. 3. Although more persons may be injured by

theft than by robbery, yet more grievous injuries may be inflicted by robbery than by theft, for which reason also robbery is more odious.

ST II–II

Question 71

Of Injustice in Judgment on the Part of Counsel

[In Four Articles, of Which Article One Is Included]

FIRST ARTICLE

Is an Advocate Bound to Defend the Suits of the Poor?

We proceed thus to the First Article:

Obj. 1. It would seem that an advocate is bound to defend the suits of the poor. For it is written: "If you see the ass of him that hates you lie underneath its burden, you shall not pass by but shall lift up the ass and its burden."[1] Now, no less a danger threatens the poor man whose suit is being unjustly hindered than if his ass were to lie underneath its burden. Therefore, an advocate is bound to defend the suits of the poor.

Obj. 2. Further, Gregory says in a homily, "Let him that has understanding beware lest he withhold his knowledge; let him that has abundance of wealth watch lest he slacken his merciful bounty; let him who is a servant to art share his skill with his neighbor; let him who has an opportunity of speaking with the wealthy plead the cause of the poor. For the slightest gift you have received will be reputed a talent."[2] Now, every man is bound not to hide but faithfully to dispense the talent committed to him, as evidenced by the punishment inflicted on the servant who hid his talent.[3] Therefore, an advocate is bound to plead for the poor.

Obj. 3. Further, the precept about performing works of mercy, being affirmative, is binding according to time and place, and this is chiefly in cases of need. Now, it seems to be a case of need when the suit of a poor man is being hindered. Therefore, it seems that in such a case an advocate is bound to defend the poor man's suit.

On the contrary, He that lacks food is no less in need than he that lacks an advocate. Yet he that is able to give food is not always bound to feed the needy. Therefore, neither is an advocate always bound to defend the suits of the poor.

I answer that, Since defense of the poor man's suit belongs to the works of mercy, the answer to this inquiry is the same as the one given above with regard to the other works of mercy.[4] Now, no man is sufficient to bestow a work of mercy on all those who need it. Wherefore, as Augustine says, "Since one cannot do good to all, we ought to consider those chiefly who by reason of place, time, or any other circumstance, by a kind of chance, are more closely united to us."[5] He says "by reason of place" because one is not bound to search throughout the world for the needy that one may succor them, and it suffices to do works of mercy to those one meets with. Hence it is written: "If you meet your enemy's ass going astray, bring it back to him."[6] He says also "by reason of time" because one is not bound to provide for the future needs of others, and it suffices to succor present needs. Hence it is written: "He that . . . shall see his brother in need and shall close his heart from him, how does the charity of God abide in him?"[7] Lastly, he says "or any other circumstance" because one ought to show kindness to those especially who are by any tie whatever united to us, according to 1 Tim. 5:8, "If any man have not care for his own, and especially for those of his house, he has denied the faith and is worse than an infidel."

It may happen, however, that these circumstances concur, and then we have to consider whether this particular man stands in such a need that it is not easy to see how he can be succored otherwise, and then one is bound to bestow the work of mercy on him. If, however, it is easy to see how he can be otherwise succored, either by himself, or by some other person still more closely united to him or in a better position to help him, one is not strictly bound to help the one in need so that it would be a sin not to do so, although it would be praiseworthy to help one in need where one is not bound to. Therefore, an advocate is not always bound to defend the suits of the poor but only when the aforesaid circumstances concur, else he would have to put aside all other business and occupy himself entirely in defending the suits of poor people. The same applies to a physician with regard to attendance on the sick.

Reply Obj. 1. So long as the ass lies under the burden, there is no means of help in this case unless those who are passing along come to the man's aid, and therefore they are bound to help. But they would not be so bound if help were possible from another quarter.

Reply Obj. 2. A man is bound to make good use of the talent bestowed on him according to the opportunities afforded by time, place, and other circumstances, as stated above.

Reply Obj. 3. Not every need is such that it is one's duty to remedy it, but only such as we have stated above.

ST II–II

Question 77

Of Cheating, Which Is Committed in Buying and Selling

*[In Four Articles, of Which
Articles One and Four Are Included]*

FIRST ARTICLE

Is It Lawful to Sell a Thing
for More Than Its Worth?

We proceed thus to the First Article:

Obj. 1. It would seem that it is lawful to sell a thing for more than its worth. In the exchanges of human life, civil laws determine that which is just. Now, according to these laws, it is just for buyer and seller to deceive one another,[1] and this occurs by the seller selling a thing for more than its worth and the buyer buying a thing for less than its worth. Therefore, it is lawful to sell a thing for more than its worth.

Obj. 2. Further, that which is common to all would seem to be natural and not sinful. Now, Augustine relates that the saying of a certain jester was accepted by all, "You wish to buy for a song and to sell at a premium,"[2] which agrees with the saying of Pr. 20:14, "It is naught, it is naught, says every buyer, and when he is gone away, then he will boast."[3] Therefore, it is lawful to sell a thing for more than its worth.

Obj. 3. Further, it does not seem unlawful if that which virtue demands be done by mutual agreement. Now, according to the Philosopher,[4] in the friendship which is based on utility, the amount of the recompense for a favor received should depend on the utility accruing to the receiver, and this utility sometimes is worth more than the thing given, for instance, if the receiver be in great need of that thing, whether for the purpose of avoiding a danger or of deriving some particular benefit. Therefore, in contracts of buying and selling, it is lawful to give a thing in return for more than its worth.

On the contrary, It is written, "All things . . . whatsoever you would that men should do to you, do you also to them."[5] But no man wishes to buy a thing for more than its worth. Therefore, no man should sell a thing to another man for more than its worth.

I answer that It is altogether sinful to have recourse to deceit in order to sell a thing for more than its just price, because this is to deceive one's neighbor so as to injure him. Hence Tully says, "Contracts should be entirely free from double-dealing; the seller must not impose upon the bidder, nor the buyer upon one that bids against him."[6]

But, apart from fraud, we may speak of buying and selling in two ways. First, as considered in themselves, and from this point of view, buying and selling seem to be established for the common advantage of both parties, one of whom requires that which belongs to the other, and vice versa, as the Philosopher states.[7] Now, whatever is established for the common advantage should not be more of a burden to one party than to another, and, consequently, all contracts between them should observe equality of thing and thing. Again, the quality of a thing that comes into human use is measured by the price given for it, for which purpose money was invented, as stated in *Eth.* V, 5.[8] Therefore, if either the price exceeds the quantity of the thing's worth or, conversely, the thing exceeds the price, there is no longer the equality of justice, and consequently, to sell a thing for more than its worth or to buy it for less than its worth is in itself unjust and unlawful.

Secondly, we may speak of buying and selling, considered as accidentally tending to the advantage of one party and to the disadvantage of the other, for instance, when one man has great need of a certain thing, while another man will suffer if he be without it. In such a case, the just price will depend not only on the thing sold but on the loss which the sale brings on the seller. And thus it will be lawful to sell a thing for more than it is worth in itself, though the price paid be not more than it is worth to the owner. Yet if the one man derive a great advantage by becoming possessed of the other man's property, and the seller be not at a loss through being without that thing, the latter ought not to raise the price, because the advantage accruing to the buyer is not due to the seller but to a circumstance affecting the buyer. Now, no man should sell what is not his, though he may charge for the loss he suffers.

On the other hand, if a man finds that he derives great advantage from something he has bought, he may, of his own accord, pay the seller something over and above, and this pertains to his virtue.

Reply Obj. 1. As stated above, human law is given to the people, among whom there are many lacking virtue, and it is not given to the virtuous alone.[9] Hence, human law was unable to forbid all that is contrary to virtue, and it suffices for it to prohibit whatever is destructive of human intercourse, while it treats other matters as though they were lawful, not by approving of them but by not punishing them. Accordingly, if, without employing deceit, the seller disposes of his goods for more than their worth or the buyer obtains them for less than their worth, the law looks upon this as licit and provides no punishment for so doing, unless the excess be too great, because then even human law demands restitution to be made, for instance, if a man be deceived in regard to more than half the amount of the just price of a thing.[10]

On the other hand, the divine law leaves nothing unpunished that is contrary to virtue. Hence, according to the divine law, it is reckoned unlawful if the equality of justice be not observed in buying and selling, and he who has received more than he ought must make compensation to him that has suffered loss if the loss be considerable. I add this condition because the just price of things is not fixed with mathematical precision but depends on a kind of estimate, so that a slight addition or subtraction would not seem to destroy the equality of justice.

Reply Obj. 2. As Augustine says, "this jester, either by looking into himself or by his experience of others, thought that all men are inclined to wish to buy for a song and sell at a premium. But since in reality this is wicked, it is in every man's power to acquire that justice whereby he may resist and overcome this inclination."[11] And then he gives the example of a man who gave the just price for a book to a man who through ignorance asked a low price for it. Hence it is evident that this common desire is not from nature but from vice; wherefore it is common to many who walk along the broad road of sin.

Reply Obj. 3. In commutative justice we consider chiefly real equality. On the other hand, in friendship based on utility we consider equality of usefulness, so that the recompense should depend on the usefulness accruing, whereas in buying it should be equal to the thing bought.

FOURTH ARTICLE

Is It, in Trading, Lawful to Sell a Thing at a Higher Price Than What Was Paid for It?

We proceed thus to the Fourth Article:

Obj. 1. It would seem that it is not lawful, in trading, to sell a thing for a higher price than we paid for it. For Chrysostom says on Mt. 21:12, "He that buys a thing in order that he may sell it, entire and unchanged, at a profit is the trader who is cast out of God's temple."[12] Cassiodorus speaks in the same sense in his commentary on Ps. 70:15, "Because I have not known learning" (or "trading" according to another version). "What is trade," says he, "but buying at a cheap price with the purpose of retailing at a higher price?" and he adds: "Such

were the tradesmen whom Our Lord cast out of the temple."[13] Now, no man is cast out of the temple except for a sin.
Therefore, such like trading is sinful.

Obj. 2. Further, it is contrary to justice to sell goods at a
higher price than their worth or to buy them for less than
their value, as shown above.[14] Now, if you sell a thing for a
higher price than you paid for it, you must either have
bought it for less than its value or sell it for more than its
value. Therefore, this cannot be done without sin.

Obj. 3. Further, Jerome says, "Shun, as you would the
plague, a cleric who from being poor has become wealthy, or
who, from being a nobody, has become a celebrity."[15] Now,
trading would not seem to be forbidden to clerics except on
account of its sinfulness. Therefore, it is a sin in trading to
buy at a low price and to sell at a higher price.

On the contrary, Augustine, commenting on Ps. 70:15,
"Because I have not known learning," says, "The greedy
tradesman blasphemes over his losses; he lies and perjures
himself over the price of his wares. But these are vices of the
man, not of the craft, which can be exercised without these
vices."[16] Therefore, trading is not in itself unlawful.

I answer that A tradesman is one whose business consists
in the exchange of things. According to the Philosopher, exchange of things is twofold; one, natural, as it were, and
necessary, whereby one commodity is exchanged for another
or money taken in exchange for a commodity, in order to
satisfy the needs of life.[17] Such like trading, properly speaking, does not belong to tradesmen but rather to housekeepers
or civil servants, who have to provide the household or the
political community with the necessaries of life. The other
kind of exchange is either that of money for money or of any
commodity for money, not on account of the necessities of
life but for profit, and this kind of exchange, properly speaking, regards tradesmen, according to the Philosopher.[18] The
former kind of exchange is commendable because it supplies
a natural need, but the latter is justly deserving of blame,
because, considered in itself, it satisfies the greed for gain,
which knows no limit and tends to infinity. Hence trading,
considered in itself, has a certain debasement attaching thereto, insofar as, by its very nature, it does not imply a virtuous
or necessary end. Nevertheless, gain, which is the end of

trading, though not implying, by its nature, anything virtuous or necessary, does not, in itself, connote anything sinful or contrary to virtue; wherefore nothing prevents gain from being directed to some necessary or even virtuous end, and thus trading becomes lawful. Thus, for instance, a man may intend the moderate gain which he seeks to acquire by trading for the upkeep of his household or for the assistance of the needy; or, again, a man may take to trade for some public advantage, for instance, lest his country lack the necessaries of life, and seek gain, not as an end, but as payment for his labor.

Reply Obj. 1. The saying of Chrysostom refers to the trading which seeks gain as a last end. This is especially the case where a man sells something at a higher price without its undergoing any change. For if he sells at a higher price something that has changed for the better, he would seem to receive the reward of his labor. Nevertheless, the gain itself may be lawfully intended, not as a last end, but for the sake of some other end which is necessary or virtuous, as stated above.

Reply Obj. 2. Not everyone that sells at a higher price than he bought is a tradesman, but only he who buys that he may sell at a profit. If, on the contrary, he buys not for sale but for possession and afterwards, for some reason, wishes to sell, it is not a trade transaction even if he sell at a profit. For he may lawfully do this, either because he has bettered the thing, or because the value of the thing has changed with the change of place or time, or on account of the danger he incurs in transferring the thing from one place to another, or again in having it carried by another. In this sense, neither buying nor selling is unjust.

Reply Obj. 3. Clerics should abstain not only from things that are evil in themselves but even from those that have an appearance of evil. This happens in trading, both because it is directed to worldly gain, which clerics should despise, and because trading is open to so many vices, since "a merchant is hardly free from sins of the lips."[19] There is also another reason: because trading engages the mind too much with worldly cares and consequently withdraws it from spiritual cares; wherefore the Apostle says, "No man being a soldier to God entangles himself with secular businesses."[20] Nevertheless, it is lawful for clerics to engage in the first mentioned kind of exchange, which is directed to supply the necessaries of life, either by buying or by selling.

ST II–II
Question 78
Of the Sin of Interest-Taking

[In Four Articles]

We must now consider the sin of usury, which is committed in loans, and under this head there are four points of inquiry: (1) Whether it is a sin to take money as a price for money lent, which is to receive interest? (2) Whether it is lawful to lend money for any other kind of consideration by way of payment for the loan? (3) Whether a man is bound to restore just gains derived from money taken in interest? (4) Whether it is lawful to borrow money under a condition of interest?

FIRST ARTICLE
Is It a Sin to Take Interest for Money Lent?

We proceed thus to the First Article:

Obj. 1. It would seem that it is not a sin to take interest for money lent. For no man sins through following the example of Christ. But Our Lord said of Himself, "At My coming, I might have exacted it," i.e., the money lent, "with interest."[1] Therefore, it is not a sin to take interest for lending money.

Obj. 2. Further, according to Ps. 18:8, "The law of the Lord is unspotted," because, to wit, it forbids sin. Now, interest of a kind is allowed in the divine law, according to Dt. 23:19–20, "You shall not lend at interest to your brother money, nor corn, nor any other thing, but to the stranger"; nay more, it is even promised as a reward for the observance of the Law, according to Dt. 28:12: "You shall lend at interest to many nations and shall not borrow of any one." Therefore, it is not a sin to take interest.

Obj. 3. Further, in human affairs justice is determined by

civil laws. Now, civil law allows interest to be taken. Therefore, it seems to be lawful.

Obj. 4. Further, the counsels are not binding under sin. But,
among other counsels we find: "Lend, hoping for nothing
thereby."[2] Therefore, it is not a sin to take interest.

Obj. 5. Further, it does not seem to be in itself sinful to
accept a price for doing what one is not bound to do. But one
who has money is not bound in every case to lend it to his
neighbor. Therefore, it is lawful for him sometimes to accept
a price for lending it.

Obj. 6. Further, silver made into coins does not differ specifically from silver made into a vessel. But it is lawful to
accept a price for the loan of a silver vessel. Therefore, it is
also lawful to accept a price for the loan of a silver coin.
Therefore, interest is not in itself a sin.

Obj. 7. Further, anyone may lawfully accept a thing which
its owner freely gives him. Now, he who accepts the loan
freely gives the interest. Therefore, he who lends may lawfully take the interest.

On the contrary, It is written: "If you lend money to any of
my people that is poor, that dwells with you, you shall not be
hard upon them as an extortioner nor oppress them with
interest."[3]

I answer that To take interest for money lent is unjust in
itself, because this is to sell what does not exist, and this
evidently leads to inequality, which is contrary to justice.

In order to make this evident, we must observe that there
are certain things the use of which consists in their consumption; thus we consume wine when we use it for drink, and we
consume wheat when we use it for food. Wherefore, in such
like things the use of the thing must not be reckoned apart
from the thing itself, and whoever is granted the use of the
thing is granted the thing itself, and for this reason, to lend
things of this kind is to transfer the ownership. Accordingly,
if a man wanted to sell wine separately from the use of the
wine, he would be selling the same thing twice, or he would
be selling what does not exist; wherefore he would evidently
commit a sin of injustice. In like manner, he commits an
injustice who lends wine or wheat and asks for double payment, viz., one, the return of the thing in equal measure; the
other, the price of the use, which is called interest.

On the other hand, there are things the use of which does not consist in their consumption; thus to use a house is to dwell in it, not to destroy it. Wherefore, in such things, both may be granted; for instance, one man may hand over to another the ownership of his house while reserving to himself the use of it for a time, or vice versa, he may grant the use of the house while retaining the ownership. For this reason, a man may lawfully make a charge for the use of his house, and, besides this, reclaim the house from the person to whom he has granted its use, as happens in renting and letting a house.

Now, money, according to the Philosopher,[4] was invented chiefly for the purpose of exchange, and, consequently, the proper and principal use of money is its consumption or alienation, whereby it is sunk in exchange. Hence, it is by its very nature unlawful to take payment for the use of money lent, which payment is known as interest, and just as a man is bound to restore other ill-gotten goods, so is he bound to restore the money which he has taken in interest.

Reply Obj. 1. In this passage, interest must be taken figuratively for the increase of spiritual goods which God exacts from us, for He wishes us ever to advance in the goods which we receive from Him, and this is for our own profit, not for His.

Reply Obj. 2. The Jews were forbidden to take interest from their brethren, i.e., from other Jews. By this we are given to understand that to take interest from any man is simply evil, because we ought to treat every man as our neighbor and brother, especially in the Evangelical community, whereto all are called. Hence it is said, without any distinction, in Ps. 14:5, "He that has not put out his money to interest," and "Who has not taken interest."[5] They were permitted, however, to take interest from foreigners, not as though it were lawful, but in order to avoid a greater evil, lest, to wit, through avarice, to which they were prone, according to Is. 56:11, they should take interest from the Jews, who were worshippers of God.

Where we find it promised to them as a reward, "You shall lend at interest to many nations," etc., lending at interest is to be taken in a broad sense for lending, as in Sir. 29:10, where we read: "Many have refused to lend at interest, not out of wickedness," i.e., they would not lend. Accordingly, the Jews are promised in reward an abundance of wealth so that they would be able to lend to others.

Reply Obj. 3. Human laws leave certain things unpunished on account of the condition of those who are imperfect and who would be deprived of many advantages if all sins were strictly forbidden and punishments appointed for them. Wherefore human law has permitted interest-taking, not that it looks upon interest-taking as harmonizing with justice, but lest the advantage of many should be hindered. Hence it is that, in civil law, it is stated that "those things according to natural reason and civil law which are consumed by being used do not admit of usufruct," and that "the Senate did not (nor could it) appoint a usufruct to such things but established a quasi-usufruct,"[6] to wit, permitting interest-taking. Moreover, the Philosopher, led by natural reason, says that "to make money by interest-taking is exceedingly unnatural."[7]

Reply Obj. 4. A man is not always bound to lend, and for this reason it is placed among the counsels. Yet it is a matter of precept not to seek profit by lending, although it may be called a matter of counsel in comparison with the maxims of the Pharisees, who deemed some kinds of interest-taking to be lawful, just as love of one's enemies is a matter of counsel. Or again, He [the Lord] speaks here not of the hope of usurious gain but of the hope which is put in man. For we ought not to lend or do any good deed through hope in man but only through hope in God.

Reply Obj. 5. He that is not bound to lend may accept repayment for what he has done, but he must not exact more. Now, he is repaid according to equality of justice if he is repaid as much as he lent. Wherefore, if he exacts more for the usufruct of a thing which has no other use but the consumption of its substance, he exacts a price of something nonexistent, and so his exaction is unjust.

Reply Obj. 6. The principal use of a silver vessel is not its consumption, and so one may lawfully sell its use while retaining one's ownership of it. On the other hand, the principal use of silver money is its division in exchanges, so that it is not lawful to sell its use and at the same time expect the restitution of the amount lent. It must be observed, however, that the secondary use of silver vessels may be an exchange, and such use may not be lawfully sold. In like manner, there may be some secondary use of silver money, for instance, a man might lend coins for show or to be used as security.

Reply Obj. 7. He who pays interest does not voluntarily give it simply but under a certain necessity, insofar as he needs to borrow money which the owner is unwilling to lend without receiving interest.

SECOND ARTICLE

Is It Lawful to Ask for Any Other Kind of Consideration for Money Lent?

We proceed thus to the Second Article:

Obj. 1. It would seem that one may ask for some other kind of consideration for money lent. For everyone may lawfully seek to indemnify himself. Now, sometimes a man suffers loss through lending money. Therefore, he may lawfully ask for or even exact something else besides the money lent.

Obj. 2. Further, as stated in *Eth.* V, 5, one is in duty bound by a point of honor to repay anyone who has done us a favor.[8] Now, to lend money to one who is in straits is to do him a favor for which he should be grateful. Therefore, the recipient of a loan is bound by a natural debt to repay something. Now, it does not seem unlawful to bind oneself to an obligation of the natural law. Therefore, it is not unlawful, in lending money to anyone, to demand some sort of compensation as a condition of the loan.

Obj. 3. Further, just as there is material remuneration, so is there verbal remuneration and remuneration by service, as a gloss says on Is. 33:15, "Blessed is he that shakes his hands from all bribes."[9] Now, it is lawful to accept service or praise from one to whom one has lent money. Therefore, in like manner, it is lawful to accept any other kind of remuneration.

Obj. 4. Further, seemingly the relation of gift to gift is the same as of loan to loan. But it is lawful to accept money for money given. Therefore, it is lawful to accept repayment by loan in return for a loan granted.

Obj. 5. Further, the lender, by transferring his ownership of a sum of money, removes the money further from himself than he who entrusts it to a merchant or craftsman. Now, it is lawful to receive interest for money entrusted to a merchant or craftsman. Therefore, it is also lawful to receive interest for money lent.

Obj. 6. Further, a man may accept a pledge for money lent, the use of which pledge he might sell for a price, as when a man mortgages his land or the house wherein he dwells. Therefore, it is lawful to receive interest for money lent.

Obj. 7. Further, it sometimes happens that a man raises the price of his goods under guise of loan, or buys another's goods at a low figure, or raises his price through delay in being paid and lowers his price that he may be paid the sooner. Now, in all these cases, there seems to be payment for a loan of money, nor does it appear to be manifestly illicit. Therefore, it seems to be lawful to expect or exact some consideration for money lent.

On the contrary, Among other conditions requisite in a just man, it is stated that he "has not taken interest and increase."[10]

I answer that, According to the Philosopher, a thing is reckoned as money "if its value can be measured by money."[11] Consequently, just as it is a sin against justice to take money, by tacit or express agreement, in return for lending money or anything else that is consumed by being used, so also is it a like sin, by tacit or express agreement, to receive anything whose price can be measured by money. Yet there would be no sin in receiving something of the kind, not as exacting it, nor yet as though it were due on account of some agreement tacit or expressed, but as a gratuity, since, even before lending the money, one could accept a gratuity, nor is one in a worse condition through lending.

On the other hand, it is lawful to exact compensation for a loan in respect to such things as are not appreciated by a measure of money, for instance, benevolence, and love for the lender, and so forth.

Reply Obj. 1. A lender may without sin enter an agreement with the borrower for compensation for the loss he incurs of something he ought to have, for this is not to sell the use of money but to avoid a loss. It may also happen that the borrower avoids a greater loss than the lender incurs, wherefore the borrower may repay the lender with what he has gained. But the lender cannot enter an agreement for compensation through the fact that he makes no profit out of his money, because he must not sell that which he has not yet and may be prevented in many ways from having.

Reply Obj. 2. Repayment for a favor may be made in two ways. In one way, as a debt of justice, and to such a debt a man may be bound by a fixed contract, and its amount is measured according to the favor received. Wherefore the borrower of money or any such thing the use of which is its consumption is not bound to repay more than he received in loan, and, consequently, it is against justice if he be obliged to pay back more. In another way, a man's obligation to repayment for favor received is based on a debt of friendship, and the nature of this debt depends more on the feeling with which the favor was conferred than on the greatness of the favor itself. This debt does not carry with it a civil obligation, which involves a kind of necessity that would exclude the spontaneous nature of such a repayment.

Reply Obj. 3. If a man were, in return for money lent, as though there had been an agreement tacit or expressed, to expect or exact repayment in the shape of some remuneration of service or words, it would be the same as if he expected or exacted some material remuneration, because both can be priced at a money value, as may be seen in the case of those who offer for hire the labor which they exercise by work or by tongue. If, on the other hand, the remuneration by service or words be given not as an obligation but as a favor, which is not to be appreciated at a money value, it is lawful to take, exact, and expect it.

Reply Obj. 4. Money cannot be sold for a greater sum than the amount lent, which has to be paid back, nor should the loan be made with a demand or expectation of aught else but of a feeling of benevolence, which cannot be priced at a pecuniary value, and which can be the basis of a spontaneous loan. Now, the obligation to lend in return at some future time is repugnant to such a feeling because an obligation of this kind also has its pecuniary value. Consequently, it is lawful for the lender to borrow something else at the same time, but it is unlawful for him to bind the borrower to grant him a loan at some future time.

Reply Obj. 5. He who lends money transfers the ownership of the money to the borrower. Hence, the borrower holds the money at his own risk and is bound to pay it all back; wherefore the lender must not exact more. On the other hand, he that entrusts his money to a merchant or craftsman, so as to form a kind of partnership, does not transfer the ownership of his money to the other, for it remains his, so that at his risk the merchant speculates with it, or the craftsman uses it for his craft, and consequently, he may lawfully demand as something belonging to him part of the profits derived from his money.

Reply Obj. 6. If a man in return for money lent to him pledges something that can be valued at a price, the lender must allow for the use of that thing towards the repayment of the loan. Else, if he wishes the gratuitous use of that thing in addition to repayment, it is the same as if he took money for lending, and that is interest-taking, unless, perhaps, it were such a thing as friends are wont to lend to one another gratis, as in the case of the loan of a book.

Reply Obj. 7. If a man wishes to sell his goods at a higher price than that which is just, in such manner that he gives the buyer time to pay, it is manifestly a case of taking interest, because this waiting for the payment of the price has the character of a loan, so that whatever he demands beyond the just price in consideration of this delay is like a price for a loan, which pertains to interest-taking. In like manner, if a buyer wishes to buy goods at a lower price than what is just, for the reason that he pays for the goods before they can be delivered, it is a sin of interest-taking, because, again, this anticipated payment of money has the character of a loan, the price of which is the rebate on the just price of the goods sold. On the other hand, if a man wishes to allow a rebate on the just price in order that he may have his money sooner, he is not guilty of the sin of interest-taking.

THIRD ARTICLE

Is a Man Bound to Restore Whatever Profits He Has Made Out of Money Gotten by Taking Interest?

We proceed thus to the Third Article:

Obj. 1. It would seem that a man is bound to restore whatever profits he has made out of money gotten by taking interest. For the Apostle says, "If the root be holy, so are the branches."[12] But the root was infected with interest-taking. Therefore, whatever profit is made therefrom is infected with it. Therefore, he is bound to restore the profit.

Obj. 2. Further, it is laid down: "Property accruing from interest-taking must be sold, and the price repaid to the persons from whom the interest was extorted."[13] Therefore, likewise, whatever else is acquired from interest money must be restored.

Obj. 3. Further, that which a man buys with the proceeds of interest-taking is due to him by reason of the money he paid for it. Therefore, he has no more right to the thing purchased than to the money he paid. But he was bound to restore the money gained through interest-taking. Therefore, he is also bound to restore what he acquired with it.

On the contrary, A man may lawfully hold what he has lawfully acquired. Now, that which is acquired by the proceeds of interest-taking is sometimes lawfully acquired. Therefore, it may be lawfully retained.

I answer that, As stated above,[14] there are certain things whose use is their consumption, and which do not admit of usufruct, according to law.[15] Wherefore, if such like things be extorted by means of interest-taking (for instance, money, wheat, wine, and so forth), the lender is not bound to restore more than he received (since what is acquired by such things is the fruit not of the thing but of human industry), unless, indeed, the other party, by losing some of his own goods, be injured through the lender retaining them, and then he is bound to make good the loss.

On the other hand, there are certain things whose use is not their consumption; such things admit of usufruct, for instance, house, land, and so forth. Wherefore, if a man has by interest-taking extorted from another his house or land, he is bound to restore not only the house or land but also the fruits accruing to him therefrom, since they are the fruits of things owned by another man and consequently are due to the other.

Reply Obj. 1. The root has not only the character of matter, as money made by interest-taking has, but has also somewhat the character of an active cause, insofar as it administers nourishment. Hence the comparison fails.

Reply Obj. 2. Further, property acquired from interest-taking does not belong to the person who paid interest but to the person who bought it. Yet he that paid interest has a certain claim on that property just as he has on the other goods of the interest-taker. Hence, it is not prescribed that such property should be assigned to the persons who paid interest, since the property is perhaps worth more than what they paid in interest, but it is commanded that the property be sold, and the price be restored, of course according to the amount taken in interest.

Reply Obj. 3. The proceeds of money taken in interest are due to the person who acquired them, not by reason of the interest money as instrumental cause but on account of his own industry as principal cause. Wherefore, he has more right to the goods acquired with interest money than to the interest money itself.

FOURTH ARTICLE

Is It Lawful to Borrow Money under a Condition of Interest?

We proceed thus to the Fourth Article:

Obj. 1. It would seem that it is not lawful to borrow money under a condition of interest. For the Apostle says that they "are worthy of death, . . . not only they that do these sins, but they also that consent to them that do them."[16] Now, he that borrows money under a condition of interest consents in the sin of the interest-taker and gives him an occasion of sin. Therefore, he sins also.

Obj. 2. Further, for no temporal advantage ought one to give another an occasion of committing a sin, for this pertains to active scandal, which is always sinful, as stated above.[17] Now, he that seeks to borrow from an interest-taker gives him an occasion of sin. Therefore, he is not to be excused on account of any temporal advantage.

Obj. 3. Further, it seems no less necessary sometimes to deposit one's money with an interest-taker than to borrow from him. Now, it seems altogether unlawful to deposit one's money with an interest-taker, even as it would be unlawful to deposit one's sword with a madman, a maiden with a libertine, or food with a glutton. Neither, therefore, is it lawful to borrow from an interest-taker.

On the contrary, He that suffers injury does not sin, according to the Philosopher,[18] wherefore justice is not a mean between two vices, as stated in the same book.[19] Now, an interest-taker sins by doing an injury to the person who borrows from him under a condition of interest. Therefore, he that accepts a loan under a condition of interest does not sin.

I answer that It is by no means lawful to induce a man to sin, yet it is lawful to make use of another's sin for a good end, since even God uses all sin for some good, since He draws some good from every evil, as stated in the *Enchiridion.*[20] Hence, when Publicola asked whether it were lawful to make use of an oath taken by a man swearing by false gods (which is a manifest sin, for he gives divine honor to them), Augustine answered that one who uses, not for a bad but for a good purpose, the oath of a man that swears by false gods is a party, not to the man's sin of swearing by demons but to his good compact whereby he kept his word. If, however, one were to induce another to swear by false gods, he would sin.[21]

Accordingly, we must also answer to the question in point that it is by no means lawful to induce a man to lend under a condition of interest, yet it is lawful to borrow at interest from a man who is ready to lend at interest and is an interest-taker by profession, provided the borrower have a good end in view, such as the relief of his own or another's need. Thus too it is lawful for a man who has fallen among thieves to point out his property to them (which they sin in taking) in order to save his life, after the example of the ten men who said to Ishmael, "Kill us not, for we have stores in the field."[22]

Reply Obj. 1. He who borrows at interest does not consent to the lender's sin but makes use of it. Nor is it the lender's acceptance of interest that pleases him, but the former's lending, which is good.

Reply Obj. 2. He who borrows at interest gives the lender an occasion, not for taking interest, but for lending; it is the interest-taker who finds an occasion of sin in the malice of his own heart. Hence there is passive scandal on his part, while there is no active scandal on the part of the person who seeks to borrow. Nor is this passive scandal a reason why the other person should desist from borrowing if he is in need,

since this passive scandal arises not from weakness or ignorance but from malice.

Reply Obj. 3. If one were to entrust one's money to an
interest-taker lacking other monies to lend at interest or with
the intention that the recipient make a greater profit through
the practice of interest-taking, one would be giving a sinner
matter for sin and so be a sharer in his guilt. If, on the other
hand, the interest-taker to whom one entrusts one's money
has other monies to lend at interest, there is no sin in entrust-
ing it to him that it be in safer keeping, since this is to use a
sinner for a good purpose.

ST II–II

Question 118

Of the Vices Opposed to Liberality
and, in the First Place, of Covetousness

*[In Eight Articles, of Which
Articles One, Three, and Seven Are Included]*

FIRST ARTICLE

Is Covetousness a Sin?

We proceed thus to the First Article:

Obj. 1. It seems that covetousness is not a sin. For covetousness is said to be almost avarice for money because, to be
sure, it consists in a desire for money, under which all external goods may be comprised. Now, it is not a sin to desire
external goods, since man desires them naturally, both because they are naturally subject to man, and because by their
means man's life is sustained (for which reason they are
spoken of as his substance). Therefore, covetousness is not a
sin.

Obj. 2. Further, every sin is against either God or one's
neighbor or oneself, as stated above.[1] But covetousness is not,
properly speaking, a sin against God, since it is opposed
neither to religion nor to the theological virtues, by which
man is directed to God. Nor again is it a sin against oneself,

for this pertains properly to gluttony and lust, of which the Apostle says, "He that commits fornication sins against his own body."[2] In like manner, neither is it apparently a sin against one's neighbor, since a man harms no one by keeping what is his own. Therefore, covetousness is not a sin.

Obj. 3. Further, things that occur naturally are not sins. Now, covetousness comes naturally to old age, and every kind of defect, according to the Philosopher.[3] Therefore, covetousness is not a sin.

On the contrary, It is written: "Let your manners be without covetousness, contented with such things as you have."[4]

I answer that, In whatever things good consists in a due measure, evil must of necessity ensue through excess or deficiency of that measure. Now, in all things that are for an end, the good consists in a certain measure, since whatever is directed to an end must needs be commensurate with the end, as, for instance, medicine is commensurate with health, as the Philosopher observes.[5] External goods come under the head of things useful for an end, as stated above.[6] Hence it must needs be that man's good in their respect consists in a certain measure; in other words, that man seeks, according to a certain measure, to have external riches insofar as they are necessary for him to live in keeping with his condition of life. Wherefore it will be a sin for him to exceed this measure, by wishing to acquire or keep them immoderately. This is what is meant by covetousness, which is defined as "immoderate love of possessing."[7] It is, therefore, evident that covetousness is a sin.

Reply Obj. 1. It is natural to man to desire external things as means to an end; wherefore this desire is devoid of sin insofar as it is held in check by a rule taken from the nature of the end. But covetousness exceeds this rule, and therefore is a sin.

Reply Obj. 2. Covetousness may signify immoderation about external things in two ways. First, so as to regard immediately the acquisition and keeping of such things, when, to wit, a man acquires or keeps them more than is due. In this way, it is a sin directly against one's neighbor, since one man cannot overabound in external riches without another man lacking them, for temporal goods cannot be possessed by many at the same time. Secondly, it may signify immoderation in the internal affection which a man has for riches, when, for instance, a man loves them, desires them, or delights in them immoderately. In this way, by covetousness a man sins against himself, because it causes disorder in his affections, though not in his body, as do the sins of the flesh.

As a consequence, however, it is a sin against God, just as all mortal sins, inasmuch as man scorns things eternal for the sake of temporal things.

Reply Obj. 3. Natural inclinations should be regulated according to reason, which is the governing power in human nature. Hence, though old people seek more greedily the aid of external things, just as everyone that is in need seeks to have his need supplied, they are not excused from sin if they exceed this due measure of reason with regard to riches.

THIRD ARTICLE
Is Covetousness Opposed to Liberality?

We proceed thus to the Third Article:

Obj. 1. It seems that covetousness is not opposed to liberality. For Chrysostom, commenting on Mt. 5:6, "Blessed are they that hunger and thirst after justice," says that there are two kinds of justice, one general and the other special, to which covetousness is opposed,[8] and the Philosopher says the same.[9] Therefore, covetousness is not opposed to liberality.

Obj. 2. Further, the sin of covetousness consists in a man's exceeding the measure in the things he possesses. But this measure is appointed by justice. Therefore, covetousness is directly opposed to justice and not to liberality.

Obj. 3. Further, liberality is a virtue that observes the mean between two contrary vices, as the Philosopher states.[10] But covetousness has no contrary and opposite sin, according to the Philosopher.[11] Therefore, covetousness is not opposed to liberality.

On the contrary, It is written: "A covetous man shall not be satisfied with money, and he that loves riches shall have no fruits from them."[12] Now, not to be satisfied with money and to love it inordinately are opposed to liberality, which observes the mean in the desire of riches. Therefore, covetousness is opposed to liberality.

I answer that Covetousness denotes immoderation with regard to riches in two ways. First, immediately in respect of the acquisition and keeping of riches. In this way a man obtains money beyond his due by stealing or retaining another's property. This is opposed to justice, and in this sense covetousness is mentioned. "Her princes in the midst of her are like wolves ravening the prey to shed blood . . . and to run after gains through covetousness."[13] Secondly, it denotes immoderation in the interior affections for riches, for instance, when a man loves or desires riches too much or takes too much pleasure in them, even if he be unwilling to steal. In this way, covetousness is opposed to liberality, which moderates these affections, as stated above.[14] In this sense, covetousness is spoken of: "That they would . . . prepare for this blessing before promised, thus to be ready as if for a blessing, not as if for covetousness," where a gloss observes, "Lest they should regret what they had given and give but little."[15]

Reply Obj. 1. Chrysostom and the Philosopher are speaking of covetousness in the first sense; covetousness in the second sense is called illiberality by the Philosopher.

Reply Obj. 2. It belongs properly to justice to appoint the measure in the acquisition and keeping of riches from the point of view of what is legally due, so that a man should neither take nor retain another's property. But liberality appoints the measure of reason principally in the interior affections and consequently in the exterior taking and keeping of money and in the spending of the same, insofar as the latter proceed from the interior affection, looking at the matter from the point of view not of the legal but of the moral debt, which depends on the rule of reason.

Reply Obj. 3. Covetousness as opposed to justice has no opposite vice, since it consists in having more than one ought according to justice, the contrary of which is to have less than one ought, and this is not a sin but a punishment. But covetousness, insofar as it is opposed to liberality, has the vice of prodigality opposed to it.

SEVENTH ARTICLE
Is Covetousness a Capital Vice?

We proceed thus to the Seventh Article:

Obj. 1. It seems that covetousness is not a capital vice. For covetousness is opposed to liberality as the mean and to prodigality as the extreme. But neither is liberality a principal virtue nor prodigality a capital vice. Therefore, covetousness also should not be reckoned a capital vice.

Obj. 2. Further, as stated above, those vices are called capital which have principal ends, to which the ends of other vices are directed.[16] But this does not apply to covetousness, since riches have the aspect, not of an end, but rather of something directed to an end, as stated in *Eth.* I, 5.[17] Therefore, covetousness is not a capital vice.

Obj. 3. Further, Gregory says that "covetousness arises sometimes from pride, sometimes from fear. For there are those who, when they think that they lack the needful for their expenses, allow the mind to give way to covetousness. And there are others who, wishing to be thought more of, are incited to greed for other people's property."[18] Therefore, covetousness arises from other vices instead of being a capital vice in respect to other vices.

On the contrary, Gregory reckons covetousness among the capital vices.[19]

I answer that, As stated in the *Second Objection,* a capital vice is one which, under the aspect of end, gives rise to other vices, because when an end is very desirable, the result is that through desire thereof man sets about doing many things either good or evil. Now, the most desirable end is happiness or felicity, which is the last end of human life, as stated above;[20] wherefore, the more a thing is furnished with the conditions of happiness, the more desirable it is. Also one of the conditions of happiness is that it be self-sufficing, else it would not set man's appetite at rest, as the last end does. Now, riches give great promise of self-sufficiency, as Boethius says,[21] the reason of which, according to the Philosopher, is that we "use money in token of taking possession of something,"[22] and again it is written: "All things obey money."[23] Therefore, covetousness, which is desire for money, is a capital vice.

Reply Obj. 1. Virtue is effected in accordance with reason, but vice is effected in accordance with the inclination of the sensitive appetite. Now, reason and sensitive appetite do not belong chiefly to the same genus, and, consequently, it does not follow that principal vice is opposed to principal virtue. Wherefore, although liberality is not a principal virtue, since it does not regard the principal good of reason, yet covetousness is a principal vice, because it regards money, which occupies a principal place among sensible goods, for the reason given in the Article.

On the other hand, prodigality is not directed to an end that is chiefly desirable; indeed, it seems rather to result from a lack of reason. Hence the Philosopher says that "a prodigal man is a fool rather than a knave."[24]

Reply Obj. 2. It is true that money is directed to something else as its end; yet, insofar as it is useful for obtaining all sensible things, it contains, in a way, all things virtually. Hence it has a certain likeness to happiness, as stated in the Article.

Reply Obj. 3. Nothing prevents a capital vice from arising sometimes out of other vices, as stated above,[25] provided that itself be frequently the source of others.

Notes to Chapter 4
ST II–II, Q. 66, AA. 1–9

1. Lk. 12:18.

2. *Hom. in Luc.* PG 31, 276.

3. *De fide* I, 1. PL 16, 530.

4. Ps. 8:8.

5. II–II, Q. 64, A. 1.

6. *Pol.* I, 8. 1256a15.

7. Gen. 1:26.

8. A. 1, *Obj.* 2.

9. *Hom. in Luc.* PG 31, 276.

10. *Decretum* I, 47, 8. RF I, 171.

11. *De haeres.* 40. PL 42, 32.

12. 1 Tim. 6:17, 18.

13. II–II, Q. 57, AA. 2, 3.

14. *Hom. in Luc.* PG 31, 276.

15. *De fide* I, 1.

16. Is. 3:9.

17. *Decretum* I, 47, 8. RF I, 171.

18. *Etym.* X. PL 82, 378.

19. I–II, Q. 1, A. 3; Q. 18, A. 6.

20. *Etym.* X. PL 82, 378.

21. *Eth.* V, 2. 1131a6.

22. 1138a12.

23. 1109b35.

24. Sir. 15:21.

25. Ex. 12:35–36.

26. *Institutes* II, 1, 18, 39, and 47. K I, 11a, 12b, 13a.

27. Ex. 20:15.

28. Wis. 10:19.

29. *Institutes* II, 1, 18. K I, 11a.

30. *Institutes* II, 1, 39. K I, 12b.

31. Mt. 13:44.

32. *Institutes* II, 1, 47. K I, 13a.

33. Ibid.

34. *Sermones ad populum,* hom. 178, 8. PL 38, 965.

35. Pr. 6:30.

36. II–II, Q. 59, A. 4; I–II, Q. 72, A. 5.

37. A. 7.

38. Pr. 6:30.

39. Pr. 6:31–32.

40. Rom. 2:2.

41. *In Joan.* 50, on 12:6. PL 35, 1762.

42. Ex. 21:16.

43. *Decretals* V, 18, 3. RF II, 810.

44. *Eth.* II, 6. 1107a9.

45. *Contra mendacium* 7. PL 40, 528.

46. *Decretum* I, 47, 8. RF I, 171.

47. A. 4.

48. *De Abraham* I, 3. PL 14, 449.

49. *Epist.* 93, 12. PL 33, 345.

50. *Sermones de vetere et novo testamento,* 82. PL 39, 1904.

51. *City of God* IV, 4. PL 41, 115.

52. Ezech. 22:27.

53. II–II, Q. 55, AA. 4, 5.

54. 1128b22.

55. AA. 4, 6.

ST II–II, Q. 71, A. 1

1. Ex. 23:5.

2. *Hom. in Evang.* I, 9. PL 76, 1109.

3. Mt. 25:30.

4. II–II, Q. 32, AA. 5, 9.

5. *De doctr. Christ.* I, 28. PL 34, 30.

6. Ex. 23:4.

7. 1 Jn. 3:17.

ST II–II, Q. 77, AA. 1, 4

1. *Codex Justinianus* IV, 44, 8 and 15. K II, 179b and 180a.

2. *De Trin.* XIII, 3. PL 42, 1017.

3. *Pr.* 20:14.

4. *Eth.* VIII, 13. 1163a16.

5. *Mt.* 7:12.

6. Cicero, *De offic.* III, 15.

7. *Pol.* I, 9. 1257a6.

8. 1133a19.

9. I–II, Q. 96, A. 2.

10. *Codex Justinianus* IV, 44, 2 and 8. K II, 179b.

11. *De Trin.* XIII, 3.

12. *Opus imperfectum in Matthaeum*, hom. 38 (apocryphal). PG 56, 840.

13. *Expos. in Psalt.* PL 70, 500.

14. A. 1.

15. *Epistola* 52, ad Nepotianum. PL 22, 531.

16. *In Ps.* PL 36, 886.

17. *Pol.* I, 3 and 9. 1253b13, 1256b40.

18. *Pol.* I, 10. 1258a38.

19. *Sir.* 26:28.

20. 2 *Tim.* 2:4.

ST II–II, Q. 78, AA. 1–4

1. *Lk.* 19:23.

2. *Lk.* 6:35.

3. *Ex.* 22:25.

4. *Eth.* V, 5. 1133a20; *Pol.* I, 9. 1257a35.

5. *Ezech.* 18:8.

6. *Institutes* II, 4, 2. K I, 13b; *Digest* VII, 5, 1 and 2. K I, 138a.

7. *Pol.* I, 10. 1258b7.

8. 1133a4.

9. *Interlin.* IV, 61a.

10. Ezech. 18:17.

11. *Eth.* IV, 1.1119b26.

12. Rom. 11:16.

13. *Decretals* V, 19,5. RF II, 813.

14. A. 1.

15. Ibid., *ad* 3.

16. Rom. 1:32.

17. II–II, Q. 43, A. 2.

18. *Eth.* V. 10. 1138a35.

19. *Eth.* V, 5. 1133b33.

20. Augustine, *Enchiridion* II. PL 40, 236.

21. *Epist.* 47, ad Publicolam. PL 33, 184.

22. Jer. 41:8.

ST II–II, Q. 118, AA. 1, 3, 7

1. I–II, Q. 72, A. 4.

2. 1 Cor. 6:18.

3. *Eth.* VI, 1. 1121b13.

4. Heb. 13:15.

5. *Pol.* I, 3. 1257b25.

6. ST II–II, Q. 117, A. 3; I–II, Q. 2, A. 1.

7. Hugh of St. Victor, *De sacramentis* II, 13, 1. Pl 176, 526.

8. *In Matt. hom.,* hom. 15. PG 57, 227.

9. *Eth.* V, 1. 1129b27; 2. 1130a14.

10. *Eth.* II, 7. 1107b8; IV, 1. 1119b22, b27.

11. *Eth.* V, 1. 1129b1.

12. Ec. 5:9.

13. Ezech. 22:27.

14. II–II, Q. 117, A. 2, *ad* 3; A. 3, *ad* 3; A. 6.

15. *Glossa*, on 2 Cor. 9:5. PL 192, 62.

16. I–II, Q. 84, AA. 3, 4.

17. 1096a5.

18. *Moral.* XV, 25. PL 75, 1096.

19. *Moral.* XXXI, 45. PL 76, 621.

20. I–II, Q. 1, AA. 4, 7, 8.

21. *De consolatione philosophiae* III, 3. PL 63, 732.

22. *Eth.* V, 5. 1133b10.

23. Ec. 10:19.

24. *Eth.* IV, 1. 1121a25.

25. II–II, Q. 36, A. 4, *ad* 1; I–II, Q. 84, A. 4.

5

War and Killing

ST II–II

Question 40
Of War

*[In Four Articles, of Which
Article One Is Included]*

FIRST ARTICLE
Is It Always Sinful to Wage War?

We proceed thus to the First Article:

Objection 1. It would seem that it is always sinful to wage war, because punishment is not inflicted except for sin. Now, those who wage war are threatened by Our Lord with punishment, according to Mt. 26:52: "All that take up the sword shall perish by the sword." Therefore, all wars are unlawful.

Obj. 2. Further, whatever is contrary to a divine precept is a sin. But war is contrary to a divine precept, for it is written: "But I say to you not to resist evil,"[1] and "Do not defend yourselves, my dearly beloved, but yield to [God's] wrath."[2] Therefore, war is always sinful.

Obj. 3. Further, nothing except sin is contrary to an act of virtue. But war is contrary to peace. Therefore, war is always a sin.

Obj. 4. Further, the exercise of a lawful thing is itself lawful, as is evident in scientific exercises. But the warlike exercises which take place in tournaments are forbidden by the Church, since those who are slain in these trials are deprived of ecclesiastical burial. Therefore, it seems that war is a sin in itself.

On the contrary, Augustine says in a sermon on the servant of the centurion, "If Christian discipline forbad war altogether, those who sought salutary counsel in the Gospel would have been advised to cast aside their arms and to give up soldiering altogether. On the contrary, they were told: 'Do violence to no man, . . . and be content with your pay.'[3] If He commanded them to be content with their pay, He did not forbid soldiering."[4]

I answer that, In order for a war to be just, three things are necessary. First, the authority of the ruler, by whose command the war is to be waged; it is not the business of a private individual to declare war, because he can seek redress of his rights from the tribunal of his superior. Similarly, it is not the business of a private individual to summon together the people, something which has to be done in wars. But since the care of the common weal is committed to those who are in authority, it is their business to watch over the common weal of the city, kingdom, or province subject to them. And just as it is lawful for them to have recourse to the sword in defending that common weal against internal disturbances, when they punish evil-doers, according to the words of the Apostle: "He bears not the sword without cause, for he is God's minister, an avenger to execute wrath upon him that does evil,"[5] so too it is their business to have recourse to the sword of war in defending the common weal against external enemies. Hence it is said to those who are in authority: "Rescue the poor and deliver the needy out of the hand of the sinner,"[6] and for this reason Augustine says, "The natural order conducive to peace among mortals demands that the power to declare and counsel war should be in the hands of those who hold the supreme authority."[7]

Secondly, a just cause is required, namely, that those who are attacked, should be attacked because they deserve it on account of some fault. Wherefore, Augustine says, "A just war is wont to be described as one that avenges wrongs, when a nation or state has to be punished for refusing to make amends for the wrongs inflicted by its subjects or to restore what it has seized unjustly."[8]

Thirdly, it is necessary that the belligerents should have a rightful intention, so that they intend the advancement of good or the avoidance of evil. Hence Augustine says, "True religion looks upon as peaceful those wars that are waged not for motives of aggrandizement or cruelty but with the object of securing peace, of punishing evil-doers, and of uplifting the good."[9] For it may happen that, even if war be declared by legitimate authority and for a just cause, it is nonetheless rendered unlawful through a wicked intention. Hence Augustine says, "The passion for inflicting harm, the cruel thirst to vengeance, an unpacific and relentless spirit, the fever of revolt, the lust of power, and such like things, all these are rightly condemned in war."[10]

Reply Obj. 1. As Augustine says, "To take up the sword is to arm oneself in order to take the life of someone without the command or permission of superior or lawful authority."[11] On the other hand, to have recourse to the sword (as a private person) by the authority of the ruler or judge or (as a public person) through zeal for justice and by the authority, so to speak, of God, is not to "take up the sword" but to use it as commissioned by another; wherefore it does not deserve punishment. And yet even those who make sinful use of the sword are not always slain by the sword, yet they always perish by their own sword, because, unless they repent, they are punished eternally for their sinful use of the sword.

Reply Obj. 2. Such like precepts, as Augustine observes,[12] should always be borne in readiness of mind, so that we be ready to obey them and, if necessary, to refrain from resistance or self-defense. Nevertheless, it is necessary sometimes for a man to act otherwise for the common good or for the good of those with whom he is fighting. Hence Augustine says, "Those whom we have to punish with a kindly severity it is necessary to handle in many ways against their will. For when we are stripping a man of the lawlessness of sin, it is good for him to be vanquished, since nothing is more hopeless than the happiness of sinners, whence arises a guilty impunity and an evil will, like an internal enemy."[13]

Reply Obj. 3. Those who wage war justly aim at peace, and so they are not opposed to peace, except to the evil peace which Our Lord "came not to send upon earth."[14] Hence Augustine says, "We do not seek peace in order to be at war, but we go to war that we may have peace. Be peaceful, therefore, in warring, so that you may vanquish those whom you war against and bring them to the prosperity of peace."[15]

Reply Obj. 4. Not all exercises by men in warlike feats of arms are forbidden but those which are inordinate and perilous and end in slaying or plundering. In older times, warlike exercises presented no such danger, and hence they were called "exercises of arms" or "bloodless wars," as Jerome states in an epistle.[16]

ST II–II

Question 64
Of Killing

*[In Eight Articles, of Which
Articles Six, Seven, and Eight Are Included]*

SIXTH ARTICLE
Is It Ever Lawful to Kill the Innocent?

We proceed thus to the Sixth Article:

Obj. 1. It would seem that in some cases it is lawful to kill the innocent. The fear of God is never manifested by sin, since, on the contrary, "the fear of the Lord drives out sin."[1] Now, Abraham was commended in that he feared the Lord, since he was willing to slay his innocent son. Therefore, one may without sin kill an innocent person.

Obj. 2. Further, among those sins that are committed against one's neighbor, the more grievous seem to be those whereby a more grievous injury is inflicted on the person sinned against. Now, to be killed is a greater injury to a sinful than to an innocent person, because the latter, by death, passes forthwith from the unhappiness of this life to the glory of heaven. Since, then, it is lawful in certain cases to kill a sinful man, much more is it lawful to slay an innocent or a righteous person.

Obj. 3. Further, what is done in keeping with the order of justice is not a sin. But sometimes a man is forced, according to the order of justice, to slay an innocent person, for instance, when a judge, who is bound to judge according to the evidence, condemns to death a man whom he knows to be innocent, but who is convicted by false witnesses, and likewise the executioner, who in obedience to the judge puts to death the man who has been unjustly sentenced.

On the contrary, It is written: "The innocent and just person you shall not put to death."[2]

I answer that An individual man may be considered in two ways: first, in himself; secondly, in relation to something else. If we consider a man in himself, it is unlawful to kill any man, since in every man, though he be sinful, we ought to love the nature which God has made and which is destroyed by slaying him. Nevertheless, as stated above, the slaying of a sinner becomes lawful in relation to the common good, which is corrupted by sin.[3] On the other hand, the life of righteous men preserves and forwards the common good, since they are the chief part of the community. Therefore, it is in no way lawful to slay the innocent.

Reply Obj. 1. God is Lord of death and life, for by His decree both the sinful and the righteous die. Hence, he who at God's command kills an innocent man does not sin, as neither does God, at Whose behest he executes; indeed, his obedience to God's commands is a proof that he fears God.

Reply Obj. 2. In weighing the gravity of a sin, we must consider the essential rather than the accidental. Wherefore, he who kills a just man sins more grievously than he who slays a sinful man: first, because he injures one whom he should love more and so acts more in opposition to charity; secondly, because he inflicts an injury on a man who is less deserving of one and so acts more in opposition to justice; thirdly, because he deprives the community of a greater good; fourthly, because he despises God more, according to Luke 10:16, "He that despises you despises Me." On the other hand, it is accidental to the slaying that the just man whose life is taken be received by God into glory.

Reply Obj. 3. If the judge knows that a man who has been convicted by false witnesses is innocent, he must, like Daniel, examine the witnesses with great care, so as to find an occasion for acquitting the innocent. But if he cannot do this, he should remit him for judgment by a higher tribunal. If even this is impossible, he does not sin if he pronounce sentence in accordance with the evidence, for it is not he that puts the innocent man to death but they who stated him to be guilty. He who is assigned to carry out the sentence of the judge who has condemned an innocent man, if the sentence contains an intolerable error, should not obey, else they would be excused who executed the martyrs. If, however, it contain no manifest injustice, he does not sin by carrying out the sentence, because he has no right to discuss the judgment of his superior, nor is it he who slays the innocent man but the judge whose minister he is.

SEVENTH ARTICLE

Is It Lawful to Kill a Man in Self-Defense?

We proceed thus to the Seventh Article:

Obj. 1. It would seem that nobody may lawfully kill a man in self-defense. For Augustine says to Publicola, "I do not agree with the opinion that one may kill a man lest one be killed by him, unless one be a soldier or hold a public office, so that one does it not for oneself but for others, having the legitimate power to do so, provided it be fitted to the person."[4] Now, he who kills a man in self-defense kills him lest he be killed by him. Therefore, this would seem to be unlawful.

Obj. 2. Further, Augustine says, "How are they free from sin in sight of divine Providence who are guilty of taking a man's life for the sake of these contemptible things?"[5] Now, among contemptible things he reckons "those which men can lose unwillingly,"[6] as appears from the context, and the chief of these is the life of the body. Therefore, it is unlawful for any man to take another's life for the sake of the life of his own body.

Obj. 3. Further, Pope Nicolas says, and we have in the *Decretum*, "Concerning the clerics about whom you have consulted us, those, namely, who have killed a pagan in self-defense, as to whether, after making amends by repenting, they may return to their former state or rise to a higher degree, know that in no case is it lawful for them to kill any man under any circumstances whatever."[7] Now, clerics and laymen are alike bound to observe the moral precepts. Therefore, neither is it lawful for laymen to kill anyone in self-defense.

Obj. 4. Further, murder is a more grievous sin than fornication or adultery. Now, nobody may lawfully commit simple fornication or adultery or any other mortal sin in order to save his own life, since the spiritual life is to be preferred to the life of the body. Therefore, no man may lawfully take another's life in self-defense in order to save his own life.

Obj. 5. Further, if the tree be evil, so is the fruit, according to Mt. 7:17. Now, self-defense itself seems to be unlawful, according to Rom. 12:19: "Do not defend yourselves, my dearly beloved." Therefore, its result, which is the slaying of a man, is also unlawful.

On the contrary, It is written: "If a thief be found breaking into a house or undermining it and be wounded so as to die, he that slew him shall not be guilty of blood."[8] Now, it is much more lawful to defend one's life than one's house. Therefore, neither is a man guilty of murder if he kill another in defense of his own life.

I answer that Nothing hinders one act from having two effects, only one of which is intended, while the other is beside the intention. Now, moral acts take their species according to what is intended and not according to what is beside the intention, since this is accidental, as explained above.[9] Accordingly, the act of self-defense may have two effects: one, the saving of one's life; the other, the slaying of the aggressor. Therefore, this act, since one's intention is to save one's own life, is not unlawful, seeing that it is natural to everything to keep itself in being as far as possible. And yet, though proceeding from a good intention, an act may be rendered unlawful if it be out of proportion to the end. Wherefore, if a man in self-defense uses more than necessary violence, it will be unlawful, whereas, if he repel force with moderation, his defense will be lawful, because according to the jurists, "It is lawful to repel force by force, provided one does not exceed the limits of a blameless defense."[10] Nor is it necessary for salvation that a man omit an act of moderate self-defense in order to avoid killing the other man, since one is bound to take more care of one's own life than of another's. But as it is unlawful to take a man's life, except by public authority acting for the common good, as stated above,[11] it is not lawful for a man to intend killing a man in self-defense, except by such as have public authority, who, while intending to kill a man in self-defense, refer this to the public good, as in the case of a soldier fighting against the foe or a judge's servant struggling with robbers, although even these sin if they be moved by private animosity.

Reply Obj. 1. The words quoted from Augustine refer to the case when one man intends to kill another to save himself from death. The passage quoted in the *Second Objection* is to be understood in the same sense. Hence he says pointedly, "for the sake of these things,"[12] whereby he indicates the intention. This suffices for the *Reply* to the *Second Objection.*

Reply Obj. 3. Irregularity results from the act, though sinless, of taking a man's life, as appears in the case of a judge who justly condemns a man to death. For this reason, a cleric, though he kill a man in self-defense, is irregular, albeit he intends not to kill him but to defend himself.

Reply Obj. 4. The act of fornication or adultery is not necessarily directed to the preservation of one's own life, as is the act whence sometimes results the taking of a man's life.

Reply Obj. 5. The defense forbidden in this passage is that which is maliciously vengeful. Hence a gloss says, "Do not defend yourselves, that is, do not strike your enemy in return."[13]

EIGHTH ARTICLE

Is One Guilty of Murder through Killing Someone by Chance?

We proceed thus to the Eighth Article:

Obj. 1. It would seem that one is guilty of murder through killing someone by chance. For we read that Lamech slew a man in mistake for a wild beast, and that he was accounted guilty of murder.[14] Therefore, one incurs the guilt of murder through killing a man by chance.

Obj. 2. Further, it is written: "If . . . one strike a woman with child, and causes a miscarriage . . . , if her death ensue thereupon, he shall render life for life."[15] Yet this may happen without any intention of causing her death. Therefore, one is guilty of murder through killing someone by chance.

Obj. 3. Further, the *Decretum* contains several canons prescribing penalties for unintentional homicide.[16] Now, penalty is not due save for guilt. Therefore, he who kills a man by chance incurs the guilt of murder.

On the contrary, Augustine says to Publicola, "When we do
a thing for a good and lawful purpose, if thereby we unintentionally cause harm to anyone, it should by no means be
imputed to us."[17] Now, it sometimes happens by chance that
a person is killed as a result of something done for a good
purpose. Therefore, the person who did it is not accounted
guilty.

I answer that, According to the Philosopher, "chance is a
cause that acts beside one's intention."[18] Hence chance happenings, strictly speaking, are neither intended nor voluntary. And, since every sin is voluntary, according to Augustine,[19] it follows that chance happenings, as such, are not
sins.

Nevertheless, it happens that what is not actually and directly voluntary and intended is accidentally voluntary and
intended, and so that which removes an obstacle is called an
accidental cause. Wherefore, he who does not remove something whence homicide results, whereas he ought to remove
it, is in a sense guilty of voluntary homicide. This happens in
two ways: first, when a man causes another's death through
occupying himself with unlawful things which he ought to
avoid; secondly, when he does not take sufficient care.
Hence, according to jurists, if a man pursue a lawful occupa-
tion and take due care, the result being that a person loses his
life, he is not guilty of that person's death, whereas, if he be
occupied with something unlawful or even with something
lawful but without due care, he does not escape being guilty
of murder if his action results in someone's death.[20]

Reply Obj. 1. Lamech did not take sufficient care to avoid
taking a man's life, and so he was not excused from being
guilty of homicide.

Reply Obj. 2. He that strikes a woman with child does
something unlawful; wherefore, if there results the death
either of the woman or of the ensouled fetus, he will not be
excused from murder, especially seeing that death is the natural result of such a blow.

Reply Obj. 3. According to the canons, a penalty is inflicted
on those who cause death unintentionally through doing
something unlawful or failing to take sufficient care.

Notes to Chapter 5

ST II–II, Q. 40, A. 1

1. Mt. 5:39.

2. Rom. 12:19.

3. Lk. 3:14.

4. *Epist.* 138, ad Marcellum, 2. PL 33, 531.

5. Rom. 13:4.

6. Ps. 81:4.

7. *Contra Faustum* XXII, 75. PL 42, 448.

8. *Quaest. Heptat.*, on Joshua 8:2. PL 34, 781.

9. St. Thomas refers to *De verbis Domini*. Actually, *Decretum* II, 23, 1 (Can. 6, *Apud veros*). RF I, 893.

10. *Contra Faustum* XXII, 74. PL 42, 447.

11. Ibid. 70. PL 42, 447.

12. *De sermone Domini in monte* I, 19. PL 34, 1260.

13. *Epist.* 138, ad Marcellum, 2. PL 33, 531.

14. Mt. 10:34.

15. *Epist.* 189, ad Bonifacium, 6. PL 33, 856.

16. Actually, Vegetius, *Instit. rei militar.* I, 928; II, 23.

ST II–II, Q. 64, AA. 6, 7, 8

1. Sir. 1:27.

2. Ex. 23:7.

3. A. 2.

4. *Epist.* 47, ad Publicolam. PL 33, 186.

5. *De lib. arb.* I, 5. PL 32, 1228.

6. Ibid.

7. *Epistola* 138, ad Osbaldum, PL 119, 1131. *Decretum* I, 50, 6. RF I, 179.

8. Ex. 22:2.

9. II–II, Q. 43, A. 3; I–II, Q. 72, A. 1.

10. *Decretals* V, 12, 18. RF II, 801.

11. A. 3.

12. *De lib. arb.* I, 5. PL 32, 1228.

13. *Glossa,* on Rom. 12:19. PL 191, 1502.

14. Gen. 4:23–24.

15. Ex. 21:22.

16. *Decretum* I, 50, 4–8. RF I, 178–80.

17. *Epist.* 47, ad Publicolam. PL 33, 187.

18. *Physics* II, 6. 197b18.

19. *De vera relig.* 14. PL 34, 133.

20. *Decretum* I, 50, 4–8. RF I, 178–80.

Sedition and Obedience

ST II–II

Question 42
Of Sedition

*[In Two Articles, of Which
Article Two Is Included]*

SECOND ARTICLE
Is Sedition Always a Mortal Sin?

We proceed thus to the Second Article:

Objection 1. It would seem that sedition is not always a mortal sin. For sedition denotes "a tumult leading to fighting," according to the gloss quoted above.[1] But fighting is not always a mortal sin; indeed, it is sometimes just and lawful, as stated above.[2] Much more, therefore, can sedition be without a mortal sin.

Obj. 2. Further, sedition is a kind of discord, as stated above.[3] Now, discord can be without mortal sin and sometimes without any sin at all. Therefore, sedition can be also.

Obj. 3. Further, it is praiseworthy to deliver a community from tyrannical rule. Yet this cannot easily be done without some dissension in the community, if one part of the community seeks to retain the tyrant, while the rest strive to dethrone him. Therefore, there can be sedition without mortal sin.

On the contrary, The Apostle forbids seditions together with other things that are mortal sins.[4] Therefore, sedition is a mortal sin.

I answer that, As stated above, sedition is contrary to the unity of the multitude, viz., the people of a political community or kingdom.[5] Now, Augustine says that "wise men understand the word 'people' to designate, not any crowd of persons, but the assembly of those who are united together in fellowship recognized by law and for the common good."[6] Wherefore it is evident that the unity to which sedition is opposed is the unity of law and the common good; whence it follows manifestly that sedition is opposed to justice and the common good. Therefore, by reason of its genus, it is a mortal sin, and its gravity will be all the greater as the common good which it assails surpasses the private good which is assailed by strife.

Accordingly, the sin of sedition is first and chiefly in its authors, who sin most grievously, and secondly, it is in those who are led by them to disturb the common good. Those, however, who defend the common good and withstand the seditious party are not themselves seditious, as neither is a man to be called quarrelsome because he defends himself, as stated above.[7]

Reply Obj. 1. It is lawful to fight, provided it be for the common good, as stated above.[8] But sedition runs counter to the common good of the multitude, so that it is always a mortal sin.

Reply Obj. 2. Discord from what is not manifestly good may be without sin, but discord from what is manifestly good cannot be without sin. And sedition is discord of this kind, for it is contrary to the unity of the multitude, which is manifestly good.

Reply Obj. 3. A tyrannical government is not just, because it is directed, not to the common good, but to the private good of the ruler, as the Philosopher states.[9] Consequently, there is no sedition in disturbing a government of this kind, unless, indeed, the tyrant's rule be disturbed so inordinately that his subjects suffer greater harm from the consequent disturbance than from the tyrant's government. Indeed, it is the tyrant, rather, that is guilty of sedition, since he encourages discord and sedition among his subjects, that he may lord over them more securely; for this is tyranny, being conducive to the private good of the ruler and to the injury of the multitude.

ST II–II
Question 104
Of Obedience

[In Six Articles]

We must now consider obedience, under which head there are six points of inquiry: (1) Whether one man is bound to obey another? (2) Whether obedience is a special virtue? (3) Its relation to other virtues; (4) Whether God must be obeyed in all things? (5) Whether subjects are bound to obey their prelates in all things? (6) Whether the faithful are bound to obey secular powers?

FIRST ARTICLE
Is One Man Bound to Obey Another?

We proceed thus to the First Article:

Obj. 1. It seems that one man is not bound to obey another, for nothing should be done contrary to the divine ordinance. Now, God has ordained that man be ruled by his own counsel, according to Sir. 15:14, "God made man from the beginning and left him in the hand of his own counsel." Therefore, one man is not bound to obey another.

Obj. 2. Further, if one man were bound to obey another, he would have to look upon the will of the person commanding him as being his own rule of conduct. Now, God's will alone, which is always right, is the rule of human conduct. Therefore, man is bound to obey none but God.

Obj. 3. Further, the more gratuitous the service, the more is it acceptable. Now, what a man does out of duty is not gratuitous. Therefore, if a man were bound in duty to obey others in doing good deeds, for this very reason his good deeds would be rendered less acceptable through being done out of obedience. Therefore, one man is not bound to obey another.

On the contrary, It is prescribed: "Obey your superiors and be subject to them."[1]

I answer that, Just as the actions of natural things proceed from natural powers, so do human actions proceed from the human will. In natural things, it behooved the higher to move the lower to their actions by the excellence of the natural power bestowed on them by God, and so, in human affairs also, the higher should move the lower by their will in virtue of divinely established authority. Now, to move by reason and will is to command. Wherefore, just as in virtue of the divinely established natural order the lower natural things need to be subject to the movement of the higher, so too in human affairs, in virtue of the order of natural and divine law, inferiors are bound to obey their superiors.

Reply Obj. 1. God left man in the hand of his own counsel, not as though it is permissible for him to do whatever he wishes, but because, unlike irrational creatures, he is not compelled by natural necessity to do what he ought to do but is left free choice proceeding from his own counsel. And just as he has to proceed on his own counsel in doing other things, so too has he in the point of obeying his superiors. For Gregory says, "When we humbly give way to another's voice, we overcome ourselves in our own hearts."[2]

Reply Obj. 2. The will of God is the first rule whereby all rational wills are regulated, to which one will approaches more than another, according to a divinely appointed order. Hence the will of the one who issues a command may be as a second rule to the will of the other man who obeys him.

Reply Obj. 3. A thing may be deemed gratuitous in two ways. In one way, on the part of the deed itself, because, to wit, one is not bound to do it; in another way, on the part of the doer, because he does it of his own free will. Now, a deed is rendered virtuous, praiseworthy, and meritorious chiefly according as it proceeds from the will. Wherefore, although obedience be a duty, if one obey with a prompt will, one's merit is not for that reason diminished, especially before God, Who sees not only the outward deed but also the inward will.

SECOND ARTICLE
Is Obedience a Special Virtue?

We proceed thus to the Second Article:

Obj. 1. It seems that obedience is not a special virtue. For disobedience is contrary to obedience. But disobedience is a general sin, because Ambrose says that "sin is to disobey the divine law."[3] Therefore, obedience is not a special virtue.

Obj. 2. Further, every special virtue is either theological or moral. But obedience is not a theological virtue, since it is not comprised under faith, hope, or charity. Nor is it a moral virtue, since it does not hold the mean between excess and deficiency, for the more obedient one is, the more is one praised. Therefore, obedience is not a special virtue.

Obj. 3. Further, Gregory says that "obedience is the more meritorious and praiseworthy the less it holds its own."[4] But every special virtue is the more to be praised the more it holds its own, since virtue requires a man to exercise his will and choice, as stated in Eth. II, 4.[5] Therefore, obedience is not a special virtue.

Obj. 4. Further, virtues differ in species according to their objects. Now, the object of obedience would seem to be the command of a superior, of which, apparently, there are as many kinds as there are degrees of superiority. Therefore, obedience is a general virtue comprising many special virtues.

On the contrary, Obedience is reckoned by some to be a part of justice, as stated above.[6]

I answer that A special virtue is assigned to all good deeds that have a special reason for praise, for it belongs properly to virtue to render a deed good. Now, obedience to a superior is due in accordance with the divinely established order of things, as shown above.[7] Therefore, it is good, since good consists in mode, species, and order, as Augustine states.[8] Again, this act has a special aspect of praiseworthiness by reason of its object. For while subjects have many obligations towards their superiors, this one, that they are bound to obey their commands, stands out as special among the rest. Wherefore obedience is a special virtue, and its specific object is a command, tacit or express. The superior's will, however it become known, is a tacit precept, and a man's obedience seems to be all the more prompt inasmuch as, by obeing, he forestalls the express command when he understands his superior's will.

Reply Obj. 1. Nothing prevents the one same material object from admitting two special aspects to which two special virtues correspond; thus a soldier, by defending his king's fortress, performs both an act of fortitude, by facing the

danger of death for a good end, and an act of justice, by
rendering due service to his lord. Accordingly, the aspect of
precept, which obedience considers, happens with acts of all
the virtues, but not with all acts of virtue, since not all acts of
virtue are a matter of precept, as stated above.[9] Moreover,
certain things are sometimes a matter of precept and pertain
to no other virtue, such things, for instance, as are not evil
except because they are forbidden. Wherefore, if obedience
be taken in its proper sense, as considering formally and
intentionally the aspect of precept, it will be a special virtue,
and disobedience a special sin, because in this way it is requisite for obedience that one perform an act of justice or of
some other virtue with the intention of fulfilling a precept,
and for disobedience that one treat the precept with actual
contempt. On the other hand, if obedience be taken in a wide
sense for the performance of any action that may be a matter
of precept, and disobedience for the omission of that action
through any intention whatever, then obedience will be a
general virtue, and disobedience a general sin.

Reply Obj. 2. Obedience is not a theological virtue, for its
direct object is not God but the precept of any superior,
whether expressed or implied, namely, the simple word of a
prelate indicating his will, which the obedient subject obeys
promptly, according to Tit. 3:2, "Admonish them to be subject to princes and to obey at a word," etc.

It is, however, a moral virtue, since it is a part of justice,
and it observes the mean between excess and deficiency. Excess thereof is measured in respect, not to quantity, but to
other circumstances, insofar as a man obeys either one whom
he ought not or in matters wherein he ought not to obey, as
we have stated above regarding religion.[10] We may also reply
that, as in justice excess is in the person who retains another's
property, and deficiency in the person who does not receive
his due, according to the Philosopher,[11] so too obedience
oberves the mean between excess on the part of him who
fails to pay due obedience to his superior, since he exceeds in
fulfilling his own will, and deficiency on the part of the
superior, who does not receive obedience. Wherefore, in this
way obedience will be a mean between two forms of wickedness, as was stated above concerning justice.[12]

Reply Obj. 3. Obedience, like every virtue, requires the will
to be prompt towards its proper object but not towards that

which is repugnant to it. Now, the proper object of obedience is a precept, and this proceeds from another's will. Wherefore obedience makes a man's will prompt in fulfilling the will of another, the maker, namely, of the precept. If that which is prescribed to him is willed by him for its own sake apart from its being prescribed, as happens in agreeable matters, he tends towards it at once by his own will and seems to comply, not on account of the precept, but on account of his own will. But if that which is prescribed is nowise willed for its own sake but, considered in itself, is repugnant to his own will, as happens in disagreeable matters, then it is quite evident that it is not fulfilled except on account of the precept. Hence Gregory says that "obedience is nil or less when it profits oneself in advantageous matters" (because, to wit, one's own will seems to tend principally, not to the accomplishment of the precept, but to the fulfillment of one's own desire), but that "it increases in disadvantageous or difficult matters" (because there one's own will tends to nothing besides the precept).[13] Yet this must be understood according to outward appearances. On the other hand, according to the judgment of God, Who searches the heart, it may happen that even in advantageous matters obedience, while profiting oneself, is no less praiseworthy, provided the will of him that obeys tends no less devotedly to the fulfillment of the precept.

Reply Obj. 4. Reverence regards directly the person that excels; wherefore it admits of various species according to the various aspects of excellence. Obedience, on the other hand, regards the precept of the person that excels and therefore admits of only one aspect. And since obedience is due to a person's precept on account of reverence to him, it follows that obedience to a man is of one species, though the causes from which it proceeds differ specifically.

THIRD ARTICLE
Is Obedience the Greatest of the Virtues?

We proceed thus to the Third Article:

Obj. 1. It seems that obedience is the greatest of the virtues. For it is written: "Obedience is better than sacrifices."[14] Now, the offering of sacrifices belongs to religion, which is the greatest of all moral virtues, as shown above.[15] Therefore, obedience is greater than all the virtues.

Obj. 2. Further, Gregory says that "obedience is the only virtue that ingrafts virtues in the soul and protects them when ingrafted."[16] Now, the cause is greater than the effect. Therefore, obedience is greater than all the virtues.

Obj. 3. Further, Gregory says that "evil should never be done out of obedience; yet sometimes for the sake of obedience we should lay aside the good we are doing."[17] Now, one does not lay aside a thing except for something better. Therefore, obedience, for whose sake the good of other virtues is set aside, is better than other virtues.

On the contrary, Obedience deserves praise because it proceeds from charity; for Gregory says that "obedience should be practiced, not out of servile fear, but from a sense of charity; not through fear of punishment, but through love of justice."[18] Therefore, charity is a greater virtue than obedience.

I answer that, Just as sin consists in man scorning God and adhering to mutable things, so the merit of a virtuous act consists in man scorning created goods and adhering to God as his end. Now, the end is greater than that which is directed to the end. Therefore, if a man scorns created goods in order that he may adhere to God, his virtue derives greater praise from his adhering to God than from his scorning earthly things. And so those, namely, the theological virtues, whereby he adheres to God in Himself, are greater than the moral virtues, whereby he holds in contempt some earthly thing in order to adhere to God.

Among the moral virtues, the greater the thing which a man holds in contempt that he may adhere to God, the greater the virtue. Now, there are three kinds of human goods that man may scorn for God's sake. The lowest of these are external goods; the goods of the body take the middle place; the highest are the goods of the soul, and among these the chief, in a way, is the will, insofar as, by his will, man makes use of all other goods. Therefore, properly speaking, the virtue of obedience, whereby we scorn our own will for God's sake, is more praiseworthy than the other moral virtues, which scorn other goods for the sake of God.

Hence, Gregory says that "obedience is rightly preferred to

sacrifices, because by sacrifices another's body is slain, whereas by obedience we slay our own will."[19] Wherefore all other acts of virtue are meritorious before God through being performed out of obedience to God's will. For one to suffer even martyrdom, or to give all one's goods to the poor, unless one directed these things to the fulfillment of the divine will, which pertains directly to obedience, they could not be meritorious, as neither would they be if they were done without charity, which cannot exist apart from obedience. For it is written: "He who says that he knows God and keeps not His commandments is a liar, . . . but he that keeps His word, in him the charity of God is truly perfect,"[20] and this because friends have the same likes and dislikes.

Reply Obj. 1. Obedience proceeds from reverence, which pays worship and honor to a superior, and in this respect it is contained under different virtues, although considered in itself, as regarding the aspect of precept, it is one special virtue. Accordingly, insofar as it proceeds from reverence for a prelate, it is contained, in a way, under respectfulness; insofar as it proceeds from reverence for one's parents, it is contained under piety; insofar as it proceeds from reverence for God, it comes under religion and pertains to devotion, which is the principal act of religion. Wherefore, from this point of view, it is more praiseworthy to obey God than to offer sacrifice. This is also because "in a sacrifice we slay another's body, whereas by obedience we slay our own will," as Gregory says.[21] As to the special case of which Samuel spoke, it would have been better for Saul to obey God than to offer in sacrifice the fat animals of the Amalekites against the commandment of God.

Reply Obj. 2. All acts of virtue, insofar as they come under a precept, pertain to obedience. Wherefore, according as acts of virtue work causally or dispositively toward the generation and preservation of virtue, obedience is said to ingraft and protect all the virtues. And yet, for two reasons, it does not follow that obedience takes precedence of all virtues absolutely. First, because, though an act of virtue come under a precept, one may nevertheless perform that act of virtue without considering the aspect of precept. Consequently, if there be any virtue whose object is naturally prior to the precept, that virtue is said to be naturally prior to obedience.

Such a virtue is faith, whereby we come to know the sublime nature of divine authority, by reason of which the power to command is competent to God. Secondly, because infusion of grace and virtues may precede, even in point of time, all virtuous acts, and in this way obedience is not prior to all virtues, neither in point of time nor by nature.[22]

Reply Obj. 3. There are two kinds of good. There is that to which we are bound of necessity, for instance, to love God, and so forth, and by no means may such a good be set aside on account of obedience. But there is another good to which man is not bound of necessity, and this good we ought sometimes to set aside for the sake of obedience to which we are bound of necessity, since we ought not to do good by falling into sin. Yet, as Gregory remarks, "He who forbids his subjects any single good must needs allow them many others, lest the souls of those who obey perish utterly from starvation, through being deprived of every good."[23] Thus the loss of one good may be compensated by obedience and other goods.

FOURTH ARTICLE
Ought God to Be Obeyed in All Things?

We proceed thus to the Fourth Article:

Obj. 1. It seems that God need not be obeyed in all things. For it is written that Our Lord, after healing the two blind men, commanded them, saying, " 'See that no man know this.' But they going out spread His fame abroad in all that country."[24] Yet they are not blamed for so doing. Therefore, it seems that we are not bound to obey God in all things.

Obj. 2. Further, no one is bound to do anything contrary to virtue. Now, we find that God commanded certain things contrary to virtue; thus He commanded Abraham to slay his innocent son,[25] and the Jews to steal the property of the Egyptians,[26] which things are contrary to justice, and Hosea to take to himself a woman who was an adulteress,[27] and this is contrary to chastity. Therefore, God is not to be obeyed in all things.

Obj. 3. Further, whoever obeys God conforms his will to the divine will even as to the thing willed. But we are not bound in all things to conform our will to the divine will as to the thing willed, as stated above.[28] Therefore, man is not bound to obey God in all things.

On the contrary, It is written: "All things that the Lord has spoken we will do, and we will be obedient."[29]

I answer that, As stated above, he who obeys is moved by the command of the person he obeys, just as natural things are moved by their moving causes.[30] Now, just as God is the first mover of all things that are moved naturally, so too is He the first mover of all wills, as shown above.[31] Therefore, just as all natural things are subject to the divine motion by a natural necessity, so too all wills, by a kind of necessity of justice, are bound to obey the divine command.

Reply Obj. 1. Our Lord in telling the blind men to conceal the miracle had no intention of binding them with the force of a divine precept, but, as Gregory says, "gave an example to His servants who follow Him, that they might wish to hide their virtue, and yet that it should be proclaimed against their will, in order that others might profit by their example."[32]

Reply Obj. 2. Even as God does nothing contrary to nature (since "the nature of a thing is what God does therein," according to a gloss on Rom. 11)[33] and yet does certain things contrary to the wonted course of nature, so too God can command nothing contrary to virtue, since virtue and rectitude of human will consist chiefly in conformity with God's will and obedience to His command, although it be contrary to the wonted mode of virtue. Accordingly, then, the command given to Abraham to slay his innocent son was not contrary to justice, since God is the author of life and death. Nor again was it contrary to justice that He commanded the Jews to take things belonging to the Egyptians, because all things are His, and He gives them to whom He will. Nor was it contrary to chastity that Hosea was commanded to take an adulteress, because God himself is the ordainer of human generation, and the right manner of intercourse with woman is that which He appoints. Hence it is evident that the persons aforesaid did not sin, either by obeying God or by willing to obey Him.

Reply Obj. 3. Though man is not always bound to will what God wills, yet he is always bound to will what God wills him to will. This comes to man's knowledge chiefly through God's command; wherefore man is bound to obey God's commands in all things.

FIFTH ARTICLE

Are Subjects Bound to Obey Their Superiors in All Things?

We proceed thus to the Fifth Article:

Obj. 1. It seems that subjects are bound to obey their superiors in all things. For the Apostle says, "Children, obey your parents in all things,"[34] and farther on: "Servants, obey in all things your masters according to the flesh."[35] Therefore, in like manner, other subjects are bound to obey their prelates in all things.

Obj. 2. Further, prelates stand between God and their subjects, according to Dt., "I was the mediator and stood between the Lord and you at that time, to show you His words."[36] Now, there is no going from extreme to extreme, except through that which stands between. Therefore, the commands of a prelate must be esteemed the commands of God; wherefore the Apostle says, "You . . . received me as an angel of God, even as Christ Jesus"[37] and "When you had received through us the word of hearing of God, you received it, not as the word of men, but, as it is indeed, the word of God."[38] Therefore, as man is bound to obey God in all things, so is he bound to obey his prelates.

Obj. 3. Further, just as religious in making their profession take vows of chastity and poverty, so do they also vow obedience. Now, a religious is bound to observe chastity and poverty in all things. Therefore, he is also bound to obey in all things.

On the contrary, It is written: "We ought to obey God rather than men."[39] Now, sometimes the things commanded by a prelate are against God. Therefore, prelates are not to be obeyed in all things.

I answer that, As stated above, he who obeys is moved at the bidding of the person who commands him by a certain necessity of justice, even as a natural thing is moved through the power of its mover by a natural necessity.[40] That a natural thing be not moved by its mover may happen in two ways. First, on account of a hindrance arising from the stronger power of some other mover; thus wood is not burnt by fire if a stronger force of water intervenes. Secondly, through lack of order in the movable with regard to its mover, since, though it is subject to the latter's action in one respect, yet it is not subject thereto in every respect. Thus, wetness is sometimes subject to the action of heat, as regards being heated, but not as regards being dried up or consumed. In like manner, there are two reasons for which a subject may not be bound to obey his superior in all things. First, on account of the command of a higher power. For as a gloss says on Rom. 13:2, "They that resist the power resist the ordinance of God. If a commissioner issue an order, are you to comply if it is contrary to the bidding of the proconsul? Again, if the proconsul command one thing, and the emperor another, will you hesitate to disregard the former and serve the latter? Therefore, if the emperor commands one thing and God another, you must disregard the former and obey God."[41] Secondly, a subject is not bound to obey his superior if the latter command him to do something wherein he is not subject to him. For Seneca says, "It is wrong to suppose that slavery falls upon the whole man, for the better part of him is excepted. His body is subjected and assigned to his master, but his soul is his own."[42] Consequently, in matters touching the internal movement of the will, man is not bound to obey his fellowman, but God alone.

Nevertheless, man is bound to obey his fellowman in things that have to be done externally by means of the body; yet, since by nature all men are equal, he is not bound to obey another man in matters touching the nature of the body, for instance, in those relating to the sustenance of his body and the begetting of children. Wherefore slaves are not bound to obey their masters, nor children their parents, in the matter of contracting marriage or of remaining in the state of virginity or the like. But in matters concerning the disposal of actions and human affairs, a subject is bound to obey his superior within the sphere of his authority; for instance, a soldier must obey his general in matters relating to war, a slave his master in matters touching the execution of the duties of his service, a son his father in matters relating to the conduct of his life and the care of the household and so forth.

Reply Obj. 1. When the Apostle says "in all things," he refers to matters within the sphere of a father's or master's authority.

Reply Obj. 2. Man is subject to God simply as regards all things, both internal and external; wherefore he is bound to obey Him in all things. On the other hand, inferiors are not subject to their superiors in all things but only in certain things and in a particular way, in respect to which the superior stands between God and his subjects, whereas in respect to other matters the subject is immediately under God, by Whom he is taught either by the natural or by the written law.

Reply Obj. 3. Religious profess obedience as to the regular mode of life, in respect to which they are subject to their prelates; wherefore they are bound to obey in those matters only which may belong to the regular mode of life, and this obedience suffices for salvation. If they be willing to obey even in other matters, this will belong to the superabundance of perfection, provided, however, such things be not contrary to God or to the rule they profess, for obedience in this case would be unlawful.

Accordingly, we may distinguish a threefold obedience: an obedience sufficient for salvation and consisting in obeying when one is bound to obey; secondly, perfect obedience, which obeys in all things lawful; thirdly, indiscriminate obedience, which obeys even in matters unlawful.

SIXTH ARTICLE
Are Christians Bound to Obey the Secular Power?

We proceed thus to the Sixth Article:

Obj. 1. It seems that Christians are not bound to obey the secular power. For a gloss on Mt. 17:25, "Then the children are free," says, "If in every kingdom the children of the king who holds sway over that kingdom are free, then the children of that King, under Whose sway are all kingdoms, should be free in every kingdom."[43] Now, Christians, by their faith in Christ, are made children of God, according to Jn. 1:12, "He gave them power to be made the sons of God, to them that believe in His name." Therefore, they are not bound to obey the secular power.

Obj. 2. Further, it is written: "You . . . are become dead to the law by the body of Christ,"[44] and the law mentioned here is the divine law of the Old Testament. Now, human law, whereby men are subject to the secular power, is of less account than the divine law of the Old Testament. Much more, therefore, since they have become members of Christ's body, are men freed from the law of subjection, whereby they were under the power of secular princes.

Obj. 3. Further, men are not bound to obey robbers, who oppress them with violence. Now, Augustine says, "Without justice, what else are kingdoms but huge robberies."[45] Since, therefore, the authority of secular princes is frequently exercised with injustice or owes its origin to some unjust usurpation, it seems that Christians ought not to obey secular princes.

On the contrary, It is written: "Admonish them to be subject to princes and powers,"[46] and: "Be you subject . . . to every human creature for God's sake, whether it be to the king as excelling or to governors as sent by him."[47]

I answer that Faith in Christ is the origin and cause of justice, according to Rom. 3:22, "The justice of God by faith in Jesus Christ"; wherefore faith in Christ does not void the order of justice but strengthens it. Now, the order of justice requires that subjects obey their superiors, else the stability of human affairs would cease. Hence faith in Christ does not excuse the faithful from the obligation of obeying secular princes.

Reply Obj. 1. As stated above, the subjection whereby one man is bound to another regards the body, not the soul, which retains its liberty.[48] Now, in this state of life, we are freed by the grace of Christ from defects of the soul but not from defects of the body, as the Apostle declares by saying of himself that "in his mind he served the law of God but in his flesh the law of sin."[49] Wherefore those that are made children of God by grace are free from the spiritual bondage of sin but not from the bodily bondage whereby they are held bound to earthly masters, as a gloss observes on 1 Tim. 6:1, "Whosoever are servants under the yoke," etc.[50]

Reply Obj. 2. The Old Law was a figure of the New Testament and, therefore, it had to cease on the advent of truth. But it is not similar concerning the human law, through which one man is subject to another. Yet man is bound even by divine law to obey his fellowman.

Reply Obj. 3. Man is bound to obey secular princes insofar as this is required by the order of justice. Wherefore, if the prince's authority is not just but usurped, or if he commands what is unjust, his subjects are not bound to obey him, except perhaps accidentally, in order to avoid scandal or danger.

Notes to Chapter 6
ST II–II, Q. 42, A. 1

1. A. 1; *Glossa*, on 2 Cor. 12:20. PL 192, 89.

2. II–II, Q. 40, A. 1.

3. A. 1, *ad 3*.

4. 2 Cor. 12:20.

5. A. 1, *ad 2*.

6. *City of God* II, 21. PL 41, 67.

7. II–II, Q. 41, A. 1.

8. II–II, Q. 40, A. 1.

9. *Pol.* III, 7. 1279b6; *Eth.* VIII, 12. 1160b8.

ST II–II, Q. 104, AA. 1–6

1. *Heb.* 13:17.

2. *Moral.* XXXV, 14. PL 76, 765.

3. *De paradiso* 8. PL 14, 309.

4. *Moral.* XXXV, 14. PL 76, 765.

5. 1105a31.

6. II–II, Q. 80.

7. A. 1.

8. *De nat. boni* 3. PL 42, 553.

9. I–II, Q. 96, A. 3.

10. I–II, Q. 92, A. 2.

11. *Eth.* V, 4. 1132a10.

12. II–II, Q. 58, A. 10.

13. *Moral.* XXXV, 14. PL 76, 766.

14. 1 Sam. 15:22.

15. II–II, Q. 81, A. 6.

16. *Moral.* XXXV, 14. PL 76, 766.

17. Ibid.

18. Ibid.

19. *Moral.* XXXV, 14. PL 76, 766.

20. 1 Jn. 2:4–5.

21. *Moral.* XXXV, 14. PL 76, 765.

22. Cf. I–II, Q. 63, A. 3.

23. *Moral.* XXXV, PL 76, 766.

24. Mt. 9:30–31.

25. Gen. 22.

26. Ex. 11.

27. Hos. 3.

28. I–II, Q. 19, A. 10.

29. Ex. 24:7.

30. A. 1.

31. I–II, Q. 9, A. 6.

32. *Moral* XIX, 23. PL 76, 120.

33. *Glossa ordin.*, on Rom. 11:24. PL 114, 508.

34. Col. 3:20.

35. Col. 3:22.

36. Dt. 5:5.

37. Gal. 4:14.

38. 1 Th. 2:13.

39. Acts 5:29.

40. AA. 1, 4.

41. *Glossa.* PL 191, 1505.

42. *De Beneficiis* III, 20.

43. *Glossa ordin.*, on Mt. 17:25. PL 114, 145.

44. Rom. 7:4.

45. *City of God* IV, 4. PL 41, 115.

46. Tit. 3:1.

47. 1 Pet. 2:13–14.

48. A. 5.

49. Rom. 7:23.

50. *Glossa*, on 1 Tim. 6:1. PL 192, 357.

Tolerance and Church-State Relations

ST II–II
Question 10
Of Unbelief in General

*[In Twelve Articles, of Which
Articles Eight, Ten, and Eleven Are Included]*

EIGHTH ARTICLE
Ought Unbelievers to Be Compelled to the Faith?

We proceed thus to the Eighth Article:

Objection 1. It would seem that unbelievers ought by no means to be compelled to the faith. For it is written that the servants of the householder, in whose field cockle had been sown, asked him, "Do you want us to go and gather it up?" and that he answered, "No, lest perhaps, gathering up the cockle, you root up the wheat also together with it";[1] on which passage Chrysostom says, "Our Lord says this so as to forbid the slaying of men. For it is not right to slay heretics, because if you do, you will necessarily slay many innocent persons."[2] Therefore, it seems that for the same reason unbelievers ought not to be compelled to the faith.

Obj. 2. Further, we read in the *Decretum*, "The holy synod prescribes, with regard to the Jews, that for the future none are to be compelled to believe."[3] Therefore, in like manner, neither should unbelievers be compelled to the faith.

Obj. 3. Further, Augustine says that "it is possible for a man to do other things against his will, but he cannot believe unless he is willing."[4] But the will cannot be compelled. Therefore, it seems that unbelievers ought not to be compelled to the faith.

Obj. 4. It is said in God's person: "I desire not the death of the sinner."[5] Now, we ought to conform our will to the divine will, as stated above.[6] Therefore, we also should not wish unbelievers to be put to death.

On the contrary, It is written: "Go out into the highways

and hedges and compel them to come in."[7] Now, men enter into the house of God, i.e., into Holy Church, by faith. Therefore, some ought to be compelled to the faith.

I answer that, Among unbelievers, there are some who have never received the faith, such as the heathens and the Jews, and these are by no means to be compelled to the faith in order that they may believe, because to believe depends on the will; nevertheless, they should be compelled by the faithful, if it be possible to do so, in order that they may not hinder the faith by their blasphemies or by their evil persuasions or even by their open persecutions. It is for this reason that Christ's faithful often wage war with unbelievers, not indeed for the purpose of forcing them to believe (because, even if they were to conquer them and take them prisoners, they should still leave them free to believe if they will), but in order to prevent them from hindering the faith of Christ.

On the other hand, there are unbelievers who at some time have accepted the faith and professed it, such as heretics and all apostates; such should be submitted even to bodily compulsion, that they may fulfill what they have promised and hold what they, at one time, undertook.

Reply Obj. 1. Some have understood the authority quoted to forbid, not the excommunication, but the slaying of heretics, as appears from the words of Chrysostom. Also, Augustine says of himself, "It was once my opinion that none should be compelled to union with Christ, that we should deal in words and fight with arguments. However, this opinion of mine is overcome, not by contradictory words, but by convincing examples, because fear of the law was so profitable that many say, 'Thanks be to the Lord Who has broken our chains asunder.' "[8] Accordingly, the meaning of Our Lord's words, "Suffer both to grow until the harvest," must be gathered from those which precede, "lest perhaps gathering up the cockle, you root up the wheat also together with it."[9] For, Augustine says, "These words show that when this is not to be feared, that is to say, when a man's crime is so publicly known and so hateful to all that he has no defenders, or none such as might cause a schism, the severity of discipline should not slacken."[10]

Reply Obj. 2. Those Jews who have in no way received the faith ought by no means to be compelled to the faith; if, however, they have received it, they ought to be compelled to keep it, as is stated in the same chapter.

Reply Obj. 3. Just as taking a vow is a matter of will, and keeping a vow a matter of obligation, so acceptance of the faith is a matter of the will, whereas keeping the faith, when once one has received it, is a matter of obligation. Wherefore heretics should be compelled to keep the faith. Thus Augustine says to the Count Boniface, "What do these people mean by crying out continually: 'We may believe or not believe just as we choose. Whom did Christ compel?' They should remember that Christ at first compelled Paul and afterwards taught Him."[11]

Reply Obj. 4. As Augustine says in the same letter, "None of us wishes any heretic to perish. But, contrariwise, the house of David did not deserve to have peace unless his son Absalom had been killed in the war which he raised against his father. Thus, if the Catholic Church by the perdition of some gathers others, she heals the sorrow of her maternal heart by the delivery of so many nations."[12]

TENTH ARTICLE

May Unbelievers Have Authority or Dominion over the Faithful?

We proceed thus to the Tenth Article:

Obj. 1. It would seem that unbelievers may have authority or dominion over the faithful. For the Apostle says, "Whosoever are servants under the yoke, let them count their masters worthy of all honor,"[13] and it is clear that he is speaking of unbelievers, since he adds, "But they that have believing masters, let them not despise them."[14] Moreover, it is written: "Servants be subject to your masters with all fear, not only to the good and gentle, but also to the demanding."[15] Now, this command would not be contained in the apostolic teaching unless unbelievers could have authority over the faithful. Therefore, it seems that unbelievers can have authority over the faithful.

Obj. 2. Further, all the members of a ruler's household are his subjects. Now, some of the faithful were members of unbelieving rulers' households, for we read in the Epistle to

the Philippians: "All of the saints salute you, especially they
that are of Caesar's household," referring to Nero, who was
an unbeliever."[16] Therefore, unbelievers can have authority
over the faithful.

Obj. 3. Further, according to the Philosopher,[17] a slave[18] is
his master's instrument in matters concerning everyday life,
even as a craftsman's servant is his instrument in matters
concerning the working of his art. Now, in such matters, a
believer can be subject to an unbeliever, for he may be an
unbeliever's peasant. Therefore, unbelievers may have authority over the faithful even as to dominion.

On the contrary, Those who are in authority can pronounce judgment on those over whom they are placed. But
unbelievers cannot pronounce judgment on the faithful, for
the Apostle says, "Dare any of you, having a matter against
another, go to be judged before the unjust," i.e., unbelievers,
"and not before the saints?"[19] Therefore, it seems that unbelievers cannot have authority over the faithful.

I answer that This question may be considered in two
ways. First, we may speak of dominion or authority of unbelievers over the faithful as of a thing to be established for the
first time. This ought by no means to be allowed, since it
would provoke scandal and endanger the faith, for subjects
are easily influenced by their superiors to comply with their
commands unless the subjects are of great virtue; moreover,
unbelievers hold the faith in contempt if they see the faithful
fall away. Hence the Apostle forbade the faithful to go to law
before an unbelieving judge. And so the Church altogether
forbids unbelievers to acquire dominion over believers or to
have authority over them in any capacity whatever.

Secondly, we may speak of dominion or authority as already in force; and here we must observe that dominion and
authority are institutions of human law, while the distinction
between faithful and unbelievers arises from the divine law.
Now the divine law, which is the law of grace, does not do
away with human law, which is the law of natural reason.
Wherefore the distinction between faithful and unbelievers,
considered in itself, does not do away with the dominion and
authority of unbelievers over the faithful.

Nevertheless, this right of dominion or authority can be
justly done away with by the sentence or ordination of the

Church, which has the authority of God, since unbelievers in virtue of their unbelief deserve to forfeit their power over the faithful, who are converted into children of God.

This the Church does sometimes and sometimes not. For among those unbelievers who are subject, even in temporal matters, to the Church and her members, the Church made the law that if the slave of a Jew became a Christian, he should forthwith receive his freedom without paying any price, if he should be an indigenous slave, i.e., one born in slavery, and likewise if, when yet an unbeliever, he had been bought for his service; if, however, he had been bought to be sold, then he should be offered for sale within three months. Nor does the Church inflict harm in this, because Jews themselves are slaves of the Church, and so she can dispose of their possessions, even as secular rulers have enacted many laws to be observed by their subjects in favor of liberty. On the other hand, the Church has not applied the above law to those unbelievers who are not subject to her or her members in temporal matters, although she has the right to do so, and this in order to avoid scandal, as also Our Lord showed that He could be excused from paying the tribute because "the children are free," but, nonetheless, ordered the tribute to be paid in order to avoid giving scandal.[20] Thus Paul too, after saying that servants should honor their masters, adds, "lest the name of the Lord and His doctrine be blasphemed."[21]

This suffices for the *Reply* to the *First Objection*.

Reply Obj. 2. The authority of Caesar preceded the distinction of faithful from unbelievers. Hence, it was not cancelled by the conversion of some to the faith. Moreover, it was a good thing that there should be a few of the faithful in the emperor's household, that they might defend the rest of the faithful. Thus the blessed Sebastian encouraged those whom he saw faltering under torture and the while remained hidden under the military cloak in the palace of Diocletian.

Reply Obj. 3. Slaves are subject to their masters for their whole lifetime and are subject to their overseers in everything, whereas the craftsman's laborer is subject to him for certain special works. Hence, it would be more dangerous for unbelievers to have dominion or authority over the faithful than that they should be allowed to employ them in some craft. Wherefore the Church permits Christians to work on

the land of Jews, because this does not entail their living
together with them. Thus Solomon besought the King of
Tyre to send master workmen to hew the trees, as related in
1 Kings 5:6. Yet, if there be reason to fear that the faithful
will be perverted by such communications and dealings, they
should be absolutely forbidden.

ELEVENTH ARTICLE
Ought the Rites of Unbelievers to Be Tolerated?

We proceed thus to the Eleventh Article:
Obj. 1. It would seem that rites of unbelievers ought not to
be tolerated. For it is evident that unbelievers sin in observing their rites, and not to prevent a sin, when one can, seems
to imply consent therein, as a gloss observes on Rom. 1:32:
"Not only they that do them, but they also that consent to
them that do them."[22] Therefore, it is a sin to tolerate their
rites.
Obj. 2. Further, the rites of the Jews are compared to idolatry, because a gloss on Gal. 5:1, "Be not held again under the
yoke of bondage," says, "The bondage of that law was not
lighter than that of idolatry."[23] But it would not be allowable
for anyone to observe the rites of idolatry; in fact, Christian
rulers at first caused the temples of idols to be closed and
afterwards to be destroyed, as Augustine relates.[24] Therefore,
it follows that even the rites of Jews ought not to be tolerated.
Obj. 3. Further, unbelief is the greatest of sins, as stated
above.[25] Now, other sins, such as adultery, theft, and the like,
are not tolerated but are punishable by law. Therefore, neither ought the rites of unbelievers to be tolerated.
On the contrary, Gregory says in the *Decretum,* speaking
of the Jews, "They should be allowed to observe all their
feasts as hitherto they and their fathers have for ages observed them."[26]
I answer that Human government is derived from the divine government and should imitate it. Now, although God
is all-powerful and supremely good, nevertheless He allows
certain evils to take place in the universe which He might
prevent, lest without them greater goods might be forfeited

or greater evils ensue. Accordingly, in human government also, those who are in authority rightly tolerate certain evils, lest certain goods be lost or certain greater evils be incurred; thus Augustine says, "If you do away with harlots, the world will be convulsed with lust."[27] Hence, though unbelievers sin in their rites, they may be tolerated either on account of some good that ensues therefrom or because of some evil avoided. Thus, from the fact that the Jews observe their rites, which of old foreshadowed the truth of the faith which we hold, there follows this good—that our very enemies bear witness to our faith, and that our faith is represented in a figure, so to speak. For this reason, they are tolerated in observance of their rites.

On the other hand, the rites of other unbelievers, which are neither truthful nor profitable, are by no means to be tolerated, except perchance in order to avoid an evil, e.g., the scandal or disturbance that might ensue or some hindrance to the salvation of those who, if they were unmolested, might gradually be converted to the faith. For this reason, the Church at times has tolerated the rites even of heretics and pagans when unbelievers were very numerous.

This suffices for the *Replies* to the *Objections*.

ST II–II

Question 11
Of Heresy

*[In Four Articles, of Which
Article Three Is Included]*

THIRD ARTICLE
Ought Heretics to Be Tolerated?

We proceed thus to the Third Article:

Obj. 1. It seems that heretics ought to be tolerated. For the Apostle says, "The servant of the Lord ought to be mild, . . . with modesty admonishing those who resist the truth, that God may at some time give them repentance to know the truth, and that they may rescue themselves from the snares of the devil."[1] Now, if heretics are not tolerated but put to death, they lose the opportunity of repentance. Therefore, it seems contrary to the Apostle's command.

Obj. 2. Further, whatever is necessary in the Church should be tolerated. Now, heresies are necessary in the Church, since the Apostle says, "There must be . . . heresies, that those . . . who are approved may be manifest among you."[2] Therefore, it seems that heretics should be tolerated.

Obj. 3. Further, the Master commanded his servants to suffer the cockle "to grow until the harvest," i.e., the end of the world, as the text indicates.[3] Now, holy men explain that the cockle denotes heretics. Therefore, heretics should be tolerated.

On the contrary, The Apostle says, "Avoid the man who is a heretic, after the first and second admonition, knowing that such a one is perverted."[4]

I answer that, With regard to heretics, two points must be observed: one, on their part; the other, on the part of the Church. On their part, there is the sin whereby they deserve not only to be separated from the Church by excommunication but also to be severed from the world by death. For it is a much graver matter to corrupt faith, which quickens the soul, than to forge money, which supports temporal life. Wherefore, if forgers of money and other evildoers are forthwith condemned to death by the secular authority, much more reason is there for heretics, as soon as they are convicted of heresy, to be not only excommunicated but even put to death.

On the part of the Church, however, there is mercy which looks to the conversion of the one who strays; wherefore she condemns not at once but "after the first and second admonition," as the Apostle directs.[5] After that, if he is yet stubborn, the Church, no longer hoping for his conversion, looks to the salvation of others by excommunicating him and separating him from the Church, and furthermore delivers him to the secular tribunal to be exterminated thereby from the world by death. For Jerome, commenting on Gal. 5:9, "A little leaven," says, "Cut off the decayed flesh, expel the mangy sheep from the fold, lest the whole house, the whole dough, the whole body, the whole flock burn, perish, rot, die. Arius was but one spark in Alexandria, but as that spark was not at once put out, the whole earth was laid waste by its flame."[6]

Reply Obj. 1. This very modesty demands that the heretic should be admonished a first and second time, and if he be unwilling to retract, he must be reckoned as already "perverted," as we may gather from the words of the Apostle quoted above.[7]

Reply Obj. 2. The profit that ensures from heresy is beside the intention of heretics, for it consists in the constancy of the faithful being put to the test, and "makes us shake off our sluggishness and search the Scriptures more carefully," as Augustine states.[8] What they really intend is the corruption of the faith, which is to inflict very great harm indeed. Consequently, we should consider what they directly intend and expel them, rather than what is beside their intention and so tolerate them.

Reply Obj. 3. According to the *Decretum,* "to be excommunicated is not to be uprooted."[9] A man is excommunicated, as the Apostle says, that his "spirit may be saved in the day of Our Lord."[10] Yet if heretics be altogether uprooted by death, this is not contrary to Our Lord's command, which is to be understood as referring to the case when the cockle cannot be plucked up without plucking up the wheat, as we explained above when treating of unbelievers in general.[11]

ST II–II
Question 60
Of Judgment

*[In Six Articles, of Which
Article Six Is Included]*

SIXTH ARTICLE
Is Judgment Rendered Perverse by Being Usurped?

We proceed thus to the Sixth Article:

Obj. 1. It would seem that judgment is not rendered perverse by being usurped. For justice is rectitude in matters of action. Now, truth is not impaired, no matter who tells it, but it may suffer from the person who ought to accept it. Therefore, again, justice loses nothing no matter who declares what is just, and this is what is meant by judgment.

Obj. 2. Further, it belongs to judgment to punish sins. Now, it is related to the praise of some that they punished sins without having authority over those whom they punished, such as Moses in slaying the Egyptian,[1] and Phineas, the son of Eleazar, in slaying Zambri, the son of Salu,[2] and "it was reputed to him for justice."[3] Therefore, usurpation of judgment pertains not to injustice.

Obj. 3. Further, spiritual power is distinct from temporal. Now, prelates having spiritual power sometimes interfere in matters concerning the secular power. Therefore, usurped judgment is not unlawful.

Obj. 4. Further, even as the judge requires authority in order to judge aright, so also does he need justice and knowledge, as shown above.[4] But a judgment is not described as unjust if he who judges lacks the habit of justice or the knowledge of the law. Neither, therefore, is it always unjust to judge by usurpation, i.e., without authority.

On the contrary, It is written: "Who are you who judge another man's servant?"[5]

I answer that, Since judgment should be pronounced according to the written law, as stated above,[6] he that pronounces judgment interprets, in a way, the letter of the law by applying it to some particular case. Now, since it belongs to the same authority to interpret and to make a law, just as a law cannot be made save by public authority, so neither can a judgment be pronounced except by public authority, which extends over those who are subject to the community. Wherefore, even as it would be unjust for one man to force another to observe a law that was not approved by public authority, so too it is unjust if a man compels another to submit to a judgment that is pronounced by other than the public authority.

Reply Obj. 1. When the truth is declared, there is no compulsion to accept it, and each one is free to receive it or not, as he wishes. On the other hand, judgment implies a compulsion; wherefore it is unjust for anyone to be judged by one who has no public authority.

Reply Obj. 2. Moses seems to have slain the Egyptian by

authority received, as it were, by divine inspiration; this seems to follow from Acts 7:24–5, where it is said that "striking the Egyptian, . . . he thought that his brethren understood that God by his hand would save Israel." Or it may be replied that Moses slew the Egyptian in order to defend the man who was unjustly attacked, without himself exceeding the limits of a blameless defense. Wherefore Ambrose says that "whoever does not ward off a blow from a fellowman when he can is as much in fault as the striker,"[7] and he quotes the example of Moses. Or we may reply with Augustine that "just as the soil gives proof of its fertility by producing useless herbs before the useful seeds have grown, so this deed of Moses was sinful although it gave a sign of great fertility,"[8] insofar, to wit, as it was a sign of the power whereby he was to deliver his people.

With regard to Phineas, the reply is that he did this out of zeal for God by divine inspiration or that, though not as yet high-priest, he was nevertheless the high-priest's son, and this judgment was his concern as also that of the other judges for whom it was a command.

Reply Obj. 3. The secular power is subject to the spiritual as the body is subject to the soul. Consequently, judgment is not usurped if a spiritual prelate interposes himself concerning temporal matters so much as for those things in which the secular power is subject to him, or which have been relinquished to him by the secular power.[9]

Reply Obj. 4. The habits of knowledge and justice are perfections of the individual, and, consequently, their absence does not make a judgment to be usurped, as does the absence of public authority which gives a judgment its coercive force.

Commentary on the Sentences II
dist. 44
expositio textus
ad 4

In reply to the fourth objection, we should say that the spiritual and the secular power alike derive from divine power, and that, as a result, secular power is subject to spiritual power insofar as God so disposes, i.e., in those things pertaining to the salvation of souls. In such matters, one should obey the spiritual rather than the secular power. But in those things which pertain to civic welfare, one should obey the secular rather than the spiritual power: "Render to Caesar the things that are Caesar's" (Mt. 22:21). Unless, per chance, the secular power is joined to the spiritual power, as in the case of the Pope, who holds the supremacy of both powers from the disposition of Him Who is both priest and king—priest forever according to the order of Melchisadech, King of kings and Lord of lords, Whose power is not taken away, and Whose kingdom is eternally indissoluble. Amen.

Notes to Chapter Seven
ST II–II, Q. 10, AA. 8, 10, 11

1. Mt. 13:28.

2. *In Matt. hom.*, hom. 46. PG 58, 477.

3. *Decretum* I, 45, 5. RF I, 161.

4. *In Joan.* 25. On Jn. 7:44. PL 35, 1607.

5. Ezech. 18:32.

6. I–II, Q. 19, AA. 9, 10.

7. Lk. 14:23.

8. *Epist.* 93, ad Vincentium, 5. PL 33, 329.

9. Mt. 13:29.

10. *Contra epistolam Parmeniani* III, 2. PL 43, 92.

11. *Epist.* 175, 6. PL 33, 803.

12. *Epist.* 175, 8. PL 33, 807.

13. 1 Tim. 6:1.

14. 1 Tim. 6:2.

15. 1 Pet. 2:18.

16. 4:22.

17. *Pol.* II, 4. 1253b32.

18. *See* Glossary, s.v. "slavery."

19. 1 Cor. 4:1.

20. Mt. 17:25–26.

21. 1 Tim. 6:1.

22. *Glossa,* on Rom. 1:32. PL 191, 1336.

23. *Glossa,* on Gal. 5:1. PL 192, 152.

24. *City of God* XVIII, 54. PL 41, 620.

25. A. 3.

26. *Decretum* I, 45, 3; RF I, 161. Gregory, *Registrum* XIII, 6; *Epistola,* ad Paschasium. PL 67, 1267.

27. *De Ordine* II, 4. PL 32, 1000.

ST II–II, Q. 11, A. 3

1. 2 Tim. 2:24–25.

2. 1 Cor. 11:19.

3. Mt. 13:30, 39.

4. Tit. 3:10–11.

5. Ibid.

6. *In Galat.* III. PL 26, 430.

7. Tit. 3:10.

8. *De Genesi contra Manichaeos* I, 1. PL 34, 173.

9. *Decretum* II, 24, 3, 37. RF I, 1000.

10. 1 Cor. 5:5.

11. II–II, Q. 10, A. 8, *ad* 1.

ST II–II, Q. 60, A. 6

1. Ex. 2:12.

2. Num. 25:7–14.

3. Ps. 105:31.

4. A. 1, *ad* 1, 3; A. 2.

5. Rom. 14:4.

6. A. 5.

7. *De officiis* I, 36. PL 16, 81.

8. *Quaest. in Heptat.* II, 2, on Ex. 2:12. PL 34, 597.

9. Italics added. Cf. ST II–II, Q. 147, A. 3: "As it belongs to secular rulers to enact legal precepts determinative of the natural law concerning those things which pertain to the common welfare in temporal matters, so also it pertains to ecclesiastical prelates to prescribe by statutes those things which pertain to the common welfare in spiritual goods."

8
Statesmanship

On Kingship
To the King of Cyprus
Book One
Chapter One

It is necessary for men living together to be ruled diligently by a king.

Our primary intention requires that we explain what is to be understood by the name "king." In all things, however, which are ordered to some goal, by which we can proceed in more than one way, there is a need for some directing principle, by which the task may be brought rightly to completion. For even a ship, randomly moved to and fro by different winds, will not reach her destined goal unless she is directed by the effort of the helmsman to her port. There is a certain goal for man toward which his whole life and deeds are ordered, since he acts by his intelligence, which is clearly to act with some goal in mind. It happens that people proceed towards their intended goal in different ways, which the very diversity of human endeavors and actions makes clear.

Therefore, man needs some directing principle to attain that goal. However, every man is endowed by nature with the light of reason, by which he may be directed in his actions to his goal. So, if it were fitting for man to live alone, as in the case of many animals, no other direction would be needed regarding that goal, but each would be a king unto himself under God, the highest king, inasmuch as in his actions he would direct himself by the light of reason divinely given to him.

Man is by nature, however, a social and political animal, living amid a multitude of his kind; more so, indeed, than is the case with all other animals, which natural necessity itself makes clear. For nature prepares for other animals their food, their covering of fur, their means of defense (such as teeth, horns, claws, or at least swiftness of flight). For man, however, none of these were provided by nature, but instead of all of these, reason was given to him, by which, through the labor of his hands, he would be able to fashion for himself all these things, but for the fashioning of all of which one man alone would not suffice. For one man alone, by his own devices, could not sufficiently make his way through life. It is, therefore, natural for man that he live in the companionship of many of his kind.

Moreover, instinct is given to other animals by which they discover all those things which are useful or dangerous, as the sheep instinctively recognizes the wolf as its enemy. Certain animals know instinctively that some herbs are medicinal and know instinctively other things necessary for their life. Man has a natural knowledge of those things which are necessary for survival, but only in a general way, insofar as, so to speak, being gifted by reason, he can pass from natural[1] principles to the recognition of those particulars which are necessary for human life. It is not possible, though, that a single person could achieve all this knowledge by his own power of reason. It is, therefore, necessary for man to live in society with his fellows, so that one may be aided by another and that different persons may be engaged in making different discoveries through their respective powers of reason; one, for example, in medicine, another in this field, another in that. This point is made most clearly evident by this—that it is man's distinctive trait to speak, whereby one man can fully express his thought to others. Other animals can express to each other in a general way their feelings, as dogs express anger when they bark and other animals express their feelings in diverse ways. Man communicates with his fellows more than any other animal we see living in a group, such as cranes, ants, and bees. Reflecting upon this Solomon says, "It is better to be two than to be one. They have been enriched in one another's company."[2] If it is natural that man live in society with his fellows, it is necessary that there be some power in men by which that group be ruled. If there be a group of people, with each one looking solely after his own interest, that group would break up into many parts unless, indeed, there were also someone taking care of those things pertaining to the good of the group, just as the body of a man or of any animal would fall apart unless there were some general ruling principle in the body which has as its interest the common good of all the members. Reflecting upon this Solomon says, "Where there is no governor, the people scatter."[3] This happens reasonably enough. The particular and the common are not the same: the particular differentiates; the common unites. Different things, however, are the result of different causes. It is necessary, therefore, that, besides that which moves each towards his own private good, there be something else that moves towards the common good of the group. Therefore, in all things which are ordered to one goal, there is to be found some ruling principle. Thus, in the universe of bodies, divine Providence rules, by a certain order, other bodies by the first (that is, the heavenly) body and by that order all bodies are ruled by the rational creature.[4] In every man, the soul rules the body, and, between the spirited and desiring parts of the soul, reason assigns an order. Again, among the members of the body, one is the chief, and it moves the others, whether it be the heart or the head. There has to be, therefore, some ruling principle in every group.

Even so, in those things which are directed to a goal, things can proceed rightly or not rightly. So, in ruling a group, it may be found that such is done rightly or not rightly. Each thing is directed rightly when it is brought to its fitting goal and not rightly when the goal is not fitting. The goal befitting a community of free men is different from that befitting a community of slaves. For the free man is the cause of his own actions; the slave, as such, belongs to another. If, therefore, a community of free men be ordered by a governor to the common good of that group, that will be a rule both right and just, as befits free men. If, in fact, his rule is directed, not to the common good of the group, but to the private advantage of the ruler, that will be a rule both unjust and perverse; wherefore the Lord warns such rulers through Ezechiel, saying, "Woe to the shepherds who feed themselves" (as if seeking their private advantage), "Should not the flocks be fed by the shepherds?"[5] However, shepherds should seek the good of the flock, and, indeed, rulers the good of that group subject to them.

If, therefore, an unjust rule is exercised by one man alone, who seeks his own advantage from that rule, not the good of the group subject to him, such a ruler is called a tyrant, a name derived from strength, since, indeed, he oppresses by his power; he does not rule by justice. Therefore, among the ancients, powerful men were called tyrants. If, though, an unjust rule be exercised not by one alone but by several who are few, it is called oligarchy, that is, rule by the few, insofar as the few indeed oppress the common people for the sake of wealth, distinguishing themselves from the tyrant solely by being more than one. If wicked rule is exercised by many, it is termed democracy, that is, rule by the people, insofar as indeed the mass of common folk, by the force of numbers, oppresses the rich. Thus the whole of the people will be, as it were, one tyrant.

We must, in like manner, distinguish different just constitutions. If things are administered by some group, it is called by the common name "polity," as, for instance, when a group of soldiers rules a city or a province. If things are administered by few, this constitution is called aristocracy, that is, the best rule or rule by the best, who, therefore, are termed "the best men." If, indeed, a just constitution is exercised by one man alone, he is properly called king; therefore, the Lord through Ezechiel says, "My servant David will be a king over all, and he will be the one shepherd of all of them."[6] Hence it is obvious that the very concept of a king entails that there be one who presides, and that he be the shepherd seeking the common good of the group and not his own advantage.

Since, then, it is necessary for man to live in society with his fellows, because by himself he could not secure those things necessary for life if he would remain in a solitary existence, it is a consequence that the companionship of many would be more complete to the extent that it will be more sufficient in itself for the necessities of life. There is, however, a certain sufficiency for life in the single family of one household (as much, that is, as suffices for the natural acts of nutrition and procreation and similar things); in one quarter of a city, there is as much sufficiency as is required for a single craft. In a city, however, (which is a complete community), there is as much as suffices for all the necessities of life, yet still much more in a province because of the need for defense and of the mutual aid of allies against the public enemy. Therefore, he who rules a complete community, that is, a city or a province, is justly termed king; he who rules a household is called father of the family, but not king.

A father has a certain likeness to a king, because of which kings are sometimes called the fathers of peoples.

It is clear from our discussion that a king is one who rules the multitude in a city or a province for the common good; therefore, Solomon says, "The king rules all lands which are subject to him."[7]

Chapter Six

The rule of one man is unqualifiedly the best. The community ought to provide that certain circumstances should be prevented, so that a king will not become a tyrant; yet, even if he does become a tyrant, this should be tolerated so that greater evils can be avoided.

Since, then, the rule of one man ought to be what we above all choose, because such a rule is the best, and since it happens that such a rule might change into tyranny, which is the worst kind of rule, as is clear from our remarks above,[1] every effort must be carefully made so that the community is provided with a king in such a way that it will not fall under a tyrant. First, it is necessary that whoever is elevated to the rank of king, by those responsible for doing so, have the kind of character that makes it unlikely that he would stoop to tyranny. Therefore Samuel, praising God's providence regarding the institution of a king, says, "The Lord sought out for Himself a man according to His heart, and the Lord commanded him to be a leader over his people."[2] Next, the governance of a kingdom must be arranged so that there is no opportunity given for a king who has been instituted to act as a tyrant. At the same time his power should be moderated so that he cannot easily stoop to tyranny. We will consider how to do this below. Finally, we certainly have to be concerned about what must be done if, nevertheless, a king lapses into behaving as a tyrant.

If, indeed, there is not an excess of tyranny, it is more profitable to put up with a milder tyranny for the time being than, by opposing the tyrant, to run into many dangers more grievous than the tyranny itself. There is a possibility that if those who oppose the tyrant do not suceed, then the enraged tyrant would become even more savage. Even if the opponents of the tyrant are successful, from this very success

most grave divisions often arise among the people: the community splinters on the question of the nature of the constitution, either during the insurrection against the tyrant or
after his overthrow. It even happens that, while the community drives out the tyrant with somebody's help, that person,
having received power, takes over the tyrant's role himself,
and fearing to suffer from someone else what he did himself
to another, oppresses his subjects with an even weightier
enslavement. Thus, then, it regularly happens in the case of
tyranny that a latter tyrant is more oppressive than his prede-
cessor, for he does not give up the preceding oppression but
rather thinks up new forms out of the malice of his heart.
This is the reason that, when at the time that everyone in
Syracuse desired the death of Dionysius, some old lady per-
sistently prayed that he might be unharmed and might out-
live her. When he found this out, he questioned her intention. She replied, "When I was a little girl we had an oppressive tyrant; I wanted him dead. He was killed, and a
somewhat more harsh tyrant succeeded him. I thought the
end of his domination would be great. We began to have a
third ruler harsher still: yourself. So if you were taken away
from us, a worse would follow you."

And if an excessive tyranny is intolerable, it has seemed to
some that the virtue of the more powerful men entitles them
to kill the tyrant and, for the sake of the liberation of the
community, to place themselves in danger of death. There is
an example of this in the Old Testament itself. For Ehud
killed a certain Eglon, King of Moab, who oppressed the
people of God with a weighty enslavement, by thrusting a
dagger into Eglon's thigh, and he was made judge of the people.[3] But this does not conform to apostolic teachings. Peter
teaches us that we ought to be reverently submissive not only
to good and gentle rulers but even to overbearing ones: "This
is indeed a grace if, because of awareness of God, someone
bears up with suffering unjustly inflicted troubles."[4] Thus,
when many Roman emperors persecuted the faith of Christ
in a tyrannical way, a great crowd (no less of the nobility than
of the common folk) were converted to the faith, making no
resistance, but they are praised for enduring death for Christ
patiently and with spirited courage. This is clearly the case
with the holy legion of Thebes. It must be judged that Ehud

killed somebody who was more the public enemy than a ruler of the people, though a tyrannical one. Thus also we read in the Old Testament that those who killed Joash, King of Juda, were killed themselves, although he had departed from the worship of God, but their children were spared according to the command of the law.[5] It would be dangerous for the community and its rulers if anybody by private initiative were to attempt to kill its public officers, even if they were tyrants. It is more often the case that evil persons expose themselves to such great dangers than do the good. For evil persons, it is common that the rule of kings is no less burdensome than is that of tyrants, since according to the saying of Solomon, "A wise king scatters the impious."[6] It is, therefore, more likely that from this sort of presumption danger to the community would occur from the loss of a king than any relief from the removal of a tyrant.

It seems, then, that actions should arise more from public authority against the brutality of tyrants than from anybody's private initiative. In the first place, if by right a certain community is entitled to provide itself with a king, it is not unjust that the installed king be deposed by that same community or that his power be curtailed, if the royal power is abused tyrannically. Nor must it be thought that such a community acts unfaithfully when it deposes a tyrant, even if it had subjected itself to him beforehand in perpetuity. For he himself deserved this: since he had not acted faithfully in discharging the royal office, so the covenant made by his subjects might likewise not be kept. Thus the Romans deposed Tarquin the Proud as king (whom they had accepted as such), because of his tyranny and that of his sons, and replaced the royal power by a lesser, that is, consular, power. Thus, also, Domitian, who succeeded the most moderate emperor, his father Vespasian, and his brother Titus, was killed by the Roman Senate when he exercised tyrannical power, and everything that he did wickedly to the Romans was justly and usefully revoked and rendered invalid by Senatorial edict. Thus it was that Blessed John the Evangelist, who was exiled by that same Domitian to the island of Patmos, was sent back to Ephesus by Senatorial edict.

If, however, by right some superior authority is entitled to provide a king for a community, the remedy for the iniquity of the tyrant must be awaited from that party. Thus the Jews deferred to Caesar Augustus in their complaint about Archelaus, who had already begun to rule in Judea in place of his father Herod, having imitated his father's malice. At first, therefore, his power was diminished when his regal title was taken from him and half his kingdom was divided up between his two brothers. Then, when this did not in fact curtail his tyranny, he was sent into exile by Tiberius Caesar to Lyons, a city in Gaul.

But if no human help at all can be gotten against a tyrant, we must turn to the king of all, God, who is an aid in times of trouble. For He has such power that He can turn the cruel heart of a tyrant to gentleness. As Solomon says, "The heart of a king is in the hand of God; . . . He will turn it wherever He wills."[7] He even turned to gentleness the cruelty of the king of Assyria, who was preparing death for the Jews. He it was who so converted cruel King Nebuchadnezzar to such piety[8] that he became a herald of divine power. "Now, therefore," he said, "I Nebuchadnezzar praise, exalt and glorify the king of heaven because all His works are true and His ways are judgments, and He is able to lay low those who walk arrogantly."[9]

The tyrant whom He indeed judges unworthy of conversion He can remove from our midst or reduce them to a state of weakness, as we learn from the Sage, "God has destroyed the thrones of proud leaders, and made the gentle to sit there in their stead."[10] He it is who, seeing the affliction of His people in Egypt and hearing their cry, cast down the tyrant Pharaoh with his army into the sea.[11] He it is who not only cast out the aforementioned Nebuchadnezzar from his regal throne because of his former arrogance but even cast him out from human society and changed him into the likeness of a beast.[12]

Nor is His hand weakened so that He cannot free His people from tyranny. He promised His people through Isaiah that He would give them rest from toil and lashings[13] and hard servitude under which they had previously served. And, through Ezechiel, He says "I will deliver My flock from their mouth,"[14] (that is, from the mouth of those who feed only themselves). But that the people should merit that such a benefit come from God, it must stop sinning, because it is by divine permission that the impious receive their rule, as a punishment for sin, as the Lord says through Hosea, "I will give you a king in my wrath,"[15] and in Job it is said, "He makes a man who is a hypocrite to reign because of the sins of the people."[16] Fault must therefore be purged away that the scourge of tyrants may cease.

ST II–II
Question 47
On Prudence

*[In Sixteen Articles, of Which
Article Eleven Is Included]*

ELEVENTH ARTICLE

Is Prudence about One's Own Good
Specifically the Same As That
Which Extends to the Common Good?

We proceed thus to the Eleventh Article:
   Obj. 1. It seems that prudence about one's own good is the same specifically as that which extends to the common good. For the Philosopher says that "political prudence and prudence are the same habit, but their essence is not the same."[1]
   Obj. 2. Further, the Philosopher says that "virtue is the same in a good man and in a good ruler."[2] Now, political prudence is chiefly in the ruler, in whom it is like master-craftsmanship. Since, then, prudence is the virtue of a good man, it seems that prudence and political prudence are the same habit.
   Obj. 3. Further, a habit is not differentiated in species or essence by things which are subordinate to one another. But the particular good, which belongs to prudence simply so called, is subordinate to the common good, which belongs to political prudence. Therefore, prudence and political prudence differ neither specifically nor essentially.
   On the contrary, Political prudence, which is directed to the common good of the political community, and domestic

economy, which is of such things as relate to the common good of the household or family, and personal economy, which is concerned with things affecting the good of one person, are all distinct sciences. Therefore, in like manner, there are different kinds of prudence, corresponding to the above differences of matter.

I answer that, As stated above, the species of habits differ according to the difference of the object when considered in its formal aspect.[3] Now, the formal aspect of all things directed to an end is taken from the end itself, as shown above;[4] wherefore the species of habits differ by their relation to different ends. Again, the individual good, the good of the family, and the good of the political community and kingdom are different ends. Wherefore there must needs be different species of prudence corresponding to these different ends, so that one is prudence simply so called, which is directed to one's own good; another, domestic prudence, which is directed to the common good of the home; a third, political prudence, which is directed to the common good of the political community or kingdom.

Reply Obj. 1. The Philosopher means, not that political prudence is substantially the same habit as any kind of prudence, but that it is the same as the prudence which is directed to the common good. This is called prudence in respect to the common note of prudence, i.e., a certain right reason applied to action, while it is called political as being directed to the common good.

Reply Obj. 2. As the Philosopher declares, "It belongs to a good man to be able to rule well and to obey well";[5] wherefore the virtue of a good man includes also that of a good ruler. Yet the virtue of the ruler and that of the subject differ specifically, even as do the virtue of a man and that of a woman, as stated by the same authority.[6]

Reply Obj. 3. Even different ends, of which one is subordinate to the other, distinguish species of a habit; thus, for instance, habits directed to riding, soldiering, and civic life differ specifically, although their ends are subordinate to one another. In like manner, though the good of the individual is subordinate to the good of the many, that does not prevent this difference from making the habits differ specifically, but it follows from this that the habit which is directed to the last end is above the other habits and commands them.

ST II–II
Question 50
On the Subjective Parts of Prudence

*[In Four Articles, of Which
Article Two Is Included]*

SECOND ARTICLE
Is Political Prudence Fittingly
Accounted a Part of Prudence?

We proceed thus to the Second Article:

Obj. 1. It would seem that political prudence is not fittingly accounted a part of prudence. For rulers' prudence is a part
of political prudence, as stated above.[1] But a part should not
be divided from the whole. Therefore, political prudence
should not be reckoned a part of prudence.

Obj. 2. Further, the species of habits are distinguished by
their various objects. Now, what the ruler has to command is
the same as what the subject has to execute. Therefore, political prudence as regards the subjects should not be reckoned a species of prudence distinct from rulers' prudence.

Obj. 3. Further, each subject is an individual person. Now,
each individual person can direct himself sufficiently by prudence commonly so called. Therefore, there is no need of a
special kind of prudence called "political."

On the contrary, The Philosopher says that "of the prudence which is concerned with the political community, one
kind is a masterbuilder's prudence and is called 'legislative';
another kind bears the common name 'political' and deals
with individuals."[2]

I answer that A slave[3] is moved by the command of his
master, and a subject by the command of his ruler, but otherwise than irrational and inanimate beings are set in motion
by their movers. For irrational and inanimate beings are
moved only by others and do not put themselves in motion,
since they have no free will whereby to be masters of their
own actions; wherefore the rectitude of their direction is not
in their power but in the power of their movers. On the other
hand, men who are slaves or subjects in any sense are moved

by the commands of others in such a way that they move themselves by their free will; wherefore some kind of rectitude of direction is required in them, so that they may direct themselves in obeying their superiors, and to this belongs that species of prudence which is called "political."

Reply Obj. 1. As stated above,[4] rulers' prudence is the most perfect species of prudence; wherefore the prudence of subjects, which falls short of rulers' prudence, retains the common name "political prudence," even as, in logic, a convertible term which does not denote the essence of a thing retains the name "proper."

Reply Obj. 2. Different aspects of the object distinguish species of a habit, as stated above.[5] Now, the same things to be done are considered by a king under a more universal aspect than should be considered by the subjects who obey, since many obey one king in various duties. Hence rulers' prudence is compared to this political prudence, of which we are speaking, as mastercraft to handicraft.

Reply Obj. 3. Man directs himself by prudence, commonly so called, in relation to his own good, but by political prudence, of which we speak, he directs himself in relation to the common good.

Notes to Chapter 8
On Kingship, Book I, Chapter 1

1. We read here "naturalibus" rather than "universalibus." The latter appears in the Vulgate edition of *On Princely Rule*. The former is the reading in all manuscripts apart from the Vulgate, as I. Th. Eschmann, O.P., demonstrates in *On Kingship*, trans. by Gerald B. Phelan and revised by Eschmann (Toronto: Pontifical Institute of Mediaeval Studies, 1946), p. 84.

2. Ec. 4:9.

3. Pr. 11:14.

4. Cf. *Summa Contra Gentiles* III, 23; 78: "The heavens impart motion to the rest of the universe, and God governs all other creatures through man."

5. 34:2.

6. 27:24.

7. Ec. 5:8.

On Kingship, Book 1, Chapter 6

1. Ch. 3.

2. 1 Sam. 13:14. Reading "Samuel" for "David." The Latin for the biblical verse differs from that of the Vulgate in all other manuscripts, as Eschmann shows.

3. Judg. 3:14. In the biblical text, Ehud hid the dagger on his thigh and thrust it into Eglon's belly.

4. 1 Pet. 2:18–19.

5. 2 Kings 14:5–6.

6. Pr. 20:26.

7. Pr. 21:1.

8. Reading with Eschmann "in tantum devotionem."

9. Dan. 4:34.

10. Sir. 10:17.

11. Ex. 14:23–28.

12. Dan. 4:30.

13. Reading with Eschmann "concussione" for "confusione"; Is. 14:3.

14. 34:10.

15. 13:11.

16. 34:30.

ST II–II, Q. 47, A. 11

1. *Eth.* VI, 8. 1141b23.

2. *Pol.* III, 4. 1277a20.

3. A. 5; I–II, Q. 54, A. 2 *ad* 1.

4. I–II, Q. 1, Intro.; Q. 102, A. 1.

5. *Pol.* III, 4. 1277a20.

6. Ibid.

ST II–II, Q. 50, A. 2

1. A. 1.

2. *Eth.* VI, 8. 1141b24.

3. *See* Glossary, s.v. "slavery."

4. A. 1.

5. I–II, Q. 54, A. 2; II–II, Q. 47, A. 5.

Selected
Bibliography

The books and articles selected here provide a background for understanding St. Thomas's moral and political thought and for applying his principles to modern contexts. The list is merely suggestive of the vast secondary literature available in many languages.

On Aristotle's philosophical system, see especially:

Grene, Marjorie. *A Portrait of Aristotle.* Chicago: University of Chicago Press, 1967.
Veatch, Henry. *Aristotle: A Contemporary Appreciation.* Bloomington, Ind.: Indiana University Press, 1974.

On Aristotle's ethics and contemporary criticism, see:

Veatch, Henry. *Rational Man: A Modern Interpretation of Aristotelian Ethics.* Bloomington, Ind.: Indiana University Press, 1962.

Especially helpful on Aristotle's politics is:

Jaffa, Harry. "Aristotle." *History of Political Philosophy.* 2nd ed. Eds. Leo Strauss and Joseph Cropsey. Chicago: University of Chicago Press, 1981, pp. 64–130.

On the encounter between Christianity and Aristotelianism, see:

Steenberghen, Fernand van. *Aristotle in the West: The Origins of Latin Aristotelianism.* Trans. L. Johnson. New York: Humanities Press, 1970.

For a full selection of medieval Islamic, Judaic, and Christian writings on political philosophy, including selections from St. Thomas's *Commentaries* on Aristotle's *Ethics* and *Politics*, see:

Medieval Political Philosophy: A Sourcebook. Eds. Ralph Lerner and Muhsin Mahdi. New York: Free Press of Glencoe, 1963.

For a well-written and concise summary of St. Thomas's times, his purpose, and the importance of his work, see:

Pieper, Josef. *Guide to Thomas Aquinas.* Trans. Richard and Clara Winston. New York: Pantheon Books, 1962.

An excellent presentation of St. Thomas's life can be found in:

Chesterton, Gilbert K. *St. Thomas Aquinas.* Garden City, N.Y.: Image Books, 1956.

For philosophical introductions to St. Thomas's system, see:

Copleston, S.J., Frederick C. *Aquinas.* Harmondsworth, Middlesex, England: Penguin Books, 1970.
Gilson, Etienne. *The Christian Philosophy of St. Thomas Aquinas.* New York: Random House, 1956.

For a solid presentation of St. Thomas's political philosophy, see:

Fortin, Ernest L. "St. Thomas Aquinas." *History of Political Philosophy.* 2nd ed. Eds. Leo Strauss and Joseph Cropsey. Chicago: University of Chicago Press, 1981, pp. 223–50.

On St. Thomas's employment of Aristotle's treatment of the virtues, see:

Jaffa, Harry. *Thomism and Aristotelianism.* Chicago: University of Chicago Press, 1952.
Sokolowski, Robert. *The God of Faith and Reason.* Notre Dame, Ind.: University of Notre Dame Press, 1982.

On St. Thomas's views on ethics, see:

McInerny, Ralph M. *Ethics Thomistica: The Moral Philosophy of Thomas Aquinas.* Washington, D.C.: The Catholic University of America, 1982.

For a Thomistic treatment of the virtues, see:

Pieper, Josef. *The Four Cardinal Virtues: Prudence, Justice, Fortitude, Temperance.* New York: Harcourt, Bruce, and World, 1965.

On the general spirit and aim of St. Thomas's ethical thought, see:

Stevens, G. "Moral Obligation in St. Thomas." *The Modern Schoolman,* 40 (1962–63):1–21.

On St. Thomas's concept of the natural law and its precepts, see:

Armstrong, Ross A. *Primary and Secondary Precepts in Thomistic Natural Law Teaching.* The Hague: Nijhoff, 1966.

D'Entrèves, Alessandro P. *Natural Law.* London: Hutchinson's University Library, 1950.

Simon, Yves. *The Tradition of Natural Law: A Philosopher's Reflections.* New York: Fordham University Press, 1965.

For attempts to treat modern political life and issues in the light of St. Thomas's principles, see:

Maritain, Jacques. *Man and the State.* Chicago: University of Chicago Press, 1951.

Regan, S. J., Richard J. *The Moral Dimensions of Politics.* New York: Oxford University Press, 1986.

Simon, Yves. *Philosophy of Democratic Government.* Chicago: University of Chicago Press, 1961.

Glossary

Accident: *an attribute which inheres in another and cannot subsist in itself.* What does not inhere in another but subsists in itself is a substance. John, e.g., is a substance, while his height is an accident; the latter cannot exist apart from the former. *See* Property, Substance.

Act: *the perfection of a being.* The act of existence is the primary perfection of every being; the specific (substantial) form perfects all material beings; particular (accidental) characteristics perfect all finite beings. Joan, e.g., is perfected or actualized by her act of existence, her human form, and her particular attributes (her knowledge, her virtue, her physical attributes). *See* Accident, Form, Matter, Potency, Substance.

Appetite: *the active tendency of things to realize their capacities.* Appetites can be conscious or unconscious, intellectual or sensible. Sensible appetites are concupiscible or irascible. *See* Concupiscible, Irascible.

Cause: *something that influences the being or the coming to be of something else.* In common parlance, the term "cause" refers primarily to the efficient cause, i.e., the agent responsible for an effect: a builder and those who work under him, e.g., are the efficient causes of a house. But there are other kinds of causes. A final cause is the end for the sake of which the efficient cause acts: a builder, e.g., builds a house to make money (subjective purpose) and to provide shelter (objective purpose). Efficient and final causes are extrinsic to the effect. Form, which makes an effect to be what it is, and matter, which receives the form, are correlative intrinsic causes: a house, e.g., is composed of bricks, wood, etc., which are given a structure and shape. *See* Form, Matter, Principle.

Concupiscence: *the (inordinate) inclination to sensuality antecedent and contrary to dictates of reason.* It is not to be identified with the concupiscible appetites as such. *See* Concupiscible.

Concupiscible: *a sensible appetite whose object is the pleasant.* Love and hate, desire and aversion, joy and sorrow are examples of movements of the concupiscible appetite. *See* Appetite, Irascible.

Constitution: *see* Polity.

Essence: *what makes things to be the substances they are.* The human essence, e.g., makes human beings to be what they are as substances, namely, rational animals. When the essence of a being is considered as the ultimate intrinsic source of the being's development, it is called its "nature"; a tadpole, e.g., develops into a frog because the former has the nature of a frog. *See* Form, Substance.

Form: *the cause responsible for the substantial character of a thing or an accidental feature.* The human form, e.g., makes John to be what he is as a substance, and other forms make him to be what he is accidentally (tall, thin, red-headed). *See* Accident, Substance.

Fomes: *see* Concupiscence.

Genus: *see* Species.

Habit: *the characteristic disposition or inclination to act in a certain way.* Habits may be of the intellect or of the will, innate or acquired, natural or supernatural, good or bad. Examples: logical argumentation is a habit of the intellect; moderation is a habit of the will; timidity may be an innate habit; cleanliness is an acquired habit; courage is a natural habit; faith is a supernatural habit. *See* Virtue.

Intellect: *the power or faculty of mind which grasps the essence of things, forms judgments, and reasons discoursively.* *See* Essence, Power.

Irascible: *a sensible appetite whose object is the useful for the individual or species.* The object does not appear as something pleasant and can be achieved only by overcoming opposition. Hope and despair, fear and anger are examples of movements of the irascible appetite. *See* Appetite, Concupiscible.

Justice: *the moral virtue whereby a person is characteristically disposed to render to other persons and the community what is their due.* Since the good of the individual is ordered to the good of the community, acts of all virtues pertain to justice. Justice so considered is general justice. It is also called "legal justice" because laws of the community order the acts of individuals to the common good. There are two particular or special forms of justice: commutative and distributive. Commutative justice is that part of justice whereby one person is characteristically disposed to render to other persons what is their due. Distributive justice is that part of justice whereby rulers of a community are characteristically disposed to regulate the distribution of benefits and burdens such that members and groups are proportionately rewarded for their contributions to the common good. *See* Right.

Matter: *the cause responsible for the "stuff" from and with which something is made.* The material causes of a house, e.g., are its bricks, wood, etc. Prime matter individualizes and so limits the substantial form of material things, and it provides the capacity for material things to change from one substance into another. *See* Form, Potency.

Nature: *see* Essence.

Political Community (Lat.: *civitas;* **Gk.:** *polis): the organized community wherein and whereby human beings are able fully to achieve their proper excellence or well-being (happiness).* Like Aristotle, Aquinas held that human beings are by their very nature social and political animals. Human beings need to associate with other human beings for self-defense and economic development, but they also and especially need to associate with others for their full intellectual and moral development. Only an organized community of a certain size can be self-sufficient enough to achieve these goals. "Political community" thus differs from the modern term "state," which signifies the supreme agency responsible for organizing the community ("society"), and from the modern term "government," which signifies the machinery and personnel of the state. Unlike Aristotle, however, Aquinas envisioned a supernatural end for human beings beyond their temporal well-being and, by reason of that supernatural end, membership of human beings in another, divinely established community, the Church. Relations between the natural and supernatural ends of human beings and between the two communities reflecting these ends were a central concern of St. Thomas. *See* Polity.

Polity: *most generally, the regime or constitution which gives to a political community its distinctive form.* It also has the specific meaning of a regime or constitution mixing monarchic (rule by one), aristocratic (rule by the few best), and democratic (rule by the people) principles. According to Aquinas, this particular regime or constitution is the best of the good forms of government, those which aim at the good of the community rather than the private interest of the ruler(s). Polity, as this specific regime or constitution, includes limited—but only limited—democratic participation. *See* Political Community.

Potency: *the capacity to be something or to become something else.* The potency of a being limits its actuality: frogs, e.g., can swim, but they cannot fly. Finite beings (beings other than God) can change accidentally: John, e.g., can go bald. Finite material beings can also change from one substance into another: grass, e.g., when consumed, becomes part of a cow. *See* Accident, Act, Matter, Power.

Power: *the active capacity to perform a certain type of activity, e.g., the power of sight. See* Potency.

Principle: *that from which something else proceeds.* The essence of a frog, specifically its form, e.g, is an ontological principle, i.e., a principle governing the frog's being and activity. Such a principle is a cause. The premises of an argument, on the other hand, are logical principles. From the premises that all men are mortal and that Socrates is a man, the intellect can conclude that Socrates is mortal. *See* Cause.

Property: *a quality or characteristic which necessarily belongs to a substance; a proper accident.* Joan's ability to use language, e.g., unlike the color of her hair, is a characteristic proper to her as a human being. *See* Accident, Substance.

Prudence: *the intellectual virtue whereby a person is characteristically disposed to reason rightly in the choice of means to achieve human excellence.* Prudence governs the moral virtues. *See* Virtue.

Regime: *see* Polity.

Right (Lat.: *jus): objectively, that which is just by nature or positive law; subjectively, what belongs to persons in their relation to other persons. See* Justice.

Slavery: *involuntary servitude.* The slavery (Lat.: *servitudo*) which Aquinas considers is the medieval variety, of which serfdom was the principal institution. The medieval slave was subject to the disposition of his master, but he enjoyed, at least in theory, rights which his master was bound to respect. This slavery should be distinguished from that of ancient Greece and Rome and from that of the antebellum American South, where slaves had no (or negligible) rights and masters had no duties toward them. So also "slave" (Lat.: *servus*).

Soul: *the substantial form of human beings.* According to Aquinas, the soul is neither material nor intrinsically dependent on matter for its existence. Hence it is immortal. *See* Form, Substance.

Species: *the substantial identity of things insofar as that identity is common to many.* The species-concept (e.g.,"man") is composed of a genus-concept (e.g., "animal"), which indicates the essence of something in an incompletely determined way, and of a specific difference between things of the same genus (e.g., "rational"). The species-concept or definition thus expresses the whole substance or essence of things.

Substance: *that which exists in itself and not in another.* Individual substances "stand under" (Lat.: *substare)* accidents and persist through accidental changes. Human beings, e.g., are composed of substance (body-soul) and accidents (size, shape, color, etc.). *See* Accident, Property.

Synderesis: the habit of first moral principles. Human beings have an innate disposition to understand the first principles of human action. Human beings are disposed by nature to recognize that they should seek the good proper to their nature and that this good includes preservation of one's life, procreation and education of children, search for truth, and community with others. *See* Habit.

Virtue: *human excellence.* Like its Greek equivalent *(aretē),* the Latin-derived term indicates a perduring quality of the human person and so a characteristic disposition to act in a properly human way. Aquinas distinguishes three kinds of virtue: intellectual, moral, and theological. Intellectual virtues have for their objects intellectual activities. Concerning theoretical truth, intellectual virtues include understanding or insight (skill in judging), science (skill in reasoning), and wisdom or contemplation (skill in understanding the ultimate causes of things). Concerning practical truth, intellectual virtues include practical wisdom or prudence (skill in making right judgments about the propriety of human actions) and art (skill in making right judgments about things to be made). Moral virtues have for their objects characteristic readiness to act in particular matters as prudence dictates; these virtues are acquired. The four cardinal virtues are prudence, fortitude, temperance, and justice. There are also for St. Thomas the theological virtues of faith, hope, and charity and the infused moral virtues. Cf. ST I–II, QQ. 49–67; II–II. QQ. 1–170. *See* Habit.

Index